W9-DAV-898

Here's to cooking Tulsa style
"In Yankee Land"!
August 1986
June & Shirley

CLEORA'S KITCHENS

CLEORA'S KITCHENS

THE MEMOIR OF A COOK

& Eight Decades of Great American Food

BY CLEORA BUTLER

COUNCIL OAK BOOKS, LTD. / TULSA, OKLAHOMA

Council Oak Books, Ltd.
Tulsa, Oklahoma 74120
© 1985 by Council Oak Books, Ltd.   All rights reserved.
ISBN 0-933031-02-5
Library of Congress Catalogue Card Number 85-072022

Manufactured in the United States of America.

Design by Carol Haralson
Photography by Gene Aker

Antique cooking implements for illustrations courtesy
of Colonial Antiques of Tulsa, Oklahoma.
Special thanks to David Cox, Phil Dutcher and A. W. Gunter.

To Allen Vernon Manning, Lucy Ann Manning, and Maggie Thomas

CONTENTS

ACKNOWLEDGMENTS

———

THIS BOOK CAME INTO BEING THROUGH THE CONTINUING encouragement of many friends and relatives. It would never have been a reality, however, without the generous help of specific individuals.

In particular, I am grateful to Donald and Barbara Simmons of Muskogee, Oklahoma, who had faith enough in my project to finance the initial typing of the notes I had made recalling various incidents in my life as well as the cost of typing my collection of over six hundred recipes.

Thanks go to Beverly Lake who accomplished all of that typing and who also executed a number of artful drawings for the early manuscript, and to my long-time friend Juanita Blakey, who worked with me testing scores of recipes included in the book.

My family was no less supportive, especially my nephews Hugh Allen Thomas and Dudley Thomas. Dudley patiently interviewed me for hours helping me to recall many important events, and devoted his time to preparing the manuscript and cataloging the vast collection of recipes in order that final selections for the book could be made.

I also pay special tribute to my good friend and former patron Mary Ann Jacobs who, as much as I ever did, cherishes a deep interest in and love for the skillful preparation of good food. We became reacquainted in 1952 when I catered an affair for over three hundred of her guests. To our mutual surprise, we realized we had known each other years before when I had worked for the George W. Snedden family. Mary Ann had been a mere thirteen years old at the time. Over the years, she too had developed more than a passing interest in cooking and determined, at the urging of her children, to one day write a cookbook. Ill health unfortunately prevented this, but she passed on to me the task of doing so. Without her continued encouragement, this book might never have been written. A number of the recipes herein come from her extensive collection, and Mary Ann Jacobs will always have my undying gratitude.

And finally, I wish to thank all those who tasted what I cooked and came back for seconds.

CLEORA BUTLER

List of Illustrations

mentioned in the Bible. European immigrants brought the potato to America where it is now such a common edible that the average citizen eats his weight in potatoes each year.

29 BREAD BOARD WITH CARVED WOODEN-HANDLED BREAD KNIFE, CA. 1900
Most bread boards were made of maple because of the density of its grain, which made the board easier to keep clean.

30 TIN PUDDING MOLD, CA. 1900
This decorative mold for custard type puddings was used by the home cook for particularly festive dinners.

31 CAST IRON MUFFIN PAN, CA.1890
A decorative muffin pan was one of the more elaborate varieties for making quick breads such as cornbread. This pattern is Victorian.

32 TINNED STEEL TUBE PAN, 1923
This professional tube pan was made of heavy tinned steel to diffuse heat rapidly through the batter. The removable bottom allows easy lifting out of the cake and the tube also conducts heat through the cake's center during baking. The pan was patented December 18, 1923 in Chicago.

33 RIBBED METAL NUTBREAD PAN, CONTEMPORARY
The classic nutbread pan dates back to Roman times and is similar to the "saddle of venison pan." Its ribbed interior makes it easier to slice the baked bread into uniform slices. This variation of the form is German.

34 STEEL-WIRED POTATO MASHER WITH WOODEN HANDLE, CA. 1920
A potato masher like this one is typical of those used in almost every American household in the first half of the century.

36 PICKLED CONDIMENTS
The art of preserving food in salt brine, vinegar and spices dates to prehistoric times. Pickles have been food for military troops since the days of Caesar. In the great period of sailing exploration, when no other imperishable food was available to prevent scurvy at sea, pickles were aboard every sailing vessel. During World War II the U.S. government commandeered forty percent of the American pickle output for the armed forces. Commercial pickling began on a wharf in Boston in 1821 when the William Underwood Company went into business.

· CLEORA'S KITCHENS ·

The Memoir of a
C · O · O · K

"Over the river and through the woods
to Grandmother's house we go."

WAYS OF COOKING AND ENTERTAINING COM-
monplace in my childhood have all but disappeared in our 1980s
world of electric ranges, food processors and exotic tidbits from
the world over. When I was a child, however, a buggy ride "over
the river and through the woods" for a home-cooked dinner at Grandmother's
was commonplace, not only for well-to-do white folks, but for the children of
ex-slaves as well.

My three brothers and I spent four or five weeks of each summer at our
grandparents' farm in Newby, Oklahoma, about twelve miles south of Bristow.
We got thoroughly dirty playing in the barnyard and miserably scratched
picking wild strawberries, blackberries, plums and possum grapes (as
Grandpa called them), so that Grandmother could make her jams and jellies—
and best of all, her exquisite wines. Yet, the time of year we most eagerly
anticipated was Thanksgiving. The jellies and jams Grandmother had made
from the fruits we picked in the summer were then to be sampled, as well as a
sip or two of that wine. It was after the big dinner, however, that Grandpa
would take all the children into the woods just south of the large two-story log
house to gather hickory nuts, walnuts and pecans. He was young and strong
then, and we'd walk for miles, Grandpa making sure everyone gathered a
respectable collection of goodies.

When the holidays were over, Grandpa would pack us off to the train station
in Bristow for the trip to Muskogee, loaded with gunny sacks filled with nuts
and other treasures. From his dugout cellar came apples, pumpkins, winter
squash, peanuts and poppin' corn. And, I must not omit this, baking-size sweet
potatoes. I mean *real yams*! When my mother baked them, the syrup actually
oozed out.

POSSUM GRAPE WINE

Squeeze the juice from the ripe possum
grapes. Add 2 gallons of cold water and
2 spoonfuls of yeast to every gallon of
grape juice. Let the mixture ferment 24
hours. Strain the mixture through a
cloth. Add 4 pounds of loaf sugar to
every gallon of liquid, stirring well. Put
the mixture in a good cask, seal tightly,
and let stand until wine looks clear.
Bottle.

Mother's Hickory Nut Cake

*Made with hickory nuts
we gathered on the mountain
behind Grandpa's house*

1   cup butter
4   eggs
2   cups sugar
3   cups all-purpose flour
1   teaspoon soda
2   teaspoons cream of tartar
1   cup cold water
2   cups hickory nutmeats
1   teaspoon lemon extract

Cream butter and sugar until light, add eggs one at a time and beat well. Sift flour, soda and cream of tartar together. Add alternately flour and water until thoroughly mixed. Add hickory nuts which have been dredged with some of the flour. Add extract and stir thoroughly. Pour into a ten-inch tube pan which has been lined with greased brown paper. Bake at 350 degrees for 45-60 minutes or until tested done. Ice with boiled icing.

Serves 12-14.

Baking Yams

Mother would choose potatoes that were a nice baking size, but not too big. She would grease them with bacon fat and put them in a baking pan, then put them in the wood-burning stove. The fire wasn't a real hot fiery fire, but it was hot enough so they would cook. I think it was the quality of the sweet potatoes that made them taste so good. Grandpa raised them. We called them "Yellow Yams."

After all the loot had been safely loaded into the baggage car, Grandpa would hand each of us a small package. We squealed in feigned surprise, knowing full well that these final expressions of his love for us were gifts of ribbon sugar cane. It had come from his last crop of the season, used for making his marvelous molasses, the sale of which contributed much to the household income. The sugar cane was usually a little dry, but we always felt delighted when Grandpa favored us with this special treat. Once back home, we strutted proudly among our playmates, offering a bite or two only to those we truly liked. None of them had a grandpa quite like Allen Vernon Manning, and few ever had the opportunity to give their teeth a good workout on a strip of ribbon sugar cane. It was a tradition he loved and one he continued with his great-grandchildren years later.

My father would meet my brothers and me at the train station in Muskogee and load us into Mr. Hudson's horse-and-buggy for the ride home. The next day, Mr. Greer, another neighbor who had a dray service, collected our loot from the depot and delivered it to our house on 15th Street at Linapaugh. As Dad unloaded the wagon, he'd shake his head in wonderment at the amount of goodies his gypsies had managed to wheedle out of his father-in-law. Of course the return home meant we also had to return to classes at Mrs. Ayres' private school on Fondulac Street, but that gave us the opportunity to tell the class about the grand manner in which we'd spent the Thanksgiving weekend.

In the winter months that followed, many happy hours were spent popping corn or picking out nutmeats for Mother to use making cookies and candies. One of her specialties was a *hickory nut cake* which she made when we were lucky enough to find a sufficient quantity of nuts.

My FIRST ATTEMPT AT COOKING CAME ON A GRAY, RAINY Sunday morning in 1911. I was only ten years old, but determined to strike out on my own. Mother had prepared and taken breakfast to Mrs. Dumas, a neighbor who was ill. My father had gone out early on some errands. With their respective tasks completed, each would return home and we'd all have breakfast.

Mother had recently started using a new baking powder called *Calumet*, because the brand she usually bought, *Dr. Price's Baking Powder*, was not available at Bonicello's grocery store over on 16th Street where she usually shopped. For an additional twenty-five cents she had also purchased a little cookbook published by *Calumet* with full-color photographs showing what each dish should look like when complete. I had never seen anything quite so beautiful. The picture of the biscuits looked temptingly real, and with Mother and Dad out of the house, I decided it was my golden opportunity.

I began to read and follow the directions in the little cookbooklet, one eye on the window, watching for Mother's return. Time was in my favor. Mother had apparently stopped to visit with Mrs. Dumas. Soon, the fire crackling in the big wood-burning stove seemed just right. Since this was my first attempt, I wasn't sure about doubling, so I made the recipe twice to be sure there'd be enough for all of us.

I had just put the biscuits in the oven when Mother rushed in and began busying herself in preparation for breakfast. Nervously, I waited for her to open the stove and discover what I had done. The ham was fried, the hash-brown potatoes and fried apples were on the back of the stove keeping warm, the eggs were all ready to scramble the minute Dad arrived, and still she hadn't started the biscuits. I could wait no longer. I proudly proclaimed, "Mother, I've made the biscuits—they're in the oven." My father arrived at that very moment, just in time to see Mother's shock. Gingerly, she bent down and opened the oven door. Surprise! My biscuits looked just like the picture in the book! Dad joked, "Get out the baking soda just in case someone gets a tummy ache." A feeling of "what if I've failed?" washed over me, but the biscuits came out tasting as good as they looked.

BAKING POWDER BISCUITS

2 cups all-purpose flour
1 teaspoon salt
1 teaspoon sugar
3 tablespoons Calumet baking powder
¾ cup milk
4 tablespoons shortening

Sift together flour, salt and baking powder. Blend shortening into sifted ingredients. Add milk to make a soft dough. Toss on floured board. Knead lightly. Roll out ½-inch thick; cut into 2-inch rounds. Place in slightly greased shallow pan. Brush tops with melted butter. Bake at 350 degrees for 10 minutes or until done.

CAREFUL ATTENTION TO THE PREPARATION OF FOOD HAS been a tradition in my family since before the Civil War. Lucy Ann Manning, my great-grandmother, spent much of her life as the house cook on a large plantation outside Waco, Texas. She and my great-grandfather, Buck Manning, had migrated with their owner from Mississippi prior to the war and by the time peace returned to the land, Buck and Lucy had brought seven children into the world.

Allen Vernon, their firstborn, was destined to become my grandfather. He grew up in the plantation "big house" amid the pots, pans and soup ladles in the kitchen where his mother worked. His father, who was overseer on the plantation, taught his son the essentials of planting and farming when time permitted, but most of Grandfather's time was spent in the house where he became familiar with food and its preparation. At fifteen, Allen developed an interest in a young girl who lived on a neighboring plantation where he often ran errands. After six years of courtship, Allen and Bettie Sadler were married on July 4, 1875.

Meanwhile, Allen had become a land owner. When slavery as an institution came to an end, Buck Manning was given a tract of land by his former owner (who was his father as well) and Buck in turn gave fifty acres to each of his children.

Allen worked diligently to till the land, developing the fledgling skills he'd acquired on the plantation. It was also necessary for him to put to use those talents learned at his mother's hand in his own kitchen, as Allen kept his youthful bride busy bearing children. When his father passed away, his mother joined the household and this lightened his load considerably. The first of Allen's children (there were to be eleven in all) was my mother, Mary Magdalena.

It was natural that, as the oldest, Maggie was required to assist in the Manning kitchen and, in time, to take full responsibility for it. Drawing upon both her grandmother's expertise and her father's knowledge, Maggie was quick in developing the talent that established her as one of the finest cooks in northeast Oklahoma. The daily burden of cooking for so many, however, though it added greatly to her culinary skills, must have been somewhat wearing on a maturing young girl. It might well have been with relief when, at eighteen, Maggie accepted the proposal of a neighboring farmhand, Joseph Thomas, who had expressed great interest in her for years. Allen Vernon Manning, however, was adamantly opposed to this young smart-aleck's designs on his eldest daughter. The one (mind you) in charge of the cooking.

At twenty, Maggie defiantly announced her intention to marry the enterprising Joe Thomas. They still had to wait three years, until October 26, 1898, for her father to begrudgingly give the hand of his daughter to my father at the local Baptist church.

Joe Thomas took his new bride to the three-room house allotted him on the farm of his new employers, Dr. and Mrs. Hugh Lovelace. His tasks included milking, caring for the livestock, and driving Dr. Lovelace around Waco on his calls. Maggie took care of the cooking, a job for which she was most certainly qualified. In fact, cooking for just the Lovelaces (and her new husband, of course) must have come as a welcome relief. The closeness in age of Joe and Maggie to their employers soon led to a friendship that transcended the normal employer/farmhand relations of the day.

In the Manning home before her marriage, Maggie had done only a small portion of the sewing, but when she saw Virginia Lovelace's hand-sewn trousseau, the exquisite needlework absolutely fascinated her. By the same token, Maggie's amazing talents in the kitchen were a marvel to Mrs. Lovelace. Thereupon was established an exchange of skills that was to last throughout the time my mother and father worked for the family. Mother became a fine seamstress, and Mrs. Lovelace an excellent cook.

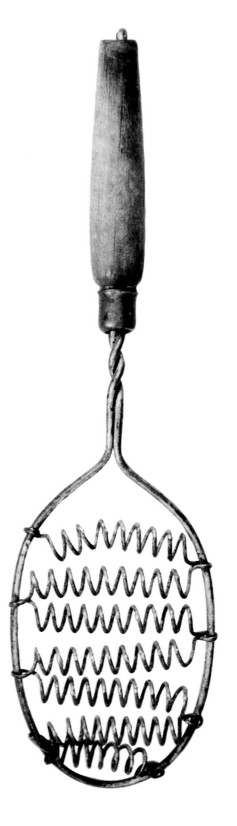

During those first years as my father drove Dr. Lovelace about while he established his new practice, the two became warm friends. So it was with a shared joy that they greeted the arrival of my elder brother, George Gilbert, born in late February of the year 1900. It was Dr. Lovelace's first experience in obstetrics. It was also timely, as about six weeks later Mrs. Lovelace gave birth to her first child, Raymond Everett.

The two couples were happy indeed. Their warm relationship had been further bonded by the births of their first heirs. Mother and Dad always recalled the events of those first years with moist eyes. When all the excitement died down, more farmhands were taken on and my father assumed the position of foreman. A young woman was hired to handle some of the household chores and help with the new Lovelace baby. The cooking/sewing exchange was also resumed.

Before long, what had started out as a small farm was taking on the atmosphere of a veritable hamlet. More land was purchased. More hands were hired. Young couples anxious to settle in the Waco area moved into small, comfortable homes that Dr. Lovelace had constructed to accommodate the growing number of employees. He named it Lovely Acres.

By now, Mother was acknowledged as an extraordinary cook and she readily shared her skills with all who wanted to learn.

The increase in workers brought a rise in the birth rate and Dr. Lovelace's work eventually led to his becoming a specialist in the field of obstetrics. Mrs. Lovelace gave birth to their second child, Marjorie Lynn, and within months I made my advent into this world. The year was 1901 and the excitement of a new century permeated the air. The one just passed, though turbulent, had stood the Manning and Thomas families well. The children coming into the world were the grandsons and granddaughters of *former* slaves. Amongst them was a future ten-year-old baker of magnificent biscuits.

It was a new era, full of promise. Joe and Maggie Thomas were beginning to build their lives together. There were the new babies, George and myself, and new relationships with the other young couples coming to Lovely Acres.

There was something else in the air as well. For a number of years, marvelous stories about people moving north to the Indian Territory had been circulating throughout the area. Land was free and the opportunities were said to be unlimited. My father, orphaned at ten, was used to making his own way and although he expected that he'd find no better employer than Dr. Lovelace, he realized that it might be years before he could become truly independent. The "Land of the Five Civilized Tribes" beckoned temptingly. For weeks, Mother and Dad talked about it. Many of their friends had already declared their intention to go. Thousands had left. Whites and blacks alike were taking advantage of the free land being offered. There were even stories about new, totally black townships like Boley and Taft with no white people living in them at all.

The decision was made. Dad was confident, as was Mother, who knew her cooking and sewing skills would always be on hand if outside income was needed. They prepared carefully, making sure that their duties at Lovely Acres were assumed by responsible people.

My grandfather watched as day by day his daughter and son-in-law made arrangements for the great trek. Several of Dad's brothers and sisters had also decided to join the caravan as had a few of Dr. Lovelace's other farmhands. To Grandad it was bad enough that Joe Thomas had taken his daughter out of the Manning kitchen. Now he was moving his favorite away to some foreign place where probably he'd never see her again. Just weeks before they were scheduled to depart, Allen Vernon Manning decided that he could not possibly stay behind in Waco. He, his wife Betty, and the remaining ten children were packed and lined up at the end of the wagon train when the large group assembled to depart.

SCOTCH SHORTBREAD

1 pound butter
½ pound lard
3 cups powdered sugar
7 cups flour

Cream lard and butter and powdered sugar thoroughly. Work flour into this with hands. Be careful not to make too stiff. Knead until dough cracks on surface and doesn't stick to the board. Divide dough into chunks that can be patted out into ½ inch thick cakes with hands. Prick with fork and bake at 300 degrees for 50 minutes. Store in tin boxes. Keeps indefinitely in refrigerator.

Baked Apple Dumplings

Apples
Sugar
Whole cloves
Lemon peel
Pastry crust

Pare apples and scoop out the cores. Fill up each hole with sugar and a clove or some grated lemon peel. Make a good pastry crust and enclose each apple in a round. Pinch the edges of the pastry closely so that no seam can be seen. Bake at 350 degrees for 20-30 minutes, until apples are done.

Eat with a rich pudding sauce or with maple syrup.

IT WAS AN EARLY SPRING MORNING IN 1902. DR. AND MRS. Lovelace, together with all the farmhands, were there to see them off. Moments before the crack of the whip that would signal the first turn of the wheels, Dr. Lovelace called my father aside and handed him an envelope containing money. They embraced briefly and Dad climbed up beside my mother and my brother George. I was snuggled in her arms (wide-eyed, it's said).

THE WAGON TRAIN SKIRTED DALLAS AND TURNED NORTH-east towards the Red River. It was known that the best farmland was in the eastern part of the territory, so it was there they were headed. Some families ended their trek when the caravan reached what looked like a good location. One of Dad's sisters branched off with another group and eventually ended up in Oklahoma City. Mother and Dad, however, kept pushing northward until they reached Muskogee. It was August.

Grandpa had by this time assumed the position of head of the clan (patriarch, if you will). Looking about the area, he proclaimed that they had

reached their destination. A parcel of land was secured and a house was built. One large room at first, then subdivisions and finally several smaller buildings to house the sixteen people who had come to this new place.

Mother put her recently acquired sewing skills to good use, making dresses and other garments for neighbors and wealthy families in the area. Her refusal, however, to turn money earned into the family coffer (for Grandfather to dispose of as he saw fit) led my father to build a small house of their own nearby. In relative harmony, the Thomases and Mannings tilled the land and lived comfortably.

I WAS FIVE AND A HALF IN 1907. ALTHOUGH STATEHOOD WAS the topic of the day, what stands out in my memory is not the transition of Indian Territory into the 46th state, but a day in early February when George, two neighborhood playmates and I decided to cook dinner. We arranged some stones and a sheet of tin into a sort of stove, and prepared several slices of pork liver left over from the day before. Mother had been ill in bed for a couple of days, so we felt safe in doing what we knew we could never receive her permission to do.

The makeshift stove was set up on the front porch. Scraps of wood had been gathered and placed carefully on the sheet of tin. We were ready to start "dinner." Just at that moment Dad came out of the front door and we scattered like gunshot. One shout from him stopped each of us dead in our tracks. We turned to face him and at his beckoning gesture shuffled slowly to the porch where he stood, his arms akimbo. After calming us and hearing our tearful explanations, as well as noting that we had been thoughtful enough to use a piece of tin to avoid burning the house down, he took out his matches and bent down to light the little fire for us.

Just then, all attention was diverted by the sound of a fast-moving buggy. With great urgency, Dr. Gregory, the family physician, pulled up to the house. Although Mother had been feeling poorly for several days we were not privy to why or just how ill she was. With scant greetings, Dr. Gregory barely missed our little stove as he rushed across the porch and into the house towards Mother's bed. My father was right behind him.

We remained quietly on the porch and, hearing no sounds from within the house, soon turned our attention back to our project. Suddenly a startling cry pierced the air. It was strangely familiar, but not having any expectation of what was at hand, we merely stared at one another in absolute amazement. A few minutes later, Dr. Gregory came out of the house, looked down at my brother and me, and with a big smile on his face proclaimed, "You've got a brand new baby brother." The four of us dashed into the house to find Mother smiling and holding our newest family member, Walter. Dad's face was one gigantic grin.

MOTHER'S MUSTARD AND/OR TURNIP GREENS

Our dad was a good gardener and always started his garden with early planting English peas (as we called them), and rows of onions, mustard greens, turnips, beets, green beans, kale and early spinach.

When the mustard greens were barely big enough to pick, Mother started testing them almost daily, until they were just right. Salt pork was cooked in one piece until it was tender, then removed from the pot and sliced. The greens, mostly mustard, were washed. The water clinging to them, when added to the liquid from the salt pork, was enough to cook a big pot of greens. Mother's greens were tender and pretty when done. She always had cornbread ready to put in the oven when the last handful of greens was put in the pot. The table was set. Our mouths were watering as we waited for the call to dinner.

The turnips were allowed to grow so we could have fresh turnips which we enjoyed eating raw. By the time the greens were ready again, young baby carrots and fresh garden onions had made their debut. Other vegetables followed—Country Gentleman sweet corn, okra, tomatoes and squash.

WHEN I WAS TWELVE, THE TIME SPENT IN THE KITCHEN AT my mother's side was the most precious to me. I watched as she magically mixed liquids and powders, added dashes of pepper and salt (plus assorted grains and crumbled leaves that I learned were called spices), placed them inside or atop the stove and produced marvelous concoctions that invariably tasted yummy. The apparent ease with which she cooked convinced me that turning out cookies and cakes must be a pushover.

One day while she was out delivering cakes she had baked, I knotted a towel around my waist and started in. I first blended some butter and sugar until the mixture was smooth and creamy. That part was simple. After all, I'd seen Mother do it hundreds of times. Then I added a few eggs to give it color, some extract and baking powder (just like Mother always did), plus milk and flour. The quantity of batter seemed to be about right. It was smooth and poured easily into the greased cake pan I had prepared. Nothing had been measured, mind you.

Having little concept of how much time was required to bake a cake, I kept peering into the oven every five minutes or so. Slowly it turned to a beautiful brown. It looked as though the kitchen magician had scored again. Within seconds of being removed from the oven, my beautiful cake began to sink, butter began oozing out from its sides, and what remained was a gooey, two-inch-high floppy discus. It didn't look too good, but it *was* a cake.

With some courage and some trepidation I tasted the results. It wasn't too bad. I then convinced my younger brothers to give it a try. (George would have none of it.) After a few bites they refused to eat any more. I had to go along with them, for I had had my fill as well. However, something had to be done with the remainder. First I cleaned all of the utensils so as to eliminate the evidence of my failure. Then I took what was left out to the back yard and buried it in a remote corner of the garden. Thus was born the dough patch.

Sometimes my experiments worked. At other times, Mother would arrive in time to salvage what I had started. Abject failures, however, found their way to the dough patch.

THEN, THERE WAS THE MOLASSES CAPER. MY EFFORTS AT blending sorghum molasses and flour to make cookies resulted in a solid sheet of gummy residue. My tasters, Walter and Joey, refused outright to even smell it. So adamant were they that they snitched to my mother about the secret dough patch. Mother was furious. She started out giving me a tongue lashing, but somewhere in the middle of it began to laugh and laughed till she was weak. She told me to stick to making good biscuits and to experiment only when she was there to guide me.

THE SORGHUM MOLASSES HAD COME FROM GRANDPA'S LAST crop of ribbon cane sugar. The first five-gallon keg was always sent to our house. While it was used in a variety of recipes, I remember especially Mother's gingerbread in which sorghum molasses was a principle ingredient. She would set this remarkably thin batter in the oven just at the time we sat down to eat. By the time dinner was over it was ready to be served. It was, and still is, one of my favorites.

The usual form of punishment in our household was a couple of sharp whacks across the bottom, but being deprived of dessert was another. Our best behavior, therefore, was very often maintained for fear of missing one of Mother's marvelous desserts. I was about four years old when something important enough occurred to make me take that risk, and it happened to be on a day Mother was to make gingerbread as the after-dinner treat.

MOLASSES

Grandpa always used red ribbon cane for his special molasses. We'd pick the cane when it was ripe, that is, when the heads went to seed. We cut the seed off, and then put the cane into the cane press, which was powered by mules. The mules walked around and around, pressing the cane juice, which ran down and was collected in a large vat. When he got enough juice, Grandpa would light the fire under the vat and cook down the juice until it tested done. It had to be fully done or it would ferment. Grandpa would test it by dipping some into a large ladle, then letting it drip. When it would drip, rather than pour from the ladle, it was done.

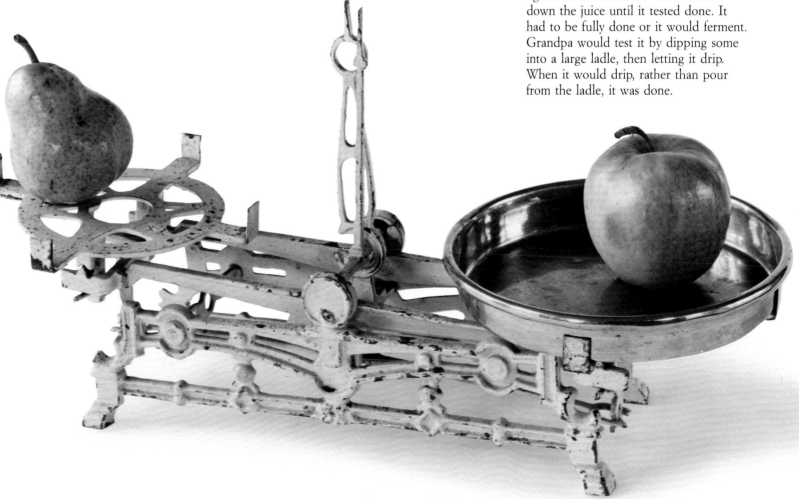

MOTHER'S GINGERBREAD

½ cup butter
1 cup sorghum molasses
½ cup sugar
2 eggs
1 cup good sorghum
2 teaspoons baking powder
1 teaspoon cinnamon
1 teaspoon ginger
2 cups flour
1 teaspoon soda
1 cup boiling water, added after all other ingredients have been blended together

Cream butter and sugar until light. Add sorghum. Sift flour with spices, baking powder and soda. Add, with eggs, to mixture. Blend thoroughly and add boiling water, stirring constantly until well mixed. Pour into a greased 9x13 inch pan. Bake in a 350 degree oven until done, about 30 minutes.

Serves 12-15.

Whenever we were having gingerbread for dessert, Mother generally set the batter in the oven just when dinner was ready to be served. By the time the meal was eaten, the gingerbread was done and cut into squares and set on the table with plenty of homemade butter and fresh whole milk. This was one of the first goodies made from the first 5-gallon keg of sorghum we received from Grandpa.

It was a beautiful spring day. It was also an especially important one. It was the day the picture-man was coming to take the annual photograph of the students attending Mrs. Ayers' school. It was my misfortune, however, to be coming down with a cold and no amount of pleading or begging could alter Mother's decision that I could not participate in the event. Not even the big tears streaming down the cheeks of a pitiful four-year-old—not even my passionate explanation of the day's significance—would change her mind.

Mrs. Ida B. Ayers ran the only private school for black children in Muskogee. In her one-room schoolhouse, she taught the first through seventh grades to thirty-five or so students. When they left Mrs. Ayers' to enter either Dunbar High School or the Manual Training High School, they were as well— if not better—prepared as the students who had attended the public school. Mrs. Ayers continued teaching until about 1922 and often visited us after our family moved to Tulsa.

On this devastating day, eight o'clock a.m. found me standing at our gate wistfully gazing at the children filing into school dressed in their very finest. The schoolhouse was but a short block and a half away and clearly visible from our yard. No lessons were taught on school picture day. I could see my classmates going in and out of the building, playing and being admonished by Mrs. Ayers not to get dirty. Occasionally one would glance in my direction and wave as I solemnly swung on the gate.

Around ten o'clock, I looked up at the sound of the trolley car over on Fondulac Street and saw the picture-man getting off. My heart pounded and my sadness deepened as he walked down the hill towards the school. I turned, looking for signs of my Mother—she was not in sight, probably cleaning or making preparations for lunch. I knew I was not properly dressed. My hair wasn't combed and in my tearful anguish that morning, I had put my shoes on the wrong feet.

No matter. This was important enough to throw all caution to the wind. Before the photographer could set up his tripod and camera, I was through the gate, across the street and standing breathless in front of Mrs. Ayers. She peered over towards our yard, looking for my Mother. Not seeing her, she gazed questioningly at me. My sadness touched her and although she knew full well that Mother would never have sent me to have a picture taken looking as I did, she nevertheless squeezed me in at the end of a long plank stretched between two chairs. Seconds later, the photographer draped his black hood over himself and his camera and began to work his magic.

Between each shot, I glanced nervously toward our yard to see if Mother had come out of the house and discovered my absence. As soon as the last picture was taken, I dashed (without goodbyes or thanks) for the house. I'm sure it must have taken a full half hour for my racing pulse to calm down, but I was safe. Mother was totally unaware that I had so flagrantly disobeyed her.

My boldness did not go undiscovered for long, however. It never occurred to me that Mrs. Ayers would bring a copy of the photo to my mother, and when she did, I was really in for it. Mother was amazed (but not a bit amused) that I had sneaked out to have my picture taken looking as I did. She was mortified and also very angry that Mrs. Ayers (who was a good friend) had allowed me to appear that way. Although they remained friends, I don't believe Mother ever truly forgave Mrs. Ayers for that. I know she never truly forgave me.

As with the biscuit incident years later, however, my dad couldn't help but be a little proud of his daughter's tenacity and boldness.

MRS. AYERS' PRIVATE SCHOOL, CLASS OF 1905. Cleora is the child farthest left in the front row of seated students.

New Potatoes with Early Green Peas in Cream Sauce

New red-skinned potatoes never had the chance to grow into big baking or boiling size in our home garden. Mother started digging around potato plants very early. When the nuggets reached the size of a half dollar or a little bigger, the new garden peas were just right and tender. She started picking and shelling to get a pint of peas, more or less, and boiled them just long enough to have a sweet crunch. The peas were added to the skinned potatoes and covered with real cream sauce, made from Jersey cow's cream, lightly salted with freshly cracked pepper.

I don't remember seeing white skinned potatoes until I was a big girl.

Our kitchen was a big area with abundant light from windows along one side of the room. Meals were taken at a round oak table which converted to an oval when leaves were set in. Against one wall sat a "safe" in which Mother's fine dishes and glasses were stored. Off of the kitchen was a closed-in and windowed back porch that stretched the width of the house. There, Mother stored foodstuffs and canned goods. One shelf was for pots and pans and the very top shelf was where preserved fruits, jams and jellies were kept. There were two iceboxes. A large one held one hundred pounds of ice and a smaller one, where milk and eggs were kept, held fifty pounds.

George and Walter milked our two cows, but additional milk was obtained from the Weeks family who employed my father as a houseman. Mr. and Mrs. Julius Weeks had no children, so we got their surplus milk and eggs as well as special treats from their kitchen. Although Mother did not work regularly for the Weeks, she pitched in whenever they wanted something special prepared or needed a temporary cook until they employed another live-in cook.

The Weeks home was on 12th street, where it still stands, just four or five blocks from where we lived. It was convenient for George or me to go every afternoon to pick up whatever milk and eggs were left over. At times I was allowed to stay over—especially if Mother was there helping out. Sometimes, as Dad passed through the swinging doors to serve dinner, I would duck under his arm and dash into the dining room before Mother could catch my skirttail. Mrs. Weeks would have Dad bring a plate, napkin and silverware and pull up a chair for me. The shining tableware and pretty plates (often with fascinating, beautiful drawings on them) captivated me. Sometimes when Mrs. Weeks was in the kitchen speaking with Mother my place would be set by invitation.

I thought Harriett Weeks was one of the nicest people in the world. She was the sister of Charles N. Haskell, Oklahoma's first governor, and she was truly an elegant lady. She was an accomplished pianist and occasionally she invited me into the living room where she'd play while Mother and Dad were finishing up to go home.

Our house, which the Weeks had originally owned and then presented to Father and Mother when they left Muskogee, was situated on the corner of 15th Street and Linapaugh. The house faced east and in back stood a barn with coops for the chickens and roaming space for our horse Daisy, our two cows, and three pigs.

The area of Muskogee where we lived was called Roberts' Addition. Mr. Roberts was a black man who had a huge tract of land in the northeast section of the city. In the early 1900s it was commonplace to see mini-farms with livestock, as we had, in sections that are now purely residential.

Behind our barn was a garden bordered with flowers which father always planted wherever we lived. Along the south and west property lines stood a row of plum, pear, and peach trees, and to the right of the house stood a lone apple tree. In addition to milking the cows, George and Walter were responsible for the garden. Young Joey was required to help wherever he could. On occasion, Dad would go down to the Katy Hotel where the Missouri, Kansas and Texas Railway pulled in. There he'd collect large tin cans which he'd sink into the ground next to the Ponderosa tomatoes so that their roots could be properly watered. Dad's principal task, however, was taking care of the livestock. He also milked cows for other families in the neighborhood. (As a matter of fact, that was what he was doing the Sunday morning I made the biscuits.)

My chores consisted of helping Mother about the house—cleaning, making the beds, washing clothes, and assisting her in the kitchen. We were pretty self-sufficient. Dad's work at the Weeks' provided cash for store-bought items and, to help along these lines, Mother baked and sold bread to families in about a five-block area around our house. Starting on Friday evenings and throughout most of Saturday, we'd all pile into the wagon and make deliveries. As we pulled up to each house, my brothers and I would run up to the door, make the delivery, and collect twenty-five cents for each loaf. This, mind you, was when a loaf of bread could be purchased for a nickel in the store.

FRIED CHICKEN

I take a 2½ to 3 pound chicken and clean it. Then I salt and pepper it and dredge it in flour seasoned with paprika. I like to use a heavy skillet. I put a good inch of oil in and brown the chicken well on both sides, turning it only once or twice. Then I put it in the oven, uncovered, for 10 minutes so that it gets cooked to the bone.

We never bought a chicken. Daddy raised them. He wouldn't raise anything that wasn't a thoroughbred. He had separate pens for the different breeds of chickens. He raised Rhode Island Reds, and for eggs, he raised the beautiful chickens called Black Minorcas. They were gorgeous—jet black with white combs. He wouldn't raise Leghorns; they were too scrawny. He liked chickens to be big enough so that when you ate one you could tell you were eating chicken.

Mother's Brandied Peaches

12 pounds peaches (freestone)
6 pounds sugar
3 pints bourbon or brandy

Peel fruit, cover with sugar and let stand several hours. Then boil until tender. Remove peaches and let juice cook until thick. Replace peaches, add whisky or brandy, and let stand in syrup overnight. Pack cold in sterilized jars. Seal.

Yields 6 quarts.

Mother had a special tub she kept only for washing vegetables and boiling jars to use for preserves. Her favorite peaches for these were the white freestone Georgia Belles which had dark red centers.

I HAD FOR THE MOST PART HEEDED MY MOTHER'S WARNING about not messing 'round her kitchen when she wasn't there to direct me. For the most part—but not wholly.

Mrs. Weeks had sent some brandy to Mother, asking her to put up some brandied peaches for the coming winter. It was midsummer when Mother started her preparations for canning. She preserved some freestone peaches from our orchard, using the brandy provided by Mrs. Weeks, and stored eight jars on the back porch behind the other items canned for the family, awaiting Mrs. Weeks' return from vacation. I chanced to discover them and, of course, sampled their unusual flavor—so different from what Mother usually made. I hit upon the extraordinary idea of making a peach cobbler. Under Mother's watchful eye I had indeed improved and was capable of preparing a variety of dishes. This, however, I wanted to be a surprise. I remember thinking that a cobbler made with those peaches would have to be a show stopper.

A show stopper it was, all right. I made a rich biscuit-dough, carefully measuring all of the ingredients this time, baked the cobbler and proudly presented it to the family at dessert time. Mother's first words on seeing my surprise was a taut, "Where did you get the peaches?" There was no laughter from her this time. She really laid it on me this time and concluded with an order for me to stay out of the kitchen except with her *express* permission.

When Mrs. Weeks learned why she only had six jars of brandied peaches instead of the eight she had expected, she took it in stride and laughingly commented, "Cleora certainly has good taste."

SANTA CAKE

1	cup butter
2	cups sugar
3	cups sifted cake flour
4	eggs separated
3	teaspoons baking powder
1	teaspoon vanilla
1	cup milk

Resift flour with baking powder. Cream butter and sugar until very light. Beat in egg yolks one at a time. Add vanilla. Add flour mixture by thirds alternately with milk. Gently fold in stiffly beaten egg whites. Bake in three greased 9-inch pans at 350 degrees for 30 to 35 minutes. Spread with boiled icing when cool.

Have all ingredients at room temperature.

Because of the quantities of the main ingredients, we used to call this the One-Two-Three-Four cake.

DURING WINTER MONTHS WHEN WE WERE HOUSEBOUND, Mother would conduct "cook-ins." She'd ask what we would like to cook for the day and we'd end up making two or three kinds of cookies or perhaps one of our favorite desserts. I was always partial to burnt-sugar ice cream. (Not surprisingly, I never suggested a dish made with peaches.) George liked rice pudding and Walter usually requested coconut cream pie. Joey, however, generally called out before anyone else with his favorite, apple dumplings. There was seldom an argument as we were all extremely fond of apple dumplings.

Joseph, Jr. was born two days before Christmas in 1910. I remember it was a day that an aunt had taken George, Walter and me into town to buy ingredients for Mother's very special Santa's cake. To us, this cake was somehow different from the numerous cakes Mother made during the rest of the year. However, when we arrived home, our mouths already watering in anticipation, we learned of the arrival of little Joey. Of course, a new baby brother was great news, but we knew that this also meant the Santa's cake would not be baked. I guess the disappointment showed on our three little faces. Mother, sensing our gloom as we gazed down at this little "troublemaker" nestled in her arms, suggested that we have Dr. Gregory take him back. The three of us looked at one another, then George heaved a sigh, looked at me and said, "We might as well keep him, Sis, since he's here."

Burnt Sugar Ice Cream

1⅓ cups half-and-half
2⅔ cups whipping cream
1 teaspoon pure vanilla
8 egg yolks
⅔ cup burnt sugar syrup (recipe to follow)

Mix together half-and-half, whipping cream and vanilla. Bring to a boil. In a separate bowl, beat the egg yolks with a wire whisk until smooth and creamy. Pour milk mixture over yolks, stirring briskly. Cook mixture over very low heat until the custard almost reaches the boiling point. Be careful that it does not boil or it will curdle. Add ⅔ cup burnt sugar syrup and blend thoroughly. Strain the custard through a fine sieve and chill quickly.

Freeze in a crank freezer until ice cream is firm. Pack well in ice and salt until ready to serve.

Burnt Sugar Syrup

2 cups granulated sugar
1 tablespoon water
2 cups hot water

Put 2 cups sugar in a heavy skillet, add 1 tablespoon water and heat, stirring continually, until it takes on a dark brown color, and, when a half teaspoonful is dropped in cold water, it makes a small ball that is brittle and bitter to the taste. Be careful not to burn it.

Slowly add 2 cups hot water, stirring constantly, and boil ten minutes. Let it cool. If the sugar candies when cool, add a bit more water and boil again. Bottle the syrup in sterilized jars when cold. If this is kept corked it will never spoil.

Yields one pint.

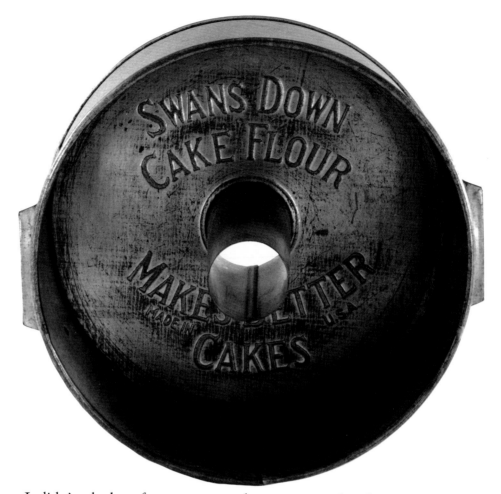

It didn't take long for us to get used to our newest brother. By the time Joey was seven or eight, he participated in Mother's cook-ins with the rest of us. Part of the learning process was having to eat what we had prepared—good or bad. Learning to be self-sufficient, especially in the kitchen, was something Mother insisted upon for all her children. We didn't mind it a bit. After all, it was a family tradition.

As the weeks and months rolled by, there were always special events like Easter with another round of culinary marvels created by Mother. I was at her side whenever possible watching and learning. In summer the menu changed. Fruits and fresh vegetables became available, and it was the season for cranking out homemade ice cream. Then, there were the periodic visits by Grandpa Manning. The most exciting of these would be the week or so before Thanksgiving when he came to butcher two of our three hogs.

Fall was the time for butchering the two large hogs that provided us with ham, bacon, and lard. The third and smaller one, a fat little porker weighing about 150 pounds, was butchered in the spring. It was used for fresh pork roasts, side meat, and for making sausage.

Grandpa arrived with his coarse salt, whole black peppercorns, home grown sage, and a canvas bag in which he crushed the peppercorns. The day before the big event, a long wooden table was constructed in the barnyard and wood was stacked by a huge iron pot filled with water. It was a great sight to see the two carcasses hanging by the barn before being cut up. If the big day was other than a Saturday (Grandpa would not butcher on a Sunday), we'd try just about any excuse to stay home from school. Of course it never worked, but we would try anyway.

I recall one of the special treats that Grandpa prepared. These were little strips of meat he called "melts." They were about three or four inches wide, ten to twelve inches long, and not over an inch and a half thick. Grandpa would skewer these on long sticks and broil them over an open fire till done. Then he'd lay them out on the long wooden table and with his large knife cut them into portions for us. If we weren't standing right there, he'd call out for us to come and get it. One summons was all it would take to bring every kid in the neighborhood, whether they were in hearing distance or not, it seemed. The "melts" looked a little like slices of liver, but oh, they tasted so deliciously different. Grandpa would say jokingly, "It's a wonder how only four grandchildren could multiply so fast."

Before he'd leave to go home, Grandpa would make his sausage. Mother would prepare sacks of cheese cloth into which the meat was packed. These would then be placed atop the other parts of the butchered hogs that had been salted and packed into boxes. I remember Grandpa's sausage as superior to any one can buy today. He made it just prior to Thanksgiving, but it was all gone by Christmas.

It was following these pre-Thanksgiving visits that all of the grandchildren would accompany Grandpa back to his farm. Besides the normal excitement of taking a vacation, there was the opportunity to see our grandmother who rarely accompanied Grandpa on his visits to Muskogee.

GRANDPA'S SAUSAGE

10	pounds fresh lean ground pork shoulder and ground tenderloin of pork, mixed
2	pounds fat trimmings off shoulder
2	tablespoons finely crumbled dried sage
2	tablespoons coarse-ground black pepper
¼	cup salt
1	(or 2) red hot peppers, finely crumbled (optional)

Place ingredients in a large bowl and mix thoroughly. If you like your sausage hot, mix in 1, or even 2 of the peppers—or take only a portion of the mixture and season it to your taste. Roll mixture into 8 to 10 foot-long sausages. Place in freezer paper, cheesecloth bags or foil. Make into patties and brown in skillet until done. Sausage can be frozen.

Each sausage serves 6-8.

GRANDMOTHER'S FRIED CORN

Use the freshest corn possible.

12 ears of fresh corn
¼ cup butter
¼ cup bacon fat
4 teaspoons sugar
  Salt and pepper

Scrape ears of corn in downward motion to get all of the milky bits usually left near the cob. Melt the butter in a large skillet and then add bacon fat. When hot, spoon in the corn and cook 15 to 20 minutes, stirring often. As corn cooks, add sugar. Add salt and pepper to taste.

Serves 8.

Betty Manning was a capable cook, although her skills never quite equalled those of her husband and daughter. But I remember especially her fried corn and her hot water cornbread, to which she sometimes added cracklin'—tiny morsels of fried pork rind.

For Grandmother's private use, Grandpa always planted eight rows of white and yellow corn in her garden just outside the farmhouse. This was, he once told us, to keep his "Betsy" (as he endearingly called her) from tearing up his field testing for the perfect ears she needed for cooking. Seems she'd just discard those that were not just right, leaving them to spoil on the ground attracting birds, squirrels and field mice.

There was an occasion when I accompanied her into her garden, holding the basket in which she collected those perfect ears. I asked her why she pulled the shuck all the way down exposing the rows of glossy kernels. Turning to face me, she pierced a grain with her thumbnail, squirting the milky fluid onto my cheek. She chuckled saying, "If'n it won't squirt, it's too old to make good fried corn." And I'll testify that her fried corn was indeed the best.

I was privileged to know and love that lady for forty-eight years of my life. She passed away in Tulsa at the age of 102.

MY MOTHER WAS NOT ONLY MY FIRST TEACHER BUT, WITHout reservation, the best. I always marveled at how she turned out so many delicious dishes on a wood-burning stove. Mother mastered things like popovers, cream puffs, all kinds of cakes—from plain pound to angel food— and won blue ribbons at the state fairs. Everything she made was produced on that unsophisticated device. Of course, I used the same kind of stove when I started, but would hesitate to do so today, now that I've become accustomed to the plethora of devices designed to help out in the kitchen. When I use my blender, mixer, or Cuisinart, I think of what a thrill Mother would have gotten using them. Late in life, long after she had established her reputation as an exquisite cook, she did use some of the appliances that became available on a limited basis when she worked as the pastry chef at Sever's Hotel in Muskogee and in the same capacity at the Ambassador Tea Room when the family moved to Tulsa in 1925.

I've always felt privileged to have her as my teacher and honored that she was my mother. I still have the flat beater she wielded so artfully while beating egg whites and boiled icings, along with many other treasured utensils she used. The tools, however, were only part of it. Throughout my young life, she filled me with confidence and taught me that cooking was a fine art. Foodstuffs were but the raw materials—the sculptor's stone, the artist's paint, the musician's instrument. Mastering the art of cooking rested on following the basic directions of a recipe (reading it four or five times if necessary), then improvising where desired. I learned early that, "dumping and stirring" could be hazardous to your results.

IMMEDIATELY FOLLOWING MY FIFTEENTH BIRTHDAY, I started my first year at Muskogee's Manual Training High School. It was a matter of course that I would take cooking, which I had decided years before was to be my profession. The freshman class in home economics was composed of about fifteen girls—five of whom were slightly older and helped cook in private homes after school and on weekends. Our teacher, Lucy Elliott, was a shy, young recent college graduate. She was known to most of the class because her brother was the proprietor of T. J. Elliott's Clothing Store where Dad bought clothes for my brothers. Mr. Elliott was also prominent in black affairs and was president of the Oklahoma State Negro Business League.

Perhaps it was the fact that there were five experienced girls in our class, coupled with the fact that we, like her, were new to the school, which prompted Miss Elliott to select our class to prepare dinner for members of the Muskogee Board of Education, who were soon to meet with our school's principals. We were very proud to have been chosen, although we had only a week to make preparations which included setting the table, serving dinner, and leaving the kitchen clean for inspection.

The classroom was equipped with a large gas range with open burners on top. Pairs of girls were assigned to smaller stoves, each equipped with two bunsen-like burners. To one side of the room was a long table for rolling out dough. Under Miss Elliott's watchful eye (most of us were unfamiliar with gas stoves), we formed teams and started our assigned tasks.

My very good friend Cynthia Mathews and I, along with Vivian Delyle, made the dinner rolls. As best as I can remember, Vivian's twin sister, Wilthian, and Edwina Nickins were responsible for the salad. Agnes Gude prepared the crabapple jelly, horseradish sauce and the other relishes required. Marie Edwards, Willie Stewart and Dorine Austine prepared the green beans while

Menu for Members of the Board of Education
Muskogee, Oklahoma
September, 1916

***

BAKED HAM
WITH HORSERADISH SAUCE
GREEN BEANS
CANDIED SWEET POTATOES
WALDORF SALAD
DINNER ROLLS
CRABAPPLE JELLY

***

LADY BALTIMORE CAKE
HOMEMADE ICE CREAM
COFFEE & TEA

VINEGAR

The H.J. Heinz Company was the first to market vinegar in individual bottles in the late 1870s. For decades afterwards, however, many women continued to make their own vinegar using "receipts" such as this one from *Woman's Favorite Cookbook* printed at the turn of the century: "Home-Made Table Vinegar. Put in an open cask four gallons of good cider and one gallon of molasses; cover the top with thin muslin and leave it in the sun, covering it up at night and when it rains. In four weeks it will be good vinegar. If Cider can not be obtained, use rainwater although it will take longer, probably four or five weeks, to make a very sharp vinegar."

another three, Ruby Smith, Delilah Manuel and Arnessa Wesley baked a ham. The ice cream and a beautiful white cake with a fruit filling topped with boiled icing was done to perfection by Quincey Glass and the Phelps twins, Vera and Era.

Friday came, the dinner was served, and we all went home knowing that we had really put on a show. We, the freshman class!

On Monday, we took our seats expectantly and awaited Miss Elliott's verdict. "Girls," she said, "your presentation at the dinner was superb. I showed you the theory and you all performed like pros." She concluded, "In fact, I believe you've secured my job."

We squealed with delight, jumped up and down and hugged each other as Miss Elliott beamed at us. I guess we strutted around that school for weeks.

MY BROTHERS, JOE AND WALTER, AND OUR COUSIN DUDE also had lessons to learn. (At fifteen, George had left home to make his own way in the world.) Their chores on our mini-farm continued, with the small garden plus the chickens, cows and hogs to be taken care of.

One autumn, just prior to Grandfather's annual hog butchering visit, Big Red, one of our two cows, had just been returned from an unsuccessful breeding attempt at a nearby stud farm. As we went to bed that evening, the sound of her continued anguish could be heard coming from the barn. While he lay in bed, my father kept one ear tuned towards Big Red, and at one point must have realized that the bell around her neck was clanging from a place somewhat more distant than the barnyard. Big Red was loose!

Dad and a neighbor, Bob Howard, combed the neighborhood. Zeroing in on the bell, they finally located Big Red and returned her to our barnyard. As Dad led her into the barn, she bolted once again. This time, however, she bolted straight into her stall with such force that she crashed head first against the far wall. Dad called out to Mr. Howard who had just reached his house down the street, and the commotion brought all of us out of the house even though it was well past midnight.

Walter and I watched as the grownups discussed the situation. Big Red was dead and Mr. Howard (a butcher by trade) suggested that she be strung up so that the carcass could be cut up as soon as possible. Mr. Howard went across the street to pick up his tools. When he returned, he had another surprise for us. His son, Wallace—who had gone to the movies with Joey and Dude much earlier—was not home. A quick search revealed that my brother and cousin were not home either.

Joe was only thirteen years old. Dude was fourteen and Wally Howard was, at fifteen, the oldest. Emulating our brother George, they had taken off to find their fortunes. Mother was in a tizzy. Dad, however, had more pressing matters at hand. Besides, he reasoned, at one or two in the morning there would be little chance of finding them. They already had a six or seven hour headstart.

It was a glum group around the breakfast table the next morning. In hushed tones, Walter and I had discussed the previous night's events as we went about our early morning chores. Now, however, we sat as silent as the two empty chairs across the table.

Mother and Dad agreed that the boys must have headed for Tulsa. If that were indeed the case, and they had in fact reached the city, it could be assumed that they were safe. A telephone call was placed to Mother's sister Minnie who worked for a family in Tulsa. She, in turn, contacted George who was employed in a factory there. Within hours, George found them, as he knew he would, wandering along Greenwood Avenue, the main street of Tulsa's famous black business district.

The three runaways started in surprise as the familiar figure of George approached them from half a block away—not sure that this meeting was by chance or, as a sinking feeling hinted, that he had been looking for them.

George took them to breakfast, knowing they couldn't have more than a few dollars between them. Being unsuccessful in dissuading the three from continuing on their unrealistic journey to Kansas City, George excused himself, promising to return in a few minutes. He returned all right, accompanied by two friends, Sam Morgan and Brit Sims—both uniformed Tulsa police officers.

As George and the police entered the restaurant, the teenagers' defiance flew out the door and they listened to the officers' simple choice: Muskogee or jail. That evening, everyone was present for dinner in the Thomas household.

There was no punishment meted out. My father simply told Joe and Dude

MOTHER'S PICKLED CAULIFLOWER AND CUCUMBERS

1   large head cauliflower
1   quart small green tomatoes, cut in wedges
3   green peppers, cut in strips
2½   cups green lima beans
1   quart pickling onions, peeled
24   cucumbers (2-inch)
1   cup coarse salt
1   cup sugar
¾   cup flour
½   cup Coleman's mustard
1   tablespoon tumeric
7   cups cider vinegar
7   cups water

Break cauliflower into flowerets. Combine with tomatoes, peppers, limas, onions and cucumbers. Cover with salt and 4 cups water. Let stand overnight. Drain. Cover with boiling water. Let stand 10 minutes. Drain. Combine remaining ingredients in preserving kettle and cool until thick. Add vegetables. Cook until just tender. Seal in sterilized jars at once.

Yields 8 pints.

that they didn't have to run away. When they again thought they were ready to go out and face the world alone, he'd not only help them pack but also see that they had enough money to get wherever they wished to go. And indeed, he did just that for each and every one of us when, over the years, our moments of departure arrived.

MUCH OF MY LEISURE TIME WAS SPENT WITH MY VERY BEST friend Eva Flowers. Eva and I had met when we joined the girl's basketball team in high school. Our backgrounds were different—she came from a very well-to-do family, while my parents enjoyed a modest, yet comfortable style of living. (Those things sometimes made a difference, even in those days, and even among blacks.) Yet, we took to one another on first sight. Neither of us played basketball well, but being on the team placed us in one another's company more often.

When time came for Eva to go away to Oberlin Junior College, my parents scraped together enough money for me to go with her, although I was unable to go back after the first year.

The warm friendship made us like sisters. We were constantly at one or the other's home, sharing stories about boyfriends, clothing styles and other important events that fill the lives of teenage girls. It was then much as it is today, sixty-four years later.

In 1921 Eva sent word from college that she and Jake Simmons of Haskell, Oklahoma had gotten married. They had been sweethearts for years so it didn't come as a surprise. Jake came from a pioneer family that had been in Oklahoma long before statehood. His great-grandfather, Cal Tom Ferguson, was of Creek Indian heritage and had been a rancher and prominent leader in local affairs.

Jacob Simmons, Sr., successfully managed the ranch and farm with his sons, including Jake, Jr., who worked long hard hours when he wasn't out courting Eva.

I was overjoyed at my best friend's fortune, but less than joyful about my own. Instead of cooking roasts, experimenting with unusual combinations of vegetables, or baking breads, cakes, and the like, as I really wanted to do, this period found me cleaning the second floor of Muskogee's Central High at the close of each school day. I helped Mother of course, endeavoring to polish my skills under her expert tutelage, but there wasn't much of a market for teenage cooks in Muskogee.

EARLY IN THE SUMMER OF 1923, MY AUNT MINNIE CAME home for a weekend visit with the news that her employer's neighbor needed someone to take over their kitchen. My heart leapt to hear that she had recommended me; and it leapt again when Dad finally gave his consent for me to go. There was some concern because of the racial disturbances in Tulsa two years earlier. But since both Aunt Minnie and my brother George would be close by, it was considered safe. I dashed over to my friend Eva's house to tell her and Jake the marvelous news. I was going to strike out on my own! Preparations were made, goodbyes were said, and the following week I boarded the train for Tulsa. Aunt Minnie met me at Union Depot and took me to her quarters at the home where she worked. On Monday morning we went to meet my employers, Mr. and Mrs. Charles Robertson. Mrs. Robertson sat and talked with me a while before taking me into the kitchen to meet the cook.

Hattie was a large woman, older than I, who was moving north. She greeted me pleasantly and did all she could during the remainder of her stay to make me feel comfortable. By the time Hattie left, I was thoroughly familiar with the kitchen and properly instructed in the ways and habits of the Robertsons. With her departure I moved into the cook's quarters over the garage. The accommodations were spacious indeed—three rooms with nice furniture.

I had truly come into my own. I was twenty-two years old, had a real job as a *cook* and was earning fourteen dollars a week!

Mrs. Robertson sensed that it might be difficult for me to adjust to being away from my family. After I had been there only a few weeks, she paid my fare home to Muskogee, possibly forestalling an onslaught of homesickness.

When I arrived back in Muskogee, everyone was thrilled at my success, especially my three closest friends, who were agog that I had really "made it" in the big city. They were so impressed that when my two-day visit was over, they were waiting at the train station with me, ready to go seek their fortunes in Tulsa. One had worked as a soda fountain clerk there the year before and was sure she could get her old job back. Another had experience as a manicurist and the third was quite accomplished in the kitchen.

The four of us showed up at the Robertson's home, baggage in hand, midday on Sunday. Mrs. Robertson was surprised, but unflappable, and she welcomed my friends into her home. When they told her they had come to Tulsa to find jobs just like I had, she invited them to stay there with me and promised to do all she could to assist them in finding employment. The very next day, she had twin beds moved into my quarters so we could sleep more comfortably.

It only took a few weeks for my friends to find situations. It was really a relief and a lot of fun having three school friends with me. Until they left, they helped about the house, cleaning, making beds and doing other household chores. Then too, I had company exploring the section around Greenwood Avenue where the majority of black Tulsans lived.

Tulsa in the mid-20s was already the social and commercial hub of northeast Oklahoma. It was *the* place to be. One black entrepreneur had reportedly moved to Tulsa and opened up a bank account with $75,000 *in cash*! Everybody was caught up in the high style of living that was characteristic of the entire nation.

After my first year, Mrs. Robertson raised my salary to $17.50 a week, explaining that it was what she had been paying Hattie before she left. She had offered me the lower salary only because she couldn't conceive that one so young and tiny, (especially compared to Hattie), could be as qualified.

In 1924 my father came to work in Tulsa as a cook for a family that had moved from Muskogee. Yes, Dad was part of the tradition too. It was unavoidable, as you might imagine, living with Mother and being around his father-in-law for so many years. Dad also had "cook-ins" with Mother—in private, you might say. He'd stay the week in Tulsa and return to Muskogee each weekend. Occasionally Mother would come back with him and stay a few days. Other times she would spend several days with me in my quarters over the garage. These visits eventually led her to pick up her sewing basket again, as Mrs. Robertson, upon learning of this "hidden" talent, paid her to make clothes for her daughter.

The entire family moved up to Tulsa in 1925. Dad went to work for the Mayo Furniture Company and Mother was hired as pastry chef at the newly opened Ambassador Tea Room. My brother George had struck out on his own several years before. Walter, who had studied music while away in school, went off to Minot, North Dakota, to join a traveling swing band. Later, Joey also took up music and moved up to New York City to join Walter.

Telltale signs of the coming economic disaster began to make themselves evident as early as 1927. The Robertsons had to dismiss me because of the failure of a silver mine in Mexico in which their money was invested. It wiped out their reserves. I spent the next few years filling in for vacationing cooks and

CLEORA BUTLER IN THE 1930s.

was able to work at elaborate parties still given by those who either did not see where the nation was heading, or refused to believe what they saw. As things got tougher, I found occasional situations as a maid. My earnings amounted to about $20 or $25 weekly, which was not bad considering the times. Mother and Dad were both working, and together we purchased a comfortable home on Kenosha Avenue in North Tulsa. It was one of the few two-story homes in the area.

THE GREAT CRASH CAME. IT BROUGHT MANY CHANGES TO the lives of Tulsa's citizens, both rich and poor. Social life, however, continued, and I free-lanced, catering private parties. However, there were significant changes in the style of entertaining. Many parties were farewell affairs—given by or on behalf of those whose fortunes had tumbled. Many well-to-do families and even a number of wealthy ones chose to leave Tulsa rather than remain living there in comparatively poorer circumstances. Many, however, managed to survive and a few even prospered to a degree.

A very good friend of mine was employed as the butler for one of the families that had managed to hold on during those desperate years. The George W. Snedden family lived in a fine, but modest, home on South Denver Avenue in Tulsa. Mr. Snedden, the son of Scotch immigrants, worked tirelessly in the oil fields outside of Tulsa and in other parts of Oklahoma. He was often away for weeks, joining his family whenever he could on weekends. The Sneddens employed only a cook and my friend the butler (who doubled as the family chauffeur). In the late 1930s when the cook announced that she would be leaving after her forthcoming marriage, my friend recommended me as her replacement.

It was good to be working full time again, especially when work of any kind was almost impossible to come by. Tulsa, despite the nation's continuing need for oil, still had its share of bread lines. My starting salary with the Sneddens was $15 weekly—a highly respectable wage in those days. Both Mother and Dad were working and my brothers helped out as much as possible, especially Walter who was playing saxophone with a band then called the Missourians, that was shortly to become the Cab Calloway Orchestra. Times may have been tough, but the Thomas/Manning clan was holding its own.

Frugality was the watchword in the early thirties and stretching the dollar was an absolute necessity for everyone. Mr. Snedden had been fortunate in his investments and had not suffered as much as most had. This factor, plus (as he used to put it) working hip-deep in oil field mud week after week, enabled his family to live comfortably and to afford a few of life's amenities. Mr. and Mrs. Snedden had two teenage children living at home and another son away for his first year of college. My responsibilities therefore were minimal. The children took care of their own room and the housecleaning chores were shared among the butler, Mrs. Snedden, and myself.

Tulsa's black community had felt the effects of the financial crash long before October of 1929. Money had already become scarce on the north side of town, where most blacks lived, and unemployment had been growing since 1927. Still everyone loved parties and a good time as much as they ever did, even though few could afford to throw a bash for even four or six friends. Our way around this was for everyone to bring something. We'd get together and brew our own beer. Then each would bring his or her share of ingredients for the planned menu. It always turned out to be an exciting evening.

After the bottom dropped out, the well-to-do (and not a few of the wealthy) followed our example. Mr. and Mrs. Snedden were part of a group of twelve couples who gathered periodically for dinner, sharing proportionately the cost of the evening. Their parties were perhaps more grandiose than those we had, but I know they were never more fun.

Mr. and Mrs. Snedden had long planned to build an elegant home on a five-acre plot they owned. This property extended from South Boston Avenue to the Arkansas River. The economic catastrophe, however, had put those plans on the shelf. In 1932, Mr. Snedden learned of the availability of an estate located on South Peoria Avenue. The owner, Arthur J. Hull, while not wiped out by the depression, had suffered a financial setback. In order to cut his family's living expenses, Mr. Hull decided to sell his estate and move to a smaller home the family owned, also on South Peoria. Mr. Hull's misfortune provided the opportunity for the Sneddens to move into a home that befitted their rising fortune. After weeks of bargaining, the Sneddens purchased the estate.

To merely describe the property as magnificent would be an injustice. South Peoria and 24th Street, while part of the City of Tulsa, was at that time pure country. The Hull estate covered thirteen acres. In addition to the eighteen-room main house, there were two greenhouses and a solarium for tropical plants. The three-car garage had a two-room apartment on the ground level and two additional apartments above for household staff. There were also two five-room cottages on the estate, a swimming pool and two barns for the stabling of horses. It was one of the most elegant homes in Tulsa, a far cry above the two bedroom house on South Denver.

Geraldine Snedden was beside herself with joy. She arranged for the Tulsa Garden Club to hold one of its monthly meetings in the new house even before they moved in. George Snedden, at all times a warm and concerned human being, was nonetheless careful when it came to spending money. Mr. Hull had employed a staff of eleven that included four gardeners, two butlers and two maids (one for upstairs and one for downstairs). They also employed a chauffeur and laundress and, naturally, there was a cook. Mr. Snedden decided that he could not maintain such a large staff lest he find himself in the same

RECIPE FOR HOME BREW

1 can Blue Ribbon light malt
10 pounds sugar
2 cakes Red Star yeast
1 cup rice
   Warm water

Pour over half the sugar into a five-gallon crock. Pour malt into the crock, rinsing the can with hot water and scraping with spatula to get all the malt out. Stir well, until sugar and malt are dissolved. Fill crock with warm water to about three inches from the top, allowing it space not to boil over. Let cool to lukewarm, dissolve yeast in a little warm water, pour into crock and stir well. When cool, put a cup of rice in. Cover the crock with newspaper and let it boil up until all the skim comes up on the newspaper. Change to clean paper. Let it set about 3 days. Add about 3 more cups of sugar. Stir carefully so the mixture doesn't splash out of the crock.

Spiced Tea

½ cup orange Pekoe tea leaves
1 tablespoon ground cinnamon
1 tablespoon ground cloves
1½ teaspoons allspice
1 cup orange juice
⅔ cup lemon juice
2 cups sugar

Mix tea and spices together; pour in 4 cups boiling water. Let stand 3 hours. Strain through a double thickness of cheesecloth. Add orange and lemon juices and sugar. Add enough boiling water to make 1 gallon.

The George W. Snedden home, ca. 1935.

predicament as had Mr. Hull. He retained one of the four gardeners and hired a new woman as laundress. He might have considered retaining the cook, a talented woman of renowned experience, but I am sure that had she been offered the position, she would have declined. You see, this amazing cook who had prepared all the meals for the Hull household was none other than Maggie Thomas, my mother.

Having visited Mother at her place of employment on many occasions, I was already somewhat familiar with the house, and with the kitchen in particular. Although the house was nicely appointed, the Sneddens decided to redecorate and hired Louis Perry, one of Tulsa's most distinguished interior decorators, to formalize their desires. Both Mr. and Mrs. Snedden involved themselves in the undertaking. Mr. Snedden had an excellent eye for color and together with Mr. Perry determined the color schemes for many of the rooms. A multi-colored carpet of soft pastel shades, woven in Australia, was Mr. Snedden's personal selection for the music and drawing rooms.

The sixteen-by-twenty-foot kitchen, however, was created by Mr. Perry from the combined ideas of Mrs. Snedden and myself, ideas that evolved through many discussions (sometimes very heated) among the three of us. Of particular

note was the magnificent professional-size restaurant range (in which I once roasted a fifteen-pound pig), the walk-in refrigerator and the butcher block worktable constructed in the center of the room with storage bins below and a rack above for hanging pots and pans. This kind of arrangement might not be uncommon today, but Louis Perry helped us create a truly professional kitchen that was unusual in its time.

Adjacent to this well arranged working space was a lounge for the servants, a butler's pantry complete with sink, utility storage space with shelves for the "good" dishes, and a closet containing a combination safe for the Snedden's collection of fine silver. One of the more unusual pieces stored there was a kidney shaped antique silver butler's tray, designed to conform to the contour of a rotund servant.

As it turned out, Mr. Snedden did not live to see the completion of his dream. That was left for Mrs. Snedden to continue. Today their home is the beautiful Tulsa Garden Center, and stands as a tribute to their painstaking efforts. I've always considered myself privileged to have lived and worked in such grand surroundings, particularly because I lovingly watched it grow into what it is today.

Of the hundreds of meals and countless parties I either prepared or supervised for the Snedden family, the most memorable occurred during the summer of 1936. It was occasioned by the presentation of the younger George Snedden's new bride, Elizabeth Borum of Cedarvale, Kansas, to Tulsa society.

Some three hundred guests had been invited to this gala tea party. Waiters from the exclusive Tulsa Club were decked out in tuxedos. A splendid variety of tea dainties had been prepared by my good friend Lucille Williams. My responsibility was limited to the preparation of two recipes that Mr. Snedden's sister brought with her from Oklahoma City. One was for *Orange Nut Bread*, and the other for *Spiced Tea*. The latter was entirely new to me, but I carefully looked over the list of ingredients and calculated what would be required to serve three hundred guests.

The preceding day, I mixed and baked fifty loaves of orange nut bread and refrigerated them along with a large quantity of fresh butter that came from a farm in nearby Broken Arrow. Then, with ground cinnamon, cloves and allspice, together with orange pekoe tea and three gallons of boiling water, I made the base for twelve gallons of spiced tea. That too was refrigerated.

Early on the eventful day, I started buttering the bread—just enough to get a bit of a jump on the crowd. Next came the tea. With a full gallon of freshly-squeezed orange juice, a half gallon of lemon juice, and twenty-four cups of sugar (all divided into portions for making one gallon of tea at a time when mixed with the base prepared the previous day), I sailed through the afternoon. Each slice of bread was served freshly buttered and the teapots were kept filled. The combination stole the show.

ORANGE NUT BREAD

6   California oranges
1   rounded teaspoon soda
1   cup sugar

BREAD:

3   eggs
1   cup sugar
2   tablespoons melted butter or margarine
1   cup broken pecan meats
3   teaspoons baking powder
1   teaspoon salt
1   cup orange rind syrup
3   cups all-purpose flour
1   cup milk

Remove orange rinds, place in kettle and cover with cold water. Add soda; let come to boil and cook for 5 minutes. Drain.

Wash rinds in cold water to remove pithy pulp inside. Cut rinds with scissors into small pieces. Use the following proportions to make syrup: 1 cup orange rind, 1 cup sugar and ½ cup water. Let mixture cook to a thick syrup. Pour in sterilized jars. Keep for Orange Nut Bread.

To prepare the bread, mix eggs, sugar and melted butter. Mix nuts with baking powder, flour and salt. Add 1 cup orange rind syrup to first mixture, then add nuts and flour alternately with milk.

Place wax paper cut to fit bottoms of 2 loaf pans. Grease sides of pans. Divide batter into pans. Bake at 350 degrees about 1 hour.

Yields 2 loaves.

WALTER THOMAS, CA. 1930.

By 1936, ECONOMIC CONDITIONS WERE BEGINNING TO improve although many were still struggling. My father still worked for the Mayo Furniture Company and Mother baked half a dozen cakes each day for the tea room at the Brown Duncan department store downtown. The band with whom brother Walter played, now called the Cab Calloway Orchestra, was becoming famous because of radio broadcasts from the well-known Cotton Club in New York City. We'd gather around the radio whenever they were on, cheering every saxophone solo, convinced it was our very own Walter being heard across the nation.

Each year, the Cab Calloway Orchestra and stage show came to town. Once they would play at the old Orpheum Theatre for Tulsa's whites, and then they would play again for the black community. As a matter of fact, all the popular bands—Ellington, Basie, Lunceford and the like—came to play at the Crystal Palace Ballroom on Greenwood Avenue just off Archer Street. The ballroom was situated upstairs over the Dixie Theatre and almost any attraction there drew a tremendous crowd.

Whenever they were in town, Walter and Cab stayed at our home on North Kenosha. While traveling about the country, Walter bragged continually about his mother's cooking to members of the orchestra. Consequently, at one point during their stay in Tulsa it was mandatory that Mother (with my assistance) put on our own show for them. Cab Calloway became one of Mother's greatest supporters, telling everyone that a body could never have a finer meal than at Maggie Thomas' home in Tulsa, Oklahoma.

In June of 1937, the band was in Tulsa for its annual visit. The event of the year, if not the decade, was at hand: the World Heavyweight Championship fight between Joe Louis and Max Schmeling. I imagine the entire country was excited because the contest was something of an international grudge match. The two had met the year before, but the win by Joe Louis after twelve rounds of fighting had been disputed by many. The earlier fight had not been for the title. This one was for the boxing championship of the world!

At least half of the orchestra members, along with their wives or girlfriends, were gathered in our front yard. Some of my friends were there and so were some of our neighbors who didn't have radios. My grandfather was also present, not as spry as he had been when my brothers and I used to visit his farm after Thanksgiving each year, but still active, and growing corn and okra in a field just down the street. My grandmother, Betty, was there and in the yard with the neighborhood children were Walter's son and daughter who lived with us in Tulsa while he and his wife toured the country.

Fried chicken and all the picnic trimmings imaginable were on hand, including homemade ice cream, to celebrate Joe Louis' certain victory.

People were still arriving when the bell sounded for the first round. Some were just milling about. Others were busy filling their paper plates with chicken and potato salad, and a few were getting settled to listen to the fight. The children were still running about, being shushed by adults intent on the unfolding event. Suddenly a loud cheer arose from those close to the radio. The fight was over! The Brown Bomber had knocked the big German out cold in the first round!

The blacks of North Tulsa literally danced in the streets. This was a most special occasion. We didn't often get a chance to cheer about anything, let alone a hero of our very own.

For a number of years I had been courted by one man in particular who at last convinced me that it was time for us to marry. I reluctantly left the Snedden family—ironically for the same reason as had my predecessor eleven years before. In 1940 I changed my name to Mrs. George R. Butler. My new husband

GEORGE R. BUTLER AND CLEORA THOMAS BUTLER IN 1940.

Coconut Torte with Butter Sauce

½   cup butter
1   cup sugar (minus 1 tablespoon)
4   egg whites
1   7-ounce package moist, shredded
    coconut
1   teaspoon vanilla

Cream the butter and sugar until light and add coconut. Fold into stiffly beaten egg whites and add vanilla. Pour into shallow 9x13-inch pan. Set pan in hot water and bake in 325 degree oven for 45 minutes. Let cool and cut into squares.

needed more time than my free hours permitted, so I had no alternative but to leave work. However, I stayed on intermittently with the Sneddens until the next year. I was, in fact, serving a dinner party for Mrs. Snedden the day the Japanese attacked Pearl Harbor.

In 1942 Tulsa was gearing up for war. There were parties galore, especially in the beginning when most everyone thought the whole thing would be over in a matter of months if not weeks. When sons and daughters, fathers, uncles and aunts were going away, people said, "Let's have a party!," so I did a lot of catering during that period. I've always felt it was a little like returning to the roaring twenties. There were parties all over the place. Parties for departing soldiers and sailors and a lot of parties given for no specific reason at all.

When I started working for the Paul J. McIntyre family in 1944 it was because they needed someone temporarily to replace their retiring cook. A few weeks later when Mrs. McIntyre left early for vacation, I was asked to remain another week or two and cook for Mr. McIntyre until he left to join the rest of the family in Colorado. This temporary situation led to many memorable years working in the McIntyre household.

When it came to entertaining, Mr. McIntyre was as much a part of the scene as was Mrs. McIntyre. He participated in the planning of most of their dinner parties. If something special could not be obtained locally, Mr. McIntyre would see to it that it was ordered from wherever in the world it was available. On one occasion the guests had devoured every one of fourteen trout shipped overnight by train from a fishery in Denver. Because none was left for the help who had expected to share at least one or two bites of this rarely served treat, Mr. McIntyre ordered another dozen the following day—just for his employees.

On another occasion, the McIntyres gave a dinner for Mr. and Mrs. Waite Phillips, who had accumulated an oil fortune in Tulsa and generously shared their wealth through numerous philanthropic projects. The Phillips were moving to California, leaving their mansion, Villa Philbrook, to the city as an art museum. For the farewell dinner party I prepared a *Coconut Torte* with a butter sauce for dessert. Following dinner, Mrs. Phillips came into the kitchen, not only to congratulate the staff on the boned squab stuffed with wild rice, but also to secure my recipe for the torte, (with her promise to never pass it on to anyone). I told her she was most welcome to pass it on to anyone she wished, explaining I felt it was little enough in return for the many wonderful things the Phillips family had done for the citizens of North Tulsa.

Christmas dinner at the McIntyre's was always a festive gathering to which twelve guests were invited. As a standard part of this occasion, a steamed fig pudding was served for dessert. The recipe had been handed down in Mrs. McIntyre's family for many generations, having been brought from Scotland by her great grandmother.

BUTTER SAUCE

½ cup butter
1 cup sugar (minus 1 tablespoon)
4 egg yolks
1 whole egg, beaten
1 teaspoon vanilla
1½ jiggers brandy (optional)
 dash of nutmeg

Combine butter and sugar as above and stir in egg yolks and beaten egg. Cook in double boiler until thick, stirring constantly. Strain to remove any bits of egg white. Stir in remaining ingredients.

Serve over torte with your favorite ice cream.

Serves 8 to 10 persons.

STEAMED FIG PUDDING

1   12-ounce package figs
1   cup milk
1   teaspoon soda
1   cup ground suet
1   cup sugar
3   eggs
2   cups bread crumbs
1   cup flour
1   teaspoon baking powder
1   teaspoon nutmeg
1   teaspoon cinnamon
½   teaspoon salt

In saucepan, heat figs, milk and soda 5 minutes. Let cool. Cream suet, sugar and egg well. Add fig mixture, crumbs, flour, baking powder, spices and salt. Mix well. Grease mold, sprinkle generously with sugar. Fill mold ⅔ full. Steam 3 hours or until done.

SAUCE:

½   cup butter
1   cup sugar
3   eggs
½   pint heavy cream, whipped
1   teaspoon vanilla
⅓   (to ½) cup bourbon or brandy

For the sauce, cream butter and sugar until light and fluffy. Add eggs, 1 at a time, beating well after each one. Fold whipped cream in butter, sugar and egg mixture. Add vanilla and bourbon with a few gratings of nutmeg.

Hamburger buns make better, fluffier crumbs.

One year, with Mrs. McIntyre's approval, I served a different dessert at this annual affair. Following the meal, however, her guest barged into the kitchen demanding an explanation for the break in tradition, exclaiming, "When we come to the McIntyre's for these special dinners, we expect fig pudding. *Always!*"

As much as I enjoyed working for the McIntyres, in the spring of 1951 I was forced to leave the family. My father-in-law had developed cancer several years before and now his condition had deteriorated to the point were he required constant care. Mrs. McIntyre expressed great sadness over the necessity of my leaving but, naturally, understood. I promised to remain available for special occasions. She, in turn, made sure all of her friends knew of my availability for catering dinner parties, luncheons or similar events.

Tears accompanied my last day at the home on Hazel Boulevard and, with their usual kindness, the McIntyres presented me with a substantial cash gift as a token of their appreciation of the seven years I had spent with them.

AMONG THE MANY GRACIOUS FAMILIES FOR WHOM I PRE-
pared special parties were the Howard J. Whitehills. There was an ease and joy
in planning affairs with Mrs. Whitehill, as she was methodical and deeply
concerned that each participant would find that which pleased him or her most
when being entertained in the Whitehill home. Entertaining for the Whitehills
ran the gamut from brunch to cocktail parties, from simple but elegant
luncheons to a black-tie bon voyage dinner party for twenty-six friends leaving
on an "Around the World in Eighty Days" sojourn. At that dinner, I recall, Mrs.
Whitehill personally mixed a special dressing at the table to serve with wedges
of lettuce.

For the Whitehills the year-end holidays were especially festive. New Year's
dinner included the traditional hog jowl with black-eyed peas, corn pone,
smoked turkey, baked ham, beef tenderloin, mustard, cheeses, both rye and
pumpernickle bread, fruitcake and eggnog (plus whatever was left over from
Christmas).

The days immediately following the holidays, however, were the ones most
eagerly awaited by those of us who had worked so diligently throughout the
year. The Whitehills annually invited their staff and their staff's families to
vacation at their estate, Clarion Ridge, on Grand Lake just northeast of Tulsa
near Grove, Oklahoma. The employees of friends of the Whitehills were also
invited to come and bring their families. My husband and I were always
included.

We'd go up on Friday. The main house, the two guest houses and the helper's
cottage were opened up to accommodate the group. A fire would be struck in
the grand fireplace and the bar and the cupboards opened—champagne, fresh
caviar and all. Dinner was usually served early (exquisitely and collectively
prepared by the best cooks in Tulsa), after which we'd play games or exchange
jokes overheard at some of the parties our employers had given.

Saturdays would be filled with individual pursuits. Those who liked fished
off the Whitehill's private dock. Others strolled along the shore of Grand Lake
or roamed the beautiful woods that adorned the estate.

Come Saturday evening, we'd all gather in the living room around a huge
basket of wrapped gifts, each with a long string attached that trailed out onto
the floor. These were "white elephant" gifts contributed by our friends,
employers and ourselves. None were identified. We merely pulled the strings in

EGGNOG

9	eggs, separated
¾	cup sugar
1	cup light cream
¾	cup rye whiskey
2	tablespoons brandy
1	cup heavy cream, whipped
	Nutmeg

Several hours before serving:
In a large bowl, with mixer at medium
speed, beat egg yolks with ½ cup of the
sugar until light and fluffy, (about 5
minutes). Now beat in light cream, then
whiskey and brandy; cover and
refrigerate. Also refrigerate egg whites.
Fifteen minutes before serving:
Beat egg whites until soft peaks are
formed; beat in ¼ cup sugar; pour egg
mixture through a strainer into egg
whites; blend thoroughly and fold in
whipped cream. Sprinkle with nutmeg
and serve in cups.

Yields 18 to 20 4-ounce cups.

*This recipe was given to me by Louise
Pacetti.*

turn until all the gifts were distributed. Each had a number on it. Three of these were lucky numbers that entitled the holder to an additional special gift. I once received a still-treasured set of crystal salt and pepper shakers.

After an early dinner on Sunday, we rested and prepared ourselves for the return home. If, as happened once in a while, the lake was not frozen over, we would get an additional treat—a boat ride on Grand Lake. The weekend was topped off with a round of songs and more jokes. Relaxed, happy, and with an optimistic outlook towards the coming year, we returned to Tulsa and our respective tasks.

I DID NOT COOK EXTENSIVELY IN THE EARLY 50S. MY HUS-band worked at the Bliss Hotel downtown at South Boston and Third Street and I enjoyed the luxury of staying at home, taking care of Papa Butler. Of course, there were the occasional catering jobs for a select group of patrons, but I spent a lot of time designing and making hats.

My career as a hatmaker resulted from an unfortunate shopping experience in the 1940s. A new and very exclusive store that had opened in downtown Tulsa was conducting a special sale on hats. Since my teens, I had had a special love of hats and was known among my friends for my collection.

While society in the 1940s had changed to the point where blacks could shop in a few white establishments, it was not usually permitted for one to try on clothing, especially hats and shoes. Occasionally, you might be permitted to try on a hat, but you were given a hand mirror and shown to a back room where "preferred" customers could not see you trying on your selection.

The hat I wanted was exquisite, so despite the horrible treatment, I purchased it. In fact, I bought two, but left the store absolutely infuriated and totally resolved never to buy another hat as long as I lived. Because of my continuing passion for hats, however, I found a way out of my problem. Research turned up a millinery correspondence school in Chicago, in which I immediately enrolled. By the time I left the McIntyres I had become quite proficient at the millinery craft and was able to sell hats to my friends in North Tulsa—often at the very respectable price of $50 apiece.

The mid-fifties found me getting restless, being home most of the day. So, when the opportunity came for me to work in a dress shop, Nan Pendleton's in downtown Tulsa, I grabbed at it. The owner of another dress shop had recommended me and following a brief interview with the owner, Maybelle Lauder, I was hired as stock clerk. The work was certainly different from any I had ever done before, but the hours were convenient and it offered me the chance to meet my husband from time to time at the newly opened lunch room in Vandevers Department Store—one of the first downtown establishments to cater to all of Tulsa's citizens.

My duties at the dress shop permitted me to continue my catering work and with Mrs. Lauder's encouragement I added several of her customers to my growing list of patrons. It was in this manner that I became acquainted with Mrs. Gifford C. Parker.

I often prepared luncheons at the Parker home for members of the various organizations to which Mrs. Parker belonged. Working for her was a pleasure because, like so many of the people for whom I had worked over the years, Gladys Parker was a perfectionist. She always made each occasion an artistic one. When serving salmon, for instance, she would have the table set with pink crystal, gold flatware, flowers and other appointments that created a totally coordinated effect. Sometimes the special look was achieved with favors such as little glass bars that magnified small print or tiny memo books for recording birthdates —always in colors that matched the overall theme. It was Mrs. Parker who recommended that I prepare a buffet dinner for her son Robert.

The Parker family owned a game preserve (in Kansas, I believe) and for this affair had chosen to serve a selection of game birds that had been caught there. To be prepared were twelve pheasants, a bevy of quail, two wild ducks and ten pigeon-like birds called chukars. The preparation of eighty birds or more required assistance, so I called on Charles Ross, one of Tulsa's finest chefs who, more than anyone else I knew, was an expert on the cooking of game.

We quartered the pheasants, halved the wild ducks and roasted them at one time. The sixty or so hand-sized quail and ten chukars were fricasseed together in a brown gravy. Each was then served on its own platter. The game birds were accompanied by wild rice, asparagus, poached pears and hot buttered rolls. Dessert was comprised of bite-sized tarts filled with lemon, chocolate and pecans.

Employing the same grand flair with which the elder Mrs. Parker presented food, Mr. Parker and his wife arranged natural settings for each of the various fowl, spread out on a sixty-foot banquet table. Lifelike pheasants, quail, ducks and chukars were stuffed in a manner that made their brilliant plumage sparkle in the light of the chandeliers. It was one of the most impressive dinner arrangements I've ever seen. Charles and I were pleased to receive accolades for the tasty game birds which had been prepared (as dictated by Parker family tradition) without the use of wine or alcohol.

My years at Nan Pendleton's Dress Shop were to lay the foundation for many things yet to come in my life. I met people from every strata of Tulsa society. When Mrs. Lauder decided to sell the shop in 1961, I determined that it was time for me to move on as well. My free-lance catering work was substantial and I felt ready to start my own business. My husband and I applied for and received one of the first Small Business Administration loans granted in North Tulsa. After selecting a promising site on bustling Pine Street and following two months of outfitting the space, we celebrated the opening of Cleora's

BAKED FUDGE

4	eggs
2	cups sugar
1	cup butter
1	cup pecans, broken in large pieces
4	heaping tablespoons cocoa
4	rounded tablespoons flour
2	teaspoon vanilla

Beat eggs well; add sugar and butter and beat well again. Sift cocoa and flour together. Add broken pecan meats. Fold into sugar, butter and egg mixture. Add vanilla. Pour in 9x12 by 3-inch Pyrex dish or tin pan. Set pan in a pan of hot water (enough to come ½ to 1 inch up on sides of pan). Bake in a 325 degree oven for 45 minutes to 1 hour. Fudge will have the consistency of firm custard and will be crusty on top. Serve with a dollop of whipped cream on each piece.

Serves 9 to 12.

Baked Fudge was a favorite dessert at Cleora's Pastry Shop, and is now served at The Garden, a Tulsa restaurant.

Pastry Shop and Catering in April of 1962.

The concept of having a pastry shop as the base for my catering business was not exactly a spur-of-the-moment idea. Back in the 40s between times I worked for the Sneddens and the McIntyres, our family income was supplemented by selling small pies in my father-in-law's billiard parlor in North Tulsa for five cents each. With my mother's help, we baked some 150 pies every day, right out of my own kitchen. Even more recently, through a contact made at the dress shop, I had been baking tarts each week for Tex Meyer, the owner of a lunch room in the Brookside section of south Tulsa.

Granted, we anticipated a lot of work, but we had no idea of what was involved in running your own business. My husband and I arrived at the shop at six a.m. every day (to open at eight) and usually did not get home until nine p.m. However, business was terrific. Among the equipment we purchased was a doughnut maker. The big shiny machine occupied a prominent spot in the front window and my husband was so busy that before long, he became an expert at the making of doughnuts. My assistant and I baked pies and cakes in the kitchen at the rear of the shop. After all these years I was now employer, rather than employee.

Soon we added chili-to-go and hamburgers to our bill of fare and upon the insistence of customers, we began to bake bread daily. One day, one of the several patrons who drove up from Tulsa's south side to shop with us came in accompanied by a friend who asked if I had ever made sourdough French bread. When I replied in the negative, she offered to obtain the necessary ingredients for making a "starter." A few weeks later Mrs. Janet Elson came in with a package she had obtained from friends in Denver.

She took time to tell me as much as she knew about baking the special bread and asked that I be certain to send her a loaf. After tasting the results of my third try, she reported that it was identical to the bread her grandmother produced from the family recipe that had been brought over from her native Poland. Janet Elson and I traded a number of recipes over the years, several of which are included in this book.

One of my North Tulsa friends would come into the shop every Thursday evening, just as our bread for the next day's sale was coming out of the oven, to purchase a loaf of our sourdough bread for the family for whom she worked. Each week she would also buy a second loaf for herself, but before she would let us wrap it, she'd break open the top of the loaf with her fingers. Reaching into her purse, she would withdraw a stick of butter, push it down into the still warm loaf and hand the bread back to us for wrapping. This, she allowed, was her weekly treat to herself.

Back when they were building the Turner Turnpike, we'd get a telephone call between ten-thirty and eleven o'clock each morning from a group of men working on the project. They'd order some twenty hamburgers, pies and doughnuts. At noon sharp, one of them would arrive and pick up their lunch. We never knew if the order was for five, ten or twenty workmen, but their business was truly appreciated. Before long, we were averaging between $500 and $800 weekly.

The catering side of the business took on a new dimension the day Mrs. Bess Rupp entered the shop to arrange for a bridal luncheon for the daughter of Mr. and Mrs. Burdette Blue. Mrs. Rupp was President of both the Tulsa Opera Guild and the Tulsa Philharmonic auxiliary. Before long we were catering all of the special parties and brunches that these organizations sponsored. These affairs often hosted celebrities such as Skitch Henderson, Peter Martin, Edward Villella, Maria and Marjorie Tallchief and Yvonne Chouteau.

It usually required two days of preparation to serve these functions. With regular business booming as it was, the shop was a madhouse just prior to the event, but I don't believe it was ever as hectic as the time immediately following the Sunday I broke my ankle. My husband and I had joined some friends fishing and disdaining a flight of stone steps, I took a short cut and fell with my foot beneath me. That Sunday evening found me on the phone with my good friend Cordelia Jenkins, who had helped me plan the brunch for two hundred

PASTRY AND PIE MAKING

In most cannister sets there is one cannister large enough to hold 5 pounds of flour. To save time, it is helpful to sift enough flour to fill this can. The amount of flour needed can be measured directly instead of sifting first, as most recipes require. For making pie crust, any good brand of all-purpose flour is suitable. Another shortcut I enjoy is making a double batch of pie crust, storing one batch in foil, waxed paper or plastic bags. Pie crust keeps a few days when wrapped well and refrigerated.

My mother was a pastry cook for many years in the Severs Hotel in Muskogee, Oklahoma. During summer vacations, I often went along to help wherever I could. I also looked for the treats that were always on hand in the pastry shop.

It was most interesting to watch Mother mix pie crust in large batches. She calculated proportions by weight instead of cupfuls. The very first thing she did to begin the morning's work was to set the sponge for breads and rolls. Next she made the pastry. Mother always mixed the flour, shortening, and salt in the big wooden bowl. She then covered the bowl and placed it in the refrigerator, where it remained until the following morning when it was mixed with ice water. She stressed the importance of handling the dough as little as possible. With the largest pastry blender I have ever seen, she cut the shortening into the large bowl of flour with the greatest of ease. Once she allowed me to try doing it. Naturally, I wanted to do it the way she did, so with fear and trembling I began. It was a great experience for a fifteen-year-old, so she guided my work carefully, but with firmness. She kept saying, "Don't be afraid. It's only flour and lard."

When the shortening was measured, half of it was blended into the flour until it looked like coarse cornmeal. Then the other half was blended in. Next came the ice cold water added gradually. The mixing was like tossing a salad. Too much liquid toughened the pastry. If the measured amount of liquid was not enough to bind the dough, more was added in spoonfuls to gather the dough from the sides of the bowl. When I found that I could make such a big batch of pastry, my fear was gone forever. I knew that if I could blend flour, shortening, salt and ice water to make pastry for a dozen or more pies, then doing it for 1 or 2 would be a cinch.

people. Fortunately, the shopping had been completed and by midday Monday, Cordelia had two relatively experienced helpers working like crazy. Cordelia stepped beautifully into the breach, I spent the two days with my hand on the telephone, and the brunch was a success.

MY HUSBAND HAD DEVELOPED DIABETES BACK IN THE MID-forties and now his condition began to worsen. It soon became apparent that my partner of twenty-eight years could not keep up with the hectic pace of the pastry shop. I was reluctant to continue without him, so in 1967 we closed our remarkably successful enterprise. Just as I had nursed my father-in-law until his passing in 1955, I remained at home with my beloved George until 1970 when he succumbed to his illness.

On a limited scale I was able to continue with some catering work out of our home on north Frankfort Place. Every week I baked sweet rolls for the students and faculty at Holland Hall High School. Eventually this led to my working a few hours, three or four days a week in the kitchen of Tulsa's Trinity Episcopal Church, preparing luncheons for special meetings. Little by little I reestablished my catering business, remodeling my kitchen to accommodate the increased activity.

I HAVE TRAVELED THE FIFTY-TWO MILES BETWEEN TULSA and Muskogee many times since leaving there in 1923, but the trip made in the late summer of 1971 was one of the most significant. Throughout the years I had maintained a close friendship with my childhood friend Eva Simmons and her husband Jake. The Simmons family's fortunes had continued to grow over the years. Oil had been discovered on their ranch in Haskell and Jake had not only prospered, but had become an international oil developer—drilling the first successful well in Africa. In addition, he was president of the Oklahoma State NAACP for many years.

Now I was called upon to prepare food for one hundred and fifty guests at Jake and Eva's home on Gerrard Street in Muskogee. All three of their sons, members of the Alpha Phi Alpha Fraternity, were hosting a dinner-style lawn picnic. Eva and Jake were present, of course, along with all the children and grandchildren. It was the first gathering of its kind since Jake and Eva had celebrated their twenty-fifth wedding anniversary at my home in Tulsa almost twenty-five years before.

Silver Anniversary Menu

CRAB MEAT CANAPES
EGG AND OLIVE SANDWICHES
OPEN FACED CHICKEN SANDWICHES
OPEN FACED HAM SANDWICHES
CELERY STUFFED WITH CREAM
CHEESE
WEDDING PUNCH OF MIXED FRUIT
JUICES
COOKIES OF SEVERAL VARIETIES
COFFEE
SPICED TEA

That summer afternoon was pure intoxication for me. I gave my utmost attention to the preparation of the baked ham, filet of beef and fried chicken, of course, but the opportunity of putting my talents to work for the children of my oldest friend gave me a complete sense of fulfillment. The lessons learned were indeed put to very good use.

Though I have cooked for seventy years, I can recall without difficulty the most memorable affair I ever catered, the twenty-fifty wedding anniversary party of Mr. and Mrs. H. T. Hutton in 1942. Mrs. Hutton had come back into my life earlier that year at the annual meeting of the Federation of Black Women's Clubs, in Langston, Oklahoma. I saw her from across the room, a gentle, elderly woman whose face was somehow familiar, and moments later we were in each other's arms. Mrs. H. T. Hutton was none other than Lucy Elliott—the woman who had taught me cooking at the Muskogee Manual Training High School twenty-six years before. Catering a party to celebrate her silver wedding anniversary gave me the pleasure of coming full circle, coming home again in my memories. The menu called for nothing extraordinary, but it was prepared with the greatest affection and appreciation.

IT IS DIFFICULT TO EXPRESS MY GRATITUDE FOR HAVING spent a lifetime doing that which seemed most appropriate—continuing a tradition that goes back one hundred years. I am pleased to include recipes offered by my niece, and my nephew (himself a capable cook) advises me that his grandson recently started experimenting on his own in the kitchen. The tradition continues.

I might sum up my attitude about the art of cooking with this verse learned somewhere, sometime ago:

*To be a good cook means
employing the economy of
great-grandmother and the
science of modern chemists.*

*It means much tasting
and no wasting.*

*It means English thoroughness,
French art and Arabian hospitality.*

*It means, in fine,
that you are to see that
everyone has something nice to eat.*

—RUSKIN

Dining Through the Decades:
The Recipes

· E A R L Y   D A Y S ·

The Early Days

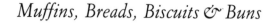

Muffins, Breads, Biscuits & Buns

CLEORA'S CORN FRITTERS

1   cup cream style corn
1   cup cracker crumbs
1   cup flour
½   teaspoon salt
½   teaspoon sugar
½   cup milk
1   teaspoon baking powder
2   eggs

Mix thoroughly. Drop spoonfuls into deep, hot fat. Brown on both sides. Drain on paper towels. Place in a low oven as fritters are fried. Serve hot with your favorite jelly or maple syrup.

Serves 6.

NOTE: *These are good late breakfasts with crisp bacon curls or thin slices of pan-broiled ham.*

FRIED CORNMEAL MUSH

1   cup yellow cornmeal moistened in 1 cup cold water
3   cups boiling water
1   teaspoon salt
     Milk
     Cornmeal and flour

Stir moistened cornmeal into boiling salted water, stirring until thick. Cover and cook over low heat 30 minutes. Stir occasionally. Pour into loaf pan rinsed with cold water. Let cool overnight. Unmold. Slice ½ inch thick. Dip first in milk, then in a mixture of cornmeal and flour. Fry in hot fat.

Serves 12.

RAISIN BREAD

2   cups milk, scalded
1½ teaspoons salt
2   tablespoons melted shortening
¼   cup molasses
1   cake yeast
¾   cup raisins, or more if you like
½   teaspoon cinnamon
6   cups flour

Combine milk, salt, shortening and molasses; cool to lukewarm. Add yeast to cooled milk mixture and allow to stand 5 minutes. Add raisins and cinnamon. Add flour, a little at a time, beating well after each addition. Mix until dough is stiff enough to knead on a lightly floured board. Knead until smooth and elastic. Cover with warm damp cloth and allow to rise until double in bulk. Form into loaves. Place in well-greased loaf pans and let rise until double in bulk. Bake at 375 degrees for 45 minutes.

Yields 2 loaves.

GRIDDLE CAKES

1   cup all-purpose flour
½   teaspoon salt
1   teaspoon sugar
2   teaspoons baking powder
1   egg, separated
2   tablespoons melted shortening
1   cup milk

Sift dry ingredients into a bowl. Add milk, egg yolk and shortening. Beat thoroughly and fold in stiffly beaten egg white. Let stand 10 minutes and do not beat any more. Cook on an ungreased griddle. Serve immediately with melted butter and your favorite syrup.

Yields 7 or 8 medium-sized griddle cakes.

GRANDMOTHER'S HOT WATER CORNBREAD

2   cups yellow or white cornmeal
1   teaspoon salt
1½ teaspoons sugar
1½ cups boiling water
3   tablespoons bacon drippings
    Bacon drippings for frying

Mix cornmeal, salt and sugar; add boiling water and 3 tablespoons melted bacon drippings and mix thoroughly. When cool enough to handle, shape into pones with wet hands, leaving fingerprints on pones. In a heavy skillet, heat bacon drippings (about ¾ cup) and fry pones until brown and crusty. Turn over and brown other side. Drain on paper towels. Serve with lots of butter.

NOTE: *Sometimes Grandmother would add ¾ cup broken cracklings to the mixture, shape into pones and fry. Her cornbread, both hot water and egg bread, were made with stoneground meal which Grandpa took to the mill; the corn was from her garden.*

Griddle cakes, Crepes and
• P A N C A K E S •

Time has eroded the once-clear distinction between griddle cakes and pancakes. Eighty years ago, griddle cakes were the familiar breakfast cakes served with butter and syrup. Pancakes were the crepes of today, baked one at a time in a small skillet and generally served rolled around a sweet or savory filling. As late as 1942 griddle cakes appeared in the index of a well-known cookbook but when the 1955 edition came out, the reference was to "griddle cakes — see Pancakes." In 1963 a new edition did not list griddle cakes at all.

Hot Cross Buns

1¼ cups milk
1 cake yeast
⅛ teaspoon salt
⅓ cup sugar
½ cup currants or raisins
¼ cup margarine
2 eggs
1 egg beaten with 2 tablespoons water

Icing:

1 cup powdered sugar
½ teaspoon vanilla
Enough water to make proper consistency

Scald milk; cool to lukewarm. Crumble in yeast; add salt, sugar, margarine, eggs and currants. Mix well. Add enough flour to make dough easy to handle. Place in greased bowl; cover and let rise in warm place until double in bulk. Pinch off rolls the size of walnuts; roll with hands to make small buns. Place on greased cooky sheet 1½ inches apart. Let rise for 30 minutes. With sharp razor blade cut top of each bun, forming a cross. Brush with egg wash, using soft pastry brush. Bake until brown at 400 degrees. When cool, fill cross with icing.

Yields 36 buns.

Note: *Mother always made these for Easter.*

Soda Biscuits

2 cups flour
½ teaspoon soda
2½ teaspoons baking powder
½ teaspoon salt
1 teaspoon sugar
⅞ cups sour milk (1 cup minus 2 tablespoons)

Sift flour with salt, sugar and baking powder. Work in shortening. Mix soda with sour milk and add to flour mixture. Knead lightly, roll, cut and bake on greased pan in 450 degree oven for 12 minutes.

Yields 12 biscuits.

Sour Cream Muffins

2 tablespoons butter or margarine
¼ cup sugar
2 eggs
2 cups flour
4 teaspoons baking powder
¼ teaspoon salt
¼ teaspoon soda
1 cup sour cream

Cream together the butter and sugar until mixture resembles whipped cream. Beat eggs until light and mix in. Sift flour, measure, then sift again with baking powder and salt. Dissolve soda in the sour cream and add to creamed mixture alternately with the dry ingredients, beating until very fluffy. Spoon into well-greased, small muffin cups. Bake at 425 degrees for 15 minutes.

Note: *The addition of a teaspoon of finely grated orange peel is suggested.*

Yields 24 small muffins.

BROWN BREAD

1¼ cups sour milk
¼ cup brown sugar
¼ teaspoon salt
½ cup molasses
1 cup raisins
1 cup nuts
2 cups graham flour or whole wheat flour
1 teaspoon soda

Combine nuts and raisins; dredge with the flour. Combine with other ingredients. Pour into 2 greased loaf pans and let set 1 hour. Bake at 275 degrees for 1 hour. Let cool before removing from pans.

Yields 2 loaves.

NOTE: *This is a different way of preparing brown bread, which is usually steamed.*

SPOON BREAD

1 cup yellow cornmeal
1 cup cold milk
2 cups scalding hot milk
1 teaspoon salt
1 teaspoon baking powder
2 tablespoons melted shortening
3 tablespoons sugar
3 egg yolks, beaten
3 egg whites, stiffly beaten

Mix cornmeal with cold milk. Stir into 2 cups scalding hot milk and cook until thick. Add the next five ingredients. Fold in stiffly-beaten egg whites. Pour into 1 ½-quart casserole which has been well greased and bake at 350 degrees for 1 hour. Serve immediately with lots of butter.

Serves 8 to 12.

BRAN MUFFINS

1 cup All-Bran
1 cup buttermilk
½ teaspoon soda
2 eggs, beaten
3 tablespoons melted shortening
1 cup white flour
3 tablespoons sugar
¼ teaspoon salt
1½ teaspoons baking powder

Pour buttermilk over All-Bran; add soda which has been dissolved in 1 tablespoon boiling water. Let stand five minutes. Add eggs and melted shortening. Blend into bran and buttermilk. Then stir in flour with sugar, salt and baking powder added. Mix thoroughly and fill well-greased muffin tins ⅔ full. Bake at 400 degrees for 20 to 30 minutes.

Yields 18 muffins.

NOTE: *Chopped dates, figs, or blueberries add variety to bran muffins. In this case, add 1 tablespoon more sugar and flour the fruit with 2 tablespoons flour before adding to batter.*

• C O R N F L A K E S •

When a patient at the Battle Creek Sanitarium broke her false teeth on a piece of zwieback, a surgeon at the "San," as it was called, developed a breakfast cereal made from thin flakes of corn. His brother, W. K. Kellogg, founded the Kellogg Company in 1906, the same year Kellogg's Corn Flakes were introduced. The regimen at the San had always included generous amounts of bran and in 1916 Kellogg marketed All-Bran for the first time. Between 1942 and 1965 the average amount of cooked cereal consumed by American families per week dropped by almost two-thirds, while the consumption of dry, boxed cereals doubled.

POPOVERS

1   cup all-purpose flour
½   teaspoon salt
⅞   cup milk (1 cup less 2 tablespoons)
3   eggs
½   teaspoon melted shortening

Sift and salt in a deep bowl; add milk, eggs and melted shortening. Beat 2 minutes with an egg beater.

Preheat iron gem pans to sizzling temperature, grease slightly and fill half full. Bake 35 minutes, starting with 350 degrees for 15 minutes; increase heat to 400 degrees and bake 20 minutes longer. Popovers should be crisp and empty. Serve immediately with plenty of butter and your favorite jam or jelly.

ORANGE BISCUITS

2   cups flour
2   teaspoons sugar
1   teaspoon salt
4   teaspoons baking powder
2   rounded tablespoons shortening
    Grated rind of 2 oranges
¾   cup milk
    Melted butter or margarine
    About 10 cocktail cubes of sugar
    Orange juice

Sift flour, sugar, salt and baking powder into a bowl. Cut shortening and orange rind into flour mixture. Add milk to make soft dough. Knead dough lightly. Roll out as for biscuits, but a little thicker. Cut biscuits with 2-inch cutter. Place closely in slightly greased shallow pan and brush slightly with melted butter or margarine. Dip each cube of sugar in orange juice and press in the center of each biscuit. Bake at 375 degrees for 10 minutes or until done.

Yields about 1 dozen.

Salads

BASIC CHICKEN SALAD

4   cups diced cooked chicken
3   cups diced celery
½   cup chopped sweet pickles
3   tablespoons vinegar
1   teaspoon salt
2   hard-cooked eggs, chopped
¾   cup mayonnaise
½   cup slivered almonds, toasted

Combine pickles, vinegar, salt, eggs, mayonnaise and almonds. Pour mixture over chicken and celery. Mix well and chill.

Serves 6 to 8.

VARIATION 1:

Add 2 cups Thompson's seedless grapes. This variation makes a festive luncheon salad served in cantaloupe rings placed on lettuce leaf or curly endive. It can also be served in ½ ripe papaya shell.

VARIATION 2:

Add 2 cups chopped tart apples and ½ teaspoon curry powder.

VARIATION 3:

Add 1 teaspoon chopped onion and 4 tablespoons chopped black olives. Serve on lettuce leaves or in ½ avocado.

NOTE: *I began using these variations in the 1960s.*

Soups, Stews & Main Dishes

MOTHER'S CHUNKY CHICKEN AND STRIP DUMPLINGS

1   chicken, 4½ to 5 pounds, cut into serving
    pieces
3   tablespoons butter
3   tablespoons oil
1   onion
2   cloves
1   carrot, halved
    Bouquet garni composed of 2 ribs celery,
    chopped, 3 sprigs parsley, 1 small bay leaf
7   cups chicken stock or chicken broth, enough
    to cover chicken

In a large heavy skillet, sauté chicken in butter and oil until it is lightly colored; add carrot, onion stuck with cloves, and bouquet garni. Add stock or broth and bring to a boil, skimming off the froth that rises to the surface. Simmer chicken, covered, for 1 hour and 30 minutes until just tender. Transfer chicken with tongs to a plate and keep it warm. Skim fat from stock. Strain stock and return it to the kettle.

DUMPLINGS:

1½ cups flour
½   teaspoon baking powder
½   teaspoon salt
1   tablespoon shortening
1   small egg, lightly beaten
⅓   cup cold water

In a large bowl, sift together flour, baking powder and salt. Cut in shortening until mixture resembles meal. Make a well in the center. Add egg and water. Stir liquid into flour mixture to form a dough.

Turn the dough out on a floured surface and knead for 10 minutes or until elastic. Chill dough, covered, for 30 minutes. Roll out half the dough very thin on a floured surface. Cut the dough into 1½-inch strips and let the dumpling noodles dry for 10 minutes. Bring stock to a boil over high heat and stir mixture with a wooden spoon. Reduce heat to low and cook dumplings for 5 to 7 minutes. Skin and bone chicken and cut into 2-inch pieces. Add chicken to kettle and simmer until it is just heated through. Garnish the dish with minced parsley and shredded carrot.

Serves 4 to 6.

OXTAIL SOUP

4½ quarts water
4   pounds oxtails
3   onions, sliced
1   can (32 ounce) tomatoes
1   can (32 ounce) tomato juice
1   bay leaf
    Salt and pepper to taste
2   parsnips, chopped
½   pound mushrooms, sliced
3   carrots, chopped
2   ribs celery, diced
2   medium zucchini, diced
3   cups corn
½   cup to ¾ cup barley

In roasting pan, combine water, oxtails, onions, tomatoes, tomato juice, bay leaf, salt and pepper. Cover and cook 8 hours at 250 degrees. Cool and refrigerate overnight. Skim off fat which has settled on top. Trim fat from oxtails, removing bones. Add vegetables and barley. Return to 250 degree oven and cook for 6 hours.

Serves 10.

OYSTER STEW

1 bottle (8 ounce) clam juice
1 pint small oysters with liquor and enough
   water to make 1 quart liquid
1 tablespoon Worcestershire sauce
1 teaspoon celery salt
1 tablespoon butter
1 pint half-and-half
   Dash *each* of paprika and nutmeg

Cook clam juice, oyster liquor, water, Worcestershire and butter over high heat until well blended. Add oysters and cook just until edges curl. Add half-and-half and more butter if desired. Season with paprika and nutmeg. Serve immediately.

Serves 4 to 6.

Vegetables

OKRA WITH CORN AND TOMATO

¼ pound okra pods, each 2 to 3 inches long
4 tomatoes, peeled, seeded and chopped
½ cup chopped onion
1 green pepper, or 1 red sweet pepper, seeded
   and chopped
¼ cup butter or margarine
   Salt and pepper to taste
2 cups fresh corn

In a skillet, sauté onion and chopped pepper until onion is softened. Stir in tomatoes, okra, salt and pepper to taste. Simmer mixture over moderate heat, stirring occasionally for 15 minutes or until vegetables are tender. Add corn and simmer 5 minutes or until most of the liquid has evaporated. Transfer vegetable mixture to a heated serving dish.

Serves 6.

MOTHER'S POTATOES WITH SALT PORK

   Small new potatoes
3 teaspoons salt
¾ pound streak-of-lean salt pork
   Spring onions, sliced thin with tops
   Freshly ground pepper

Dig enough small new potatoes to make 3 quarts or more. Wash well but do not peel. Cover with cold water and add salt. Bring the water to a boil, and boil the potatoes until they are just tender when tested with point of paring knife. Drain the potatoes. While potatoes are cooking, cut salt pork and fry until crisp. Set aside pork, retaining bacon fat and brown pan bits. Add onions to bacon fat and cook until tender. Remove onions; combine with crisp, crumbled salt pork and add the potatoes. Pepper to taste. Serve hot.

Serves 6.

NOTE: *If you have a potato patch in your garden use the first ones harvested for this marvelous treat.*

The Origin of

• M A R G A R I N E •

During the Franco-Prussian War of 1870 Napoleon III conducted a contest to find a cheap substitute for butter. A French chemist, Hippolyte Mège-Mouries, churned together a mixture of chopped beef suet, milk, water, and other ingredients to create margarine — and to win the prize. Margarine was introduced to the United States in 1874.

Puddings, Pies & Cakes

INDIAN PUDDING

2   cups milk
⅓   cup yellow cornmeal
3   tablespoons dark molasses
3   tablespoons brown sugar
1   tablespoon butter
½   teaspoon cinnamon
½   teaspoon ginger
¼   teaspoon salt
½   cup raisins or chopped nuts
    Soft vanilla ice cream

Scald 1 cup milk in the top of a double boiler over direct heat and slowly shake in cornmeal, stirring until the mixture begins to boil. Set the pan over boiling water and cook for 15 minutes, stirring occasionally. Add molasses, sugar, butter, seasoning and raisins. Mix well and pour into a buttered, 1-quart baking dish. Pour remaining cold milk over the top. Bake at 300 degrees for 1½ to 2 hours. Serve the pudding warm with the softened ice cream as a sauce.

Serves 4 to 6.

PEACH CRUMB PUDDING

FILLING:

½   cup sugar
3   tablespoons flour
5   pounds ripe peaches, peeled and sliced

Combine 3 tablespoons flour and ½ cup sugar; mix gently with the peaches. Put in a buttered 9-inch square baking dish.

FOR CRUST:

½   cup sugar
1   cup flour
½   cup butter

With a pastry blender, mix until crumbly ½ cup sugar, 1 cup flour and butter for crust; sprinkle over the peaches. Bake at 350 degrees until the peaches are tender and the crumbs brown (about 1 hour). Serve warm with thick unwhipped cream.

Serves 8.

GRATED SWEET POTATO PUDDING

4   cups grated raw sweet potatoes
½   cup sugar
½   cup light corn syrup
1½   cups milk
⅓   cup melted butter or margarine
3   eggs, beaten
1   teaspoon ground nutmeg
1   teaspoon ground cinnamon
½   teaspoon salt

Combine all ingredients, mixing well. Spoon mixture into a lightly greased 2-quart casserole. Bake at 325 degrees for 1½ hours or until slightly firm.

Serves 6 to 8.

SPICY MINCE PIE

Pastry for double pie crust
1⅓ cups sugar
½ teaspoon salt
½ teaspoon ground cinnamon
¼ teaspoon ground cloves
1½ cups chopped apples
1 cup dark raisins
½ cup jellied cranberry sauce
⅓ cup chopped walnuts
1 teaspoon grated orange peel
½ teaspoon grated lemon peel
¼ cup freshly squeezed lemon juice
1 tablespoon butter

Combine sugar, salt and spices. Add apples, raisins, cranberry sauce, walnuts, orange peel, lemon peel and lemon juice. Pour into pastry-lined 9-inch pie plate. Dot with butter. Add top crust. Bake at 400 degrees for 30 to 35 minutes. Serve warm.

Serves 6.

MOTHER'S BLUEBERRY CAKE
A BREAKFAST DESSERT

1½ cups fresh blueberries
1 cup sugar, divided
1 teaspoon cornstarch
2 tablespoons lemon juice
4 tablespoons water
¼ cup butter
1 egg, beaten
¾ cup plus 2 tablespoons cake flour
¼ teaspoon salt
1 teaspoon baking powder
¼ teaspoon nutmeg
¼ cup milk

Cook together for 10 minutes blueberries, ½ cup sugar, cornstarch, lemon juice and water; cool. Meanwhile, using the rest of the ingredients, make a plain cake batter in the usual manner. Pour blueberries in a greased 8-inch cake pan or deep-dish pie pan and cover with the cake batter. Bake at 350 degrees for 25 to 30 minutes. Serve warm with sweet or sour cream.

Serves 6.

NOTE: *Originally Mother used wild huckleberries whenever we were fortunate enough to find a sufficient quantity in the woods.*

CONCORD GRAPE PIE

4 cups Concord grapes
1 cup sugar
2 tablespoons cornstarch
3 tablespoons butter
Flaky pastry for 2-crust pie
Egg wash (1 egg yolk beaten with 2 tablespoons milk)

Line a 9-inch pie tin with flaky pastry and chill. Prepare grape filling as follows: Wash and drain grapes. Squeeze pulp out of grapes into a saucepan, placing skins in a bowl. Place saucepan over medium heat and cook to a pulp. Sieve grape pulp into the bowl with the removed skins. Heat grapes to boiling. Add sugar, sifted and thoroughly blended with cornstarch, to grapes. Add 3 tablespoons butter; cook until thickened. Cool but do not chill. Pour into unbaked pastry shell. Roll out top crust. Moisten edge of bottom crust and seal with egg wash. Sprinkle lightly with sugar. Slash top crust several times if a solid top is used. Bake at 400 degrees for 10 minutes. Reduce heat to 350 degrees and continue baking for 30 minutes longer.

Serves 6 to 8.

MOTHER'S ANGEL FOOD CAKE

1¼ cups cake flour
½ cup sugar (extra)
1½ cups egg whites, room temperature
¼ teaspoon salt
1¼ teaspoons cream of tartar
1⅓ cups sugar
1 teaspoon almond extract
½ teaspoon vanilla

Sift flour. Measure flour and sift together with ½ cup sugar three times. Add salt and cream of tartar to egg whites and beat until stiff, but not dry. Fold in 1⅓ cups sugar, 2 tablespoons at a time, using a wire whip. Add extracts. Fold in flour and sugar mixture gently, 4 tablespoons at a time, using about 10 turns at a time with a wire whip. Spoon into 10-inch tube pan. Bake for 35 to 40 minutes at 375 degrees. Remove from oven. Turn upside down. Let cool completely. Frost with favorite icing.

BOILED ICING

1½ cups granulated sugar
¾ cup water
1 tablespoon white corn syrup
2 egg whites, beaten until stiff
1 teaspoon vanilla

Let sugar, water and corn syrup cook until it spins thread. Pour syrup in fine stream over stiffly beaten egg whites and beat until cold. Add 1 teaspoon vanilla. When fluffy and glossy, spread on cake.

NOTE: *Mother would whip the egg whites for the cake and beat the corn syrup into the egg whites on her turkey platter, using her whip.*

Soft wheat flour called Queen of the Pantry was Mother's choice for this cake.

Relishes & Preserves

CLEORA'S PEAR PRESERVES

24 Bartlett pears
2 lemons
  Cold water
  Sugar
1 small stick cinnamon (optional)
  Whole cloves (optional)

Wash and peel pears. Wash and remove seeds from lemons and slice very thin. Place pears in a large kettle, and barely cover with cold water. Let come to boil and cook twenty minutes.

Let stand in juice overnight. Next morning, measure pears and add ¾ cup sugar for each 1 cup pears. Cook with cinnamon and cloves, if desired, until transparent. Add sliced lemons which have been boiled separately then drained. Seal in sterilized jars.

Yields about 6 pints.

NOTE: *I always let the pears sit overnight in water instead of sugar because they stay tender that way. Simmering the lemons separately keeps the pear preserves from taking on a bitter flavor.*

MOTHER'S CORN RELISH

2 quarts sweet corn, cut from cob
2 quarts ripe tomatoes
1 quart onions (4 medium)
1 quart cucumbers (3 large)
1 quart celery (1 small bunch, without leaves)
2 sweet green peppers
½ cup salt
3 cups white vinegar
2 cups sugar
2 cups water
2 teaspoons mustard seed
¼ teaspoon tumeric
1 tablespoon Coleman's mustard
1 tablespoon celery seed

Scald, peel and chop tomatoes. Peel and slice onions and cucumbers. Chop celery. Boil corn on cob for 3 minutes. Cool and cut from cob. Measure 2 quarts. Chop green peppers coarsely. Combine all ingredients. Cook in preserving kettle 40 to 50 minutes. Pack in sterilized jars. Seal.

Yields 12 pints.

Making a Plain
• C A K E •

"Make a plain cake in the usual manner" was a well-understood directive in the days before packaged cake mixes. It meant to cream butter and sugar until they were fluffy and then beat in eggs or egg yolks one at a time, followed by any flavorings to be used. Next milk was added and (if the eggs had been separated) beaten egg whites were folded in. Last, the flour (sifted with salt and leavening) was beaten in "by degrees." The cook was required to beat continuously from beginning to end of the process.

MOTHER'S CHOW CHOW

2½ quarts chopped green tomatoes
2½ quarts chopped white cabbage
2½ quarts chopped cucumbers
1¼ quarts chopped onions
3 cups chopped green beans
   Pickling salt
4 red sweet peppers, chopped
4 tablespoons white mustard seed
2 tablespoons celery seed
2 tablespoons whole allspice
1 tablespoon whole cloves
1 hot pepper (optional)
2½ cups sugar
2½ cups cider vinegar

Prepare vegetables, except hot pepper, and put them in a stone crock in layers with a sprinkling of salt (about 2 tablespoons) between each layer. Let stand 12 hours, then drain off the brine. Put vegetables in a preserving kettle over the fire. Sprinkle 1 hot pepper, if used, spices, sugar and vinegar over vegetables. Cover tightly and simmer until thoroughly cooked. Pour in sterilized jars while hot.

Yields 12 pints.

· T W E N T I E S ·

The Twenties

Cocktails & Hors d'oeuvres

OLD-FASHIONED COCKTAIL

½   cube sugar
2   dashes angostura bitters
2   tablespoons water
1   jigger bourbon
1   large lump ice

Muddle well and add bourbon and ice. Stir very well. Decorate with slice of orange, twist of lemon peel and a cherry. Serve in old-fashioned glasses.

CLOVER CLUB

3   parts gin
1   part French vermouth
1   part grenadine syrup
    White of 1 egg
    Cracked ice

Shake well and serve.

Yields 4 cocktails.

SIDE CAR

1   part lemon juice
1   part Cointreau
2   parts brandy

Shake well with ice. Pour in cocktail glasses and serve. Do not serve with a fruit appetizer.

THE OLD ARMY COCKTAIL

2   parts gin
1   part Italian vermouth
    Thin zest (peel) of 2 lemons and 1 orange
    Cracked ice
    Pickled onions

Put in shaker and shake. Pour into glasses of cracked ice and garnish with pickled onion.

SWEDISH LIVER LOAF

1   pound beef or pork liver, chopped fine
¼   cup chopped onion, fried tender in 2 tablespoons fat
½   pound ground sausage
2   eggs
2   cups thin cream
1   teaspoon pepper
3   teaspoons salt
1   teaspoon sugar
¼   teaspoon *each* cinnamon, cloves, nutmeg and allspice
2   cups flour
2   to 3 cups chopped nuts

Mix ingredients thoroughly in the order given. Press through a colander. Bake in a well-greased, covered loaf pan or ring mold set in pan of hot water in a 350 degree oven for 2 hours. Remove cover after first hour. Roll liver loaf in chopped nuts; wrap in waxed paper and chill thoroughly. Cut in thin slices and arrange on a chilled platter around a center of deviled eggs and olive-filled cornucopias of thin-sliced boiled ham, minced ham loaf or other lunch meat.

Serves 10.

NOTE: *Accompany with rye bread and butter sandwiches, potato chips or hot French fries, and cole slaw.*

Prohibition and the

• C O C K T A I L •

In the years following the founding of the Women's Christian Temperance Union in 1874, prohibition forces in the United States gathered strength. By July 1, 1914, 31 states were "dry" or committed to prohibition soon. In January, 1920, the 18th Amendment went into effect, prohibiting the "manufacture or transportation of intoxicating liquor within the United States."

However, prohibition did not greatly affect Tulsa, which had already been "dry" in theory and fully "wet" in fact. In 1930 Tulsa had more millionaires per capita than any other American city and liquor flowed like black gold for those who could afford it.

PICKLED EGGS

2   teaspoons ground ginger
2   teaspoons pickling spices
12   peppercorns
3½   cups white vinegar
12   hard-cooked eggs, peeled
2   medium onions, sliced
3   cloves garlic
½   teaspoon dill weed

Combine ginger, pickling spices, peppercorns and vinegar in a saucepan. Bring to a boil; reduce heat and simmer 5 minutes. Place eggs in a crock or glass jar. Pour hot liquid over eggs; add water if necessary to cover. Add onion, garlic and dill weed. Cover and refrigerate at least 4 days. Serve in wedges with salt and pepper to taste.

Serves 12 to 24.

NOTE: *Eggs may be kept in pickling liquid several months.*

CELERY STICKS

Fill 2-inch lengths of crisp tender celery with a mixture of cream cheese seasoned to taste with blue cheese, onion juice and a dash of Tabasco. Sprinkle with paprika.

HERB STUFFED EGGS

9   hard-cooked eggs
½   cup sour cream
3   tablespoons dill weed
1   tablespoon *each* mashed anchovy fillet, snipped chives and minced parsley
    Salt and pepper to taste

Halve eggs lengthwise. Force yolks through a sieve into a bowl; blend in sour cream, dill, mashed anchovy, chives and parsley, salt and pepper. Chill the mixture, covered, for 30 minutes. Fill 12 of the reserved halves with the mixture, mounding it, and garnish the eggs with the remaining whites, minced.

Yields 12 stuffed eggs.

CHEESE ROLL

1   pound sharp or American cheese, grated
5   blocks Roquefort cheese
1   package (3 ounce) cream cheese
    Orange juice to taste
    Dash Tabasco
1   teaspoon Worcestershire sauce
    Paprika

Combine first 6 ingredients. Shape into log. Roll in paprika. Roll in waxed paper. Chill and slice.

DEVILED EGGS

12   eggs
1½   cups soft cream cheese
4   tablespoons mayonnaise
1   tablespoon prepared mustard
¾   teaspoon salt
4   teaspoons vinegar
     Dash cayenne
     Dash garlic salt — or any other seasoning you desire

Put eggs in simmering, not boiling, water and let them simmer for 15 minutes if medium eggs, 20 minutes for large ones. Move the eggs around with a spoon for the first 7 or 8 minutes; this keeps the yolks in the center where they should be. When eggs are done, pour cold water on them immediately and let them stand until they are cooled. Peel and cut them in half lengthwise. Put the yolks through a food mill or a sieve. Add softened cream cheese, mayonnaise and other seasonings. Blend well and fill the whites. Decorate each one with 1 caper, a bit of pimiento or a bit of anchovy.

VARIATIONS FOR FILLINGS:

Remove the yolks from the eggs; mash them up with mayonnaise; salt and pepper to taste. Fill whites with flaked crab meat, then pile yolk mixture on top. Sprinkle with chopped chives.

Mash yolks with mayonnaise and then add chopped lobster meat and season with a little curry powder.

Serves 12 to 24.

BACONED OLIVES

Wrap giant stuffed olives with strips of bacon. Secure bacon with round toothpicks and fry in deep fat. Powder with pulverized roasted peanuts.

Soups & Salads

RED CABBAGE SLAW

1   medium red cabbage
2   (or 3) tablespoons tarragon vinegar
4   teaspoons sugar
    Salt
½   teaspoon celery seed
⅛   teaspoon cayenne or more to taste
½   (to ¾) cup sour cream
2   (to 3) tablespoons top milk (according to
    desired consistency)

Shred cabbage fine and toss with rest of ingredients.
Chill and serve.

Serves 6.

NOTE: *This slaw is colorful with pale meats and very
good with fish.*

EDITOR'S NOTE: *Use cream or half-and-half for the
"top milk."*

Rich Milk, Skim Milk and
• T O P   M I L K •

The earliest machine designed to homogenize milk
was developed in France in 1899 and brought to the
United States in 1905. Homogenizers were used to
solve a marketing problem created by poor sales of
skim milk. Surplus butter was mixed with the milk
under pressure to create a milk which had the fat
content of whole milk and which would not separate. Whole unhomogenized milk continued to be
widely available for another fifty years, however,
providing "top milk" and "rich milk" for use in
custards and cream sauces.

BOILED SALAD DRESSING

1   teaspoon dry mustard
1   teaspoon salt
¼   teaspoon paprika
2   tablespoons sugar
3   egg yolks
4   tablespoons melted butter
2   tablespoons vinegar
2   tablespoons lemon juice
½   cup cream (whipped)

Mix seasonings; add egg yolks. Mix well; add liquids
and cook in double boiler. Cool. Add whipped cream
and mix thoroughly. Refrigerate. Use for slaw.

Yields 1½ cups dressing.

CALIFORNIA FRENCH DRESSING

1   cup salad oil (not olive)
1   tablespoon vinegar
½   cup orange juice
2   teaspoons onion, grated
2   teaspoons sugar
1   teaspoon salt
1   teaspoon dry mustard
1   clove garlic, grated (optional)
1   teaspoon A-1 Sauce
1   heaping teaspoon paprika
¼   teaspoon cayenne pepper

Mix all ingredients and beat with electric beater. Pour
in bottle. Always shake well before serving.

CLEORA'S AVOCADO DRESSING

1   large avocado
2   tablespoons lime juice
1½ tablespoons finely chopped onion
1   garlic clove, minced
1   teaspoon salt
1   large tomato, peeled, seeded and finely
    chopped
    Minced jalapeño pepper to taste

Mash the pulp of the avocado using a silver fork to keep avocado from darkening. Add lime juice, onion, garlic and salt. Blend well. Add tomato and chill. Add jalapeño pepper to taste.

Yields 1½ to 2 cups.

NOTE: *The first avocado I ever saw was brought from Mexico by my employer, Charles Robertson. Mrs. Robertson and I studied this unusual piece of fruit, and when we cut it open to find the enormous seed inside, we couldn't decide which was the part to be eaten, the pulp or the seed. Finally we decided we had best wait until Mr. Robertson returned home. He called it an Alligator Pear but, of course, we know it as an avocado. Mr. Robertson raved over its delicate flavor, and the above dressing, save for the jalapeño peppers which I've since added for zip, was concocted from his description. Since then, I've used avocados in everything from soup to desserts.*

THOUSAND ISLAND DRESSING

1   cup homemade mayonnaise
¼   cup chili sauce
1   hard-cooked egg, chopped fine
3   tablespoon green pepper, chopped fine
2   tablespoons onion, diced fine
4   tablespoons pimento-stuffed olives, chopped
    fine
1   teaspoon paprika
1   to 2 tablespoons minced fresh herbs
    (optional)
3   tablespoons celery, chopped fine

Stir together and refrigerate.

OYSTER BISQUE

1   pint oysters with liquor
2   tablespoons butter
    Chicken broth
1   cup milk
2   cups light cream
½   teaspoon paprika
2   tablespoons flour
3   egg yolks
2   tablespoons water
    Dash nutmeg
1   teaspoon salt

Heat oysters but do not boil. Drain and reserve liquor. Chop oysters until they are fine. Melt butter; blend in flour. Stir in the oyster liquor with enough chicken broth to make 1 cup liquor, the milk, cream and seasonings. When soup boils gently, add chopped oysters. Add egg yolks, beaten with water, and heat for another minute. If too thick, add a little more chicken broth. Sprinkle about 3 tablespoons chopped parsley over soup and serve immediately.

Serves 6.

PEASANT SOUP

5   large, peeled potatoes in chunks
4   large onions, in chunks
½   bunch parsley
1   outside rib celery or outside leaves of a head
    of lettuce
1   clove garlic
½   stick butter
    Salt and pepper to taste
½   teaspoon paprika
1   pint milk or light cream
    Chives

Put first 8 ingredients in 6 to 8 cups chicken broth and cook 1½ hours. Then mash through a coarse strainer. Add 1 pint milk or cream. Sprinkle chives on top.

Serves 6 to 8.

SPRING SOUP

1   pound spinach
2   ribs celery
1   onion
1   bunch sorrel
1   teaspoon salt
¼   teaspoon pepper
¼   cup water
4   cups chicken broth
    Thin slices of lemon

Put vegetables and ¼ cup water in heavy pot with tight lid and cook until they are soft. Add chicken broth, salt and pepper and bring to boil. Let simmer over low heat for 10 minutes. Strain. Serve with a garnish of thin slices of lemon.

Serves 4.

NOTE: *If sorrel is unavailable, substitute another pound of spinach.*

Breads & Stuffings

SPOON BREAD SOUFFLÉ

1   cup yellow cornmeal
4   cups milk
¼   cup chopped onion
¼   cup chopped celery
1   teaspoon salt
1   tablespoon sugar
½   teaspoon pepper
3   egg yolks, well beaten
3   egg whites, stiffly beaten
1   tablespoon butter

Combine cornmeal, milk, onion, celery, salt, sugar and pepper. Cook 10 minutes, stirring constantly. Remove from heat. Add small amount of hot mixture to egg yolks; add this mixture to remaining hot mixture. Fold in beaten egg whites. Pour into a 2-quart, greased casserole. Dot with butter. Bake at 325 degrees for 1 hour. Serve with plenty of butter.

Serves 6 or 8.

• C O R N M E A L •

Southern cooks prefer "water-ground" corn meal, the whole grain meal made the old-fashioned way by grinding dried corn between water-driven mill-stones. It is widely available throughout the South and in specialty stores in the rest of the country. Most cornmeal marketed today is labeled "degerminated," indicating that the germ has been sifted out in order to improve the keeping qualties of the cornmeal.

CORNMEAL PUFFS

½ cup yellow cornmeal
½ cup cold milk
1 cup scalding hot milk
1 teaspoon sugar
1 tablespoon melted shortening
½ teaspoon salt
½ teaspoon baking powder
1 egg yolk
1 egg white, beaten

Mix cornmeal and cold milk. Stir into the hot milk. Cook over moderate heat until thick. Let cool 5 or 10 minutes. Then add sugar, shortening, salt, baking powder and egg yolk. Fold in egg white. Let sit 10 minutes to absorb moisture of egg. Form into walnut-sized balls. Fry in deep hot fat until golden.

Serves 4.

NOTE: *Cornmeal Puffs are delicious served with Spanish omelettes, sausage and syrup or with thin slices of sautéed ham, apple rings and scrambled eggs. This recipe is easily doubled.*

CHESTNUT STUFFING

3 pounds shelled chestnuts
1 quart stale bread crumbs
¾ cup butter
1 lemon, juice and rind
1 tablespoon chopped parsley
⅛ teaspoon nutmeg
   Salt and pepper to taste

Boil chestnuts in salted water, then mash. Fry bread crumbs in butter which has been slightly browned; mix with chestnuts. Add seasonings and enough stock until it is of desired consistency.

Yields enough stuffing for a 5 to 6 pound bird.

HUSH PUPPIES

1 cup cornmeal
2 tablespoons flour
1½ teaspoons salt
1 teaspoon baking powder
¼ teaspoon soda
3 tablespoons chopped onion
2 eggs
½ cup buttermilk
¼ cup sweet milk

Sift meal, then sift together other dry ingredients. Add onion, eggs and milk gradually. Beat well. Drop by spoonfuls (dessert size) into deep fat heated to 350 degrees. Cook until brown and drain on paper towels.

Yields 2 dozen.

POTATO STUFFING

2 cups hot mashed potatoes
1 egg, beaten
1 tablespoon minced parsley
½ teaspoon poultry seasoning
1 onion, chopped fine
½ cup chopped celery
1 loaf stale dry bread, cut in cubes
   Salt and pepper to taste

Add beaten egg to mashed potatoes. Mix into this parsley, poultry seasoning, onion and celery. Pour cold water over bread for an instant; squeeze dry and add to mixture. Season with salt, pepper and more poultry seasoning if desired.

Yields enough stuffing for a 10 pound turkey.

NOTE: *Use for stuffing fowl or roast.*

ROLLED OATS GRIDDLE CAKES

2 cups rolled oats
2 cups buttermilk
4 egg yolks, well beaten
4 tablespoons melted butter
⅔ cup all-purpose flour
½ teaspoon salt
3 teaspoons baking powder
4 egg whites, stiffly beaten

Mix oats with buttermilk. Cover and let stand overnight at room temperature.

Next morning, add egg yolks and butter. Mix well and sift together flour, salt and baking powder. Add to the oats and egg mixture. Last, fold in egg whites. Drop by spoonfuls onto a hot griddle that has been lightly greased. Serve with your favorite syrup and plenty of melted butter, bacon and/or sausage, and coffee or tea.

Serves 6.

NOTE: *These are particularly good served during Lent on Shrove Tuesday.*

FANCY BRAN MUFFINS

1¼ cups all purpose flour
3 teaspoons baking powder
½ cup sugar
2½ cups 40% Bran Flakes
1¼ cups milk
½ teaspoon nutmeg
½ teaspoon allspice
½ teaspoon cinnamon
1 large, tart apple, including skin, rather coarsely grated or 2 medium carrots, rather coarsely grated
⅓ cup vegetable oil or sunflower oil
1 egg
½ cup nuts
½ cup raisins

Sift together flour, baking powder and sugar. Set aside.

Mix together bran flakes and milk in a large bowl. Let stand a minute or two. Stir to soften bran flakes. Add spices. Grate apple or carrots into mixture. Add oil. Beat in egg and mix well. Stir in nuts and raisins.

Add dry ingredients to cereal mixture, stirring only until combined. Divide batter evenly into 12 greased 2½-inch muffin pan cups. Bake in 400 degree oven for about 25 minutes or until golden brown. Serve warm.

Yields 12 muffins.

Late-Night Suppers & Side Dishes

BLINTZES

½ cup flour
¼ teaspoon salt
3 eggs
1 cup milk

FILLING:

1 pint cottage cheese, sieved
1 egg
3 tablespoons sugar
  Grated rind of 1 lemon
  Dash of cinnamon
1 tablespoon butter

Beat egg; add milk, then flour. Beat again until well blended. Bake like crepes in a greased 6-inch skillet on one side only.

Beat filling ingredients until smooth. Lay pancakes browned side up and place 2 tablespoons of filling near top edge. Fold like an envelope. Add butter to a larger skillet and brown filled blintzes on both sides. Serve with plenty of crisp bacon and cherry preserves or your favorite jam.

Yields about 14 blintzes.

The Marketing of

• M A R G A R I N E •

Margarine production increased greatly after 1910 when the process for hardening vegetable fats by hydrogenation was developed. From its introduction, margarine was vigorously opposed by dairy farmers and even as late as the 1960s some states did not allow it to be sold except in its bleached form. A small capsule of artificial yellow food coloring was packaged with the margarine and the purchaser mixed the two together.

MIDNIGHT SCRAMBLED EGGS

½ cup onions, chopped
1 cup boiled ham, chopped
½ cup green peppers, chopped
12 eggs
3 tablespoons butter or margarine
Salt
Pepper

Chop the onions, ham and peppers quite fine and mix together in a bowl. Break the eggs in a bowl and beat a few seconds with a fork. Melt the butter in a big frying pan and pour in the eggs. After they have cooked a minute or two, stir in the ham and vegetables. Season with salt and pepper and continue to stir slowly until the eggs are cooked to a nice soft consistency. Then have buttered toast and warm plates ready and serve at once with coffee.

Serves 8.

NOTE: *This scrambled egg dish is a very popular snack following a night on the town. It can be prepared in a chafing dish right before your guests in the dining room.*

BUCKWHEAT CAKES WITH CHICKEN LIVERS

BUCKWHEAT CAKES:

1 cup unsifted buckwheat flour
2 teaspoons baking powder
1 teaspoon granulated sugar
½ teaspoon salt
1 egg, well beaten
¾ cup milk
2 tablespoons melted butter or margarine

Combine and sift buckwheat flour, baking powder, sugar and ½ teaspoon salt. Stir in combined egg and milk. Add 2 tablespoons melted butter or margarine and combine thoroughly. Pour batter in 5-inch cakes on a hot, greased griddle. When puffed and cooked on edges, turn and cook on other side.

CHICKEN LIVERS:

1 pound chicken livers
4 tablespoons melted butter or margarine
4 tablespoons flour
2 cups hot water
2 tablespoons Worcestershire sauce
1 teaspoon salt

Sauté chicken livers in 4 tablespoons butter until browned. Remove livers and add 4 tablespoons flour to gravy, blending well. Stir in water and heat until thickened, stirring constantly. Add Worcestershire sauce and salt. Add the chicken livers to the gravy. Spoon over buckwheat cakes.

Serves 6.

MEXICAN RAREBIT

1   small green pepper, chopped
1   small onion, chopped
2   tablespoons margarine
1   can (17 ounce) corn
½   cup tomato, peeled
⅓   pound Cheddar cheese, cubed
⅛   teaspoon salt
1   teaspoon chili powder
2   eggs

Wash pepper, remove seeds and chop fine. Chop onion fine and cook slowly in margarine until softened. Heat pepper, onion, corn, tomato, cheese, salt and chili powder together in double boiler until cheese melts. Remove from fire. Beat eggs; add to hot mixture, stirring constantly, and return to fire until mixture is hot and thickened. Serve from chafing dish on crisp crackers.

Serves 6 to 8.

OKRA WITH TOMATO AND GREEN PEPPER

1   pound okra
¼   cup olive oil
½   cup chopped onion
1   green pepper, chopped
1   garlic clove, minced
2   tomatoes, peeled, seeded and chopped
1   teaspoon ground coriander
    Salt and pepper to taste

Rinse and trim okra 2 to 3 inches long. In a skillet sauté okra in olive oil until it is lightly browned. Stir in onion, green pepper and garlic and sauté mixture until the onion is softened. Stir in tomatoes, coriander, salt and pepper and simmer mixture, covered, stirring occasionally for 15 minutes or until the okra is tender.

Serves 4 to 6.

STUFFED POTATOES CREOLE

6   baking potatoes
1   medium green pepper, diced
⅓   cup butter or margarine, diced
2   tablespoons minced onions
1   medium tomato, peeled and diced
1   (to 2) tablespoons milk
2   teaspoons salt
¼   teaspoon ground white pepper
1   teaspoon paprika
¼   teaspoon crumbled whole rosemary leaves
    Paprika for garnish

Bake potatoes at 425 degrees for 1 hour or until done. Sauté green pepper in 3 tablespoons of the butter until limp. Add onion and tomato. Cook 1 minute longer. Cut potatoes in half lengthwise and scoop out centers, leaving shells intact. Add milk and seasonings to potato mixture and mash well. Blend in sautéed vegetables. Fill shells with mixture and dot tops with remaining butter. Bake at 400 degrees for 20 minutes. Garnish with paprika. Serve at once.

Serves 6.

CORN PUDDING

    Kernels from 6 ears corn, grated
3   eggs, separated
1   cup milk
2   tablespoons butter
1   teaspoon salt
1   teaspoon flour
½   teaspoon baking powder
1   cup grated American cheese (optional)

Mix butter well, then add beaten egg yolks, grated corn and other ingredients, adding stiffly-beaten egg whites last. Bake at 350 degrees for 30 minutes. Grated American cheese (about 1 cup) may be added.

Serves 6.

Entrées

FLAKED FISH ASPIC
WITH BLACKSTONE DRESSING

2   tablespoons gelatin
¾   cup clear chicken broth
1   cup hot chicken broth
    Juice of 1 lemon
½   cup chili sauce
2   chopped dill pickles
1   cup diced celery
1   pound flaked crab meat or shrimp
    Lettuce leaves

BLACKSTONE DRESSING

1   cup mayonnaise
⅔   cup olive oil
⅓   cup vinegar
¼   teaspoon salt
3   canned pimentos, finely chopped
1   tablespoon onion, finely chopped
3   tablespoons chili sauce
    Pepper to taste

Soak gelatin in cold broth 5 minutes; add to hot broth and stir until dissolved. Let cool. Add lemon juice, chili sauce, and salt to taste. Set in refrigerator. Just when it begins to thicken, add pickles, celery and flaked fish. Place in molds and set in refrigerator to harden. Serve on lettuce leaves with Blackstone Dressing.

Make boiled salad dressing (see index) and when cool, mix with the dressing ingredients in order given and serve over aspic, or quartered lettuce or tomatoes.

Yields 4 to 6 servings.

BRAISED SHORT RIBS

2   onions
4   carrots
2   cloves garlic
½   cup bacon fat
½   teaspoon crushed rosemary
2   bay leaves
6   pounds meaty short ribs
    Flour seasoned with salt, pepper and garlic powder
3   cups beef broth
½   cup dry red wine

Sauté onions, carrots and garlic in bacon fat until vegetables are softened. Add rosemary and bay leaves and sauté mixture for 1 minute. Using a slotted spoon transfer vegetables to a baking pan. Dredge short ribs in seasoned flour and brown them in the fat remaining in skillet; transfer them as they are browned to the baking pan. Discard the fat from the skillet; add 3 cups beef broth and ½ cup dry red wine and bring the liquid to a boil, stirring in the brown bits clinging to the bottom and sides of the skillet. Pour the liquid into the baking pan; bring it to a boil and braise the ribs, covered, in a preheated oven of 300 degrees for 2 hours, or until they are very tender. Transfer the ribs to a heated serving dish and keep them warm. Skim the fat from the pan juices and discard the bay leaves. Sprinkle the ribs with salt and pepper to taste and pour the pan juices over them.

Serves 6.

NOTE: *Serve the ribs with buttered noodles or parsleyed new potatoes.*

TONGUE WITH RAISIN SAUCE

1   beef tongue (2½ to 3 pounds)
1   carrot, sliced
2   large onions, sliced
     Small piece of bay leaf
½   teaspoon pepper
1   teaspoon salt

Scrub the tongue. Place in a kettle with carrot, onion, bay leaf and pepper. Cover with cold water. Bring slowly to boiling point and let simmer without boiling until tender (2 to 3 hours). Do not add the salt until the last few minutes of cooking.

Strain off stock and set aside to cool. Remove skin from tongue and set aside to cool.

SAUCE:

1   cup red wine vinegar
1   cup brown sugar
½   cup seedless raisins
1   glass (8 ounce) currant jelly
2   tablespoons orange marmalade
1   lemon, sliced very thin
½   teaspoon whole cloves
½   inch stick cinnamon
½   cup stock from tongue
     Parsley

Mix vinegar, brown sugar, raisins, jelly, marmalade, lemon, spices and stock from tongue together. Heat until jelly melts. Put tongue in a covered roaster. Pour sauce around tongue and place in a 250 degree oven. Let simmer slowly for 1 hour or more.

Uncover roaster about 20 minutes before serving so that the sauce will thicken. It should be rather syrupy. If it is too thin, let it cook down for a few minutes on top of the stove until it is as thick as you like. Pour around tongue and garnish with parsley or watercress.

Serves 6.

POT ROAST OF LAMB

5½   pound boned lamb shoulder
¼   cup lemon juice
2   tablespoons butter or margarine
1   can (10½ ounce) condensed beef broth, undiluted
1   bay leaf
2   pounds new potatoes (12)
8   medium onions, peeled
½   cup fresh mint or 1 tablespoon dried mint
2   tablespoons flour

FILLING:

1   cup finely chopped onion
½   cup chopped parsley
½   teaspoon dried marjoram leaves
2   cloves of chopped garlic
1½   teaspoons salt
1   teaspoon dried basil leaves

Untie lamb and place on cutting board. Pound with mallet until meat is all the same thickness. Pour lemon juice over meat. Combine filling ingredients and spread over meat and roll up as for a jelly roll. Re-tie meat and brown roast well in butter in Dutch oven (about 25 minutes.). Spoon off excess fat from drippings and add beef broth mixed with water to make 1½ cups liquid. Add liquid and bay leaf and cover. Simmer 1½ hours, turning roast once. Add onions and potatoes and cook 40 minutes until meat and vegetables are tender. Remove to serving platter.

Skim fat from liquid; measure and add water to make 1¾ cups. Mix flour with ¼ cup water and stir into pan liquid. Add mint and bring to boil. Then simmer until thickened. Remove string from roast. Cut meat into slices. Pass gravy to be spooned over meat.

Serves 8.

Desserts

BANANA FRITTERS

4 bananas
¼ cup brandy
3 tablespoons sugar
½ teaspoon grated lemon rind
Flour

Quarter bananas by splitting in half lengthwise and then cutting across each length. Mix in brandy with sugar and lemon rind. Soak bananas in brandy mixture. Drain, dip in flour, shake off surplus, then dip in batter.

BATTER:

2 egg yolks
¾ cup milk or water
½ teaspoon salt
1 cup sifted flour
1 tablespoon oil
2 egg whites, stiffly beaten

Make the batter by beating the egg yolks well and adding the milk or water, a tablespoon of the brandy in which the bananas soaked, salt, flour and oil. Mix well, then fold in stiffly-beaten egg whites. Pan fry in butter or fry in deep fat at 360 degrees until brown. Serve with brandy sauce or whipped cream.

Serves 4 to 6.

PEACH KUCHEN

½ cup butter or margarine
2 tablespoons sugar
1 egg, slightly beaten
½ teaspoon baking powder
8 medium peaches, peeled and sliced
½ cup sugar
1 tablespoon cornstarch
¼ teaspoon cinnamon
⅛ teaspoon *each* salt, nutmeg
1 cup sour cream

Mix butter, 2 tablespoons sugar, egg, flour and baking powder together like pie dough. Pat dough with hands into a 9x13x2 baking pan. Top with peaches mixed with sugar, cornstarch, cinnamon, salt and nutmeg. Cover with sour cream. Bake at 350 degrees for 35 minutes.

Serves 8 to 10.

DOVIE'S APPLESAUCE CAKE
DOVIE MOORE

½ cup butter or margarine
1 cup sugar
1 egg, beaten with ¼ teaspoon salt
1 cup applesauce
2 cups flour
1 teaspoon soda, dissolved in 2 tablespoons hot water
1 teaspoon *each* cinnamon, cloves and allspice
1 cup seedless raisins
½ cup chopped nuts (optional)

Cream butter and sugar. Add beaten egg. Add applesauce, soda and water mixture. Mix flour, spices, raisins and nuts, if used. Mix well and put in greased 8-inch pan. Bake 25 or 30 minutes in 350 degree oven. Sprinkle with powdered sugar or frost with buttercream frosting.

GREEN TOMATO PIE

4   cups sliced green tomatoes
2   tablespoons flour
½   cup sugar
    Grated rind of 1 lemon
¼   teaspoon allspice
¼   teaspoon salt
1   teaspoon lemon juice
3   tablespoons butter or margarine
    Pastry for 9-inch pie and lattice top

Line a pie pan with your favorite pie dough. Mix flour, sugar, lemon rind, spices and salt together. Sprinkle a little on the bottom of pie shell. Add a layer of green tomatoes. Cover each layer with sugar mixture, lemon juice and dot with butter. Repeat this sequence until pie is filled. Cover with lattice crust and bake at 350 degrees for 45 minutes.

Serves 6 to 8.

MEATLESS MINCE PIE

8   cups chopped green tomatoes
¼   cup vinegar
1½   cups sugar
1   teaspoon salt
1   teaspoon cinnamon
1   teaspoon cloves
1   cup raisins
3   tablespoons butter or margarine
    Pastry for 8-inch pie with top crust

Place tomatoes in a saucepan and add just enough water to cover. Cook 30 minutes. Drain off juice thoroughly. Add the remaining ingredients. Continue to cook until mixture thickens (about 20 minutes). Cool. Pour mixture into pie shell. Cover with a top crust and bake in a 375 degree oven for 30 minutes.

Serves 6 to 8.

Pickles & Mincemeat

KOSHER DILL PICKLES

20   to 25 pickling cucumbers
⅛   teaspoon powdered alum for each quart
6   (to 8) cloves garlic
12   (to 14) heads dill
6   (to 8) hot red peppers
1   quart vinegar
1   cup Kosher salt
3   quarts water
    Grape leaves

Wash cucumbers; let stand in cold water overnight. Pack in sterilized jars. To each quart add ⅛ teaspoon alum, 1 clove garlic, 2 heads dill and 1 red pepper. Combine vinegar, salt and water; bring to a boil. Fill jars. Place grape leaf in each jar and seal.

Yields 6 to 8 quarts, depending on size of cucumbers.

CLEORA'S HAMBURGER ONIONS

1   quart sliced Bermuda onions

PICKLE JUICE OF:

¾   cup white vinegar
½   cup sugar
2   teaspoons salt
1¼   cups cold water
⅛   teaspoon cracked pepper (optional)

Peel and slice medium thin enough Bermuda onions to fill a quart jar. In saucepan, cover onions with cold water and bring to the boiling point but *do not boil.* Remove from fire; drain and immediately cover with ice cubes to prevent further cooking.
    Drain and pour pickle juice over onions.

OIL PICKLES

4   quarts cucumbers, sliced
    Pickling salt
½   teaspoon cloves
½   teaspoon allspice
2   teaspoons cinnamon
½   teaspoon celery seed
½   cup mustard seed
½   cup sugar
1   dozen onions, thinly sliced
½   cup olive oil (more if you like)
    Cold vinegar

Cover sliced cucumbers with boiling water. When cold, drain and cover with weak brine (¼ cup pickling salt to each quart water). Let stand overnight. Next morning, combine cloves, allspice, celery seed, cinnamon, mustard seed and sugar. Drain cucumbers; mix with onions, then mix with spices. Pour olive oil and enough cold vinegar to cover. Mix well and seal.

Yields 5 quarts.

NOTE: *Store 2 weeks before using. Oil will rise to top and seal jars. Shake before opening to distribute oil.*

CASSIA BUD OR 12-DAY PICKLES

75 cucumbers (2 to 3 inch)
4   quarts boiling water
2   cups coarse-medium salt
1   teaspoon alum
6   cups vinegar
8   cups sugar
1   ounce (4 tablespoons) celery seed
1   ounce (4 tablespoons) cassia buds

Cut cucumbers in sliced rounds. Bring the salted water to a boil; cool. Pour over cucumbers placed in a crock; cover. Let stand 1 week.

Drain; cover with boiling water; add alum; let stand 24 hours.

Drain; cover with hot syrup made with the vinegar, 5 cups sugar, celery seed and cassia buds. For 3 successive days drain off syrup; add 1 cup sugar to syrup; pour syrup over pickles (total 8 cups sugar).

On the third day, drain and pack in sterilized jars; pour hot syrup over top. Seal.

Yields 14 pints.

NOTE: *You forget the 12 days with the first bite.*

EDITOR'S NOTE: *You will have to look in a specialty store for the cassia buds which are the small, unopened flower buds of one variety of cassia, a relative of the tree from which cinnamon is derived.*

ELVIRA'S MINCEMEAT

1   large beef tongue
2   pounds beef suet
12 Winesap apples
1   pound citron
1   pound raisins
1   pound currants
2   pounds sugar
½   ounce (2 teaspoons) cinnamon
¼   ounce (1¼ teaspoons) mace
¼   ounce (¾ teaspoon) nutmeg
¼   ounce (1 teaspoon) ground cloves
1   teaspoon salt
1   quart dry sherry
1   pint bourbon

Cover tongue with water and cook slowly until very tender. Let cool in liquid and skin. Shred suet and chop it fine. Peel, core and chop apples. Shred citron. Grind tongue in meat grinder or put in blender. Mix all ingredients; add spices, bourbon and wine. Mix thoroughly. Pack in stone jar. Cover closely and store in cool place. Keeps well for months.

· T H I R T I E S ·

The Thirties

Canapés

SEASONED PECANS

4   cups large shelled pecans
10 dashes Worcestershire sauce
3   dashes Tabasco sauce
⅔   cup butter
    Coarse salt

Melt butter in pan. Pour in mixing bowl all but the milky substance in melted butter. Add Tabasco sauce and Worcestershire sauce and mix well. Add pecans and stir well until all the nuts are coated. Put nuts in shallow pan and heat in a slow oven at 275 degrees until nuts are crisp. Watch last few minutes to prevent burning. Sprinkle with coarse salt and store in paper bag.

PICKLED SHRIMP

2½ pounds cooked shrimp, peeled and deveined
2   large onions, sliced into rings
1½ cups salad oil
½   cup white vinegar
½   cup lemon juice
2½ teaspoons celery seed
⅓   cup sugar
    Salt to taste
1   tablespoon capers and juice
    Several dashes of Tabasco
4   bay leaves

Layer shrimp and onions in glass bowl. Combine remaining ingredients and pour over shrimp and onions. Refrigerate at least 24 hours. Drain well and serve with toothpicks.

Serves 6.

ARTICHOKE CANAPÉS

24 rounds (2-inch) of white bread
    Softened butter
1   cup mayonnaise
¾   cup Parmesan cheese, grated
    Salt and pepper to taste
¼   cup minced onion
    Lemon juice to taste
1   can (8½ ounce) artichoke hearts, drained

Butter the bread. Mix together mayonnaise and
cheese; season with salt, pepper, onion and lemon
juice. Slice artichoke hearts in ⅜-inch slices. Place 2
slices of artichoke heart on each buttered bread
round; spread with cheese mixture to cover. Put on
cookie sheet. Broil until melted and golden. Watch
carefully! Serve hot.

Yields 24 canapés.

NOTE: *Canapés can be made in the morning — cover
and refrigerate until ready to broil and serve. Delicious!*

OYSTERS WRAPPED WITH BACON

Raw oysters (allow 2 to 3 per guest)
Bacon (1 strip per 2 oysters)

Drain raw oysters, but do not wash them. Season
with salt and pepper. Then cut bacon strips in half.
Wrap 1 oyster in ½ bacon strip. Use a toothpick to
hold them in shape. Place oysters on a sheet pan and
put them in a 350 degree oven until brown and
slightly crisp. Remove from pan. Put in a chafing dish
or on a platter. Serve hot.

NOTE: *Pitted olives may be done the same way, only
omit salt and pepper.*

BACONED PRUNES

½   pound large prunes
½   pound sliced bacon
    Toothpicks

Soak prunes in hot water to cover for 3 hours.
Carefully remove pits without marring shape of
prunes.
    Cut bacon strips in half crosswise; then roll each
prune in one of these bacon strips. Secure with a
toothpick.
    Broil under a low broiler 8 minutes, turning once
or twice.

DRIED BEEF AND ARICHOKE DIP

5   ounces dried beef
¼   cup butter or margarine
3   tablespoons flour
2   pints sour cream
2   cans (14 ounce) artichoke hearts
¼   cup Parmesan cheese
½   cup dry white wine
1   can (4 ounce) of mushrooms, drained and
    chopped coarsely
1   tablespoon Worcestershire sauce
    Dash pepper
    Dash Tabasco

Tear dried beef into bite-size pieces. Sauté in butter
or margarine. Sprinkle with flour; stir well and add
sour cream. (Milk may be added if mixture is too
thick.) Add remaining ingredients and mix well. Serve
in chafing dish with Melba toast rounds.

Yields 6 to 7 cups.

GINGER CHICKEN ROLLS

¾ cup sesame seeds
1 tablespoon sugar
12 ounces cooked chicken
½ cup chopped candied ginger
½ cup ground almonds
2 fresh shallots, minced
2 teaspoons curry powder
  Salt and pepper to taste
2 teaspoons lemon juice
1 package (8 ounce) cream cheese
4 tablespoons softened butter

Toast sesame seeds with sugar in a heavy skillet over a medium fire until crisp but not dark. Let cool. Chop chicken very fine. In mortar, combine remaining ingredients with the butter and cream cheese. Shape mixture into four rolls. Coat with sesame seeds. Wrap in wax paper, twist ends of paper together, wrap in foil and freeze. When ready to use, bring to room temperature and serve with sesame seed crackers or melba toast.

• W A X E D   P A P E R •

In 1877 an American candlemaker came up with the idea of coating newspaper with wax to make it a tidier wrap for fresh fish. By 1884 paraffin-coated paper was used to line cracker boxes. Housewives of 1902 could buy bread wrapped in waxed paper, and in the same year rolls of waxed paper in cutter-edged boxes were first marketed.

HAWAIIAN MEAT STICKS

2 pounds sirloin tip, cut very thin (like bacon) across the grain 1½ or 2 inch by 4 inch strips

MARINADE:

½ cup soy sauce
1 clove of garlic, crushed
1 small piece of fresh ginger or ½ teaspoon ground ginger
3 tablespoons brown sugar
¼ teaspoon coarse-ground pepper

Combine ingredients for marinade. Soak steak in marinade for 3 or 4 hours. Thread strips of steak on bamboo skewers which have been soaked in water. Broil over hibachi coals to degree of doneness desired.

Serves 8.

NOTE: *This recipe came from Hawaii in 1938.*

SAVITA DIP

½ cup roquefort or blue cheese
1 tablespoon Savita
1 package (8 ounce) cream cheese
  Juice of one lemon
  Juice of one onion
1 pint mayonnaise

Mix all ingredients together until smooth. Use as dip with raw vegetables or on chunks of lettuce.

EDITOR'S NOTE: *Savita was a brand of concentrated brewer's yeast in paste form used to flavor soups, sauces, and dips. It is no longer marketed. A similar product, imported from France under the name Marmite, is available in 5.2-ounce jars in specialty stores.*

CHEESE FINGERS

1 cup flour
¼ teaspoon salt
 Dash of cayenne
2 tablespoons shortening
½ teaspoon baking powder
 Ice water
½ cup grated cheese

Mix flour, salt, cayenne, shortening and baking powder. Add cheese and enough ice water to make pastry-like dough. Roll out into thin sheet. Cut in ½-inch strips with jagging iron and bake at 400 degrees for 8 to 10 minutes.

Cheese fingers can be brushed with a little egg wash and sprinkled with paprika before baking.

Serves 6 to 8.

VARIATION: *Use ¼ cup each bleu cheese and Cheddar cheese.*

NOTE: *A jagging iron was an old-fashioned kind of pastry wheel for cutting a decorative edge on pastry.*

Light Suppers & Casseroles

POTATO CHOWDER

2 tablespoons butter
2 tablespoons flour
1 pint milk
1 pint cream
1 pint chicken broth
6 slices bacon
1 large onion, finely chopped
6 diced cold potatoes
 Chopped parsley

Make a sauce with the flour, melted butter, milk, cream and chicken broth. Chop and fry the bacon and onions and add them to the sauce with potatoes and chopped parsley. Cook 45 minutes over a low fire.

Serves 6.

EGGPLANT SOUFFLÉ

3 pounds eggplant
3 cups water
1 tablespoon vinegar
3 tablespoons butter
2 tablespoons flour
1 cup milk
1 cup fine bread crumbs
3 egg yolks, slightly beaten
1 cup chopped pecans
1 large green pepper, finely chopped
½ pound aged Cheddar cheese
½ teaspoon coarse black pepper
¼ teaspoon cayenne
3 egg whites, stiffly beaten

Pare, cube and boil eggplant in water with vinegar for 30 minutes. Pour into a colander and drain well. Make cream sauce of butter, flour and milk. Add sauce to well-drained eggplant, mixing thoroughly. Add bread crumbs, egg yolks, pecans and green pepper to eggplant mixture.

Grate cheese, reserving ½ cup to sprinkle on top of soufflé. Stir balance of cheese into mixture. Season to taste with pepper and cayenne. Fold in egg whites. Pour into well-buttered 3-quart casserole and bake in 350 degree oven for 45 minutes.

Serves 8 to 10.

NOTE: *This dish is a delicious vegetable for a buffet supper.*

CELERY RAREBIT

2 tablespoons margarine
2 tablespoons flour
1½ cups milk
  Salt
  Pepper
1 cup sharp Cheddar cheese
1 whole egg
1 egg yolk
1 cup diced celery

Cook celery in a small amount of water until tender and drain. Make white sauce of next 5 ingredients and when thoroughly cooked, add cheese and beaten eggs. Stir until well blended. Add celery. Serve on crackers or toast.

Serves 6.

• OLEO •

The name margarine is derived from *margarites,* the Greek word for "pearly." Early margarines were called "oleomargarine" because beef oleo oil, a component of beef tallow, was one of their principal ingredients. Throughout the first half of the present century, margarine was commonly referred to as "oleo."

HAM LOAF SUPREME

1 pound ground ham
1 pound ground lean pork
1 cup soft bread crumbs
1 egg, beaten
1 cup sour cream
½ cup chopped green pepper
1 teaspoon dry mustard
½ teapsoon salt

Lightly mix all ingredients just until blended. Shape into loaf in a shallow baking pan. Bake at 350 degrees for 1½ hours. Allow to stand 10 minutes before removing to serving platter.

Serves 8.

NOTE: *Serve this loaf with horseradish-flavored cheese sauce.*

BAKED LIMA BEANS
LELA GOFF

1 pound baby lima beans
3 teaspoons salt
¾ cup butter
¾ cup brown sugar
1 tablespoon dry mustard
1 tablespoon Grandma's molasses
1 cup sour cream

Soak beans overnight, then drain. Cover with fresh water. Add 1 teaspoon salt and cook until tender (30 to 40 minutes). Drain. Rinse under hot water and put into medium-sized casserole. Dab butter over the hot beans. Now mix brown sugar, dry mustard and remaining salt in a bowl and sprinkle over beans. Stir in molasses. Finally, pour sour cream over beans and mix tenderly. Bake at 350 degrees for 1 hour.

Serves 6.

SALMON BAKE

1   can (16 ounce) red salmon
1   tablespoon lemon juice
1   cup grated raw carrots
1   small green pepper, sliced
½   cup mayonnaise or salad dressing
    Butter or margarine
1   tablespoon flour
½   cup milk
⅛   teaspoon pepper
⅛   teaspoon paprika
1   egg, beaten
2   slices white bread, crusts trimmed

Drain salmon well; remove backbone and skin; arrange in 1½-quart casserole. Then sprinkle with lemon juice. Start heating oven to 350 degrees. Fold in carrots, green pepper and mayonnaise. In small saucepan, over low heat, melt 1 tablespoon butter; stir in flour until smooth. Then add milk, stirring until thickened. Remove from heat; stir in pepper, paprika and egg; fold into salmon mixture. Butter bread and cut into squares. Arrange over top of casserole. Bake 25 to 30 minutes until bubbly hot and golden. Let cool about 5 minutes; then serve garnished with lemon slices or parsley sprigs if desired.

FRESH PORK AND BEAN CASSEROLE

1½ cups small pink beans
5   cups water
2   large pork chops
1   clove garlic, minced
1   medium onion, chopped
2   medium tomatoes, or 1 cup canned tomatoes
1   can (4 ounce) green chili peppers
½   pound (2 cups) grated Cheddar cheese
2   teaspoons salt
¼   teaspoon pepper
2   tablespoons butter or margarine

Cook dried beans in water until tender (no need to soak first). Remove fat from chops and render in frying pan. Cut pork meat into cubes and brown in pork fat with the garlic and onion. Cut tomatoes and green chili peppers into small pieces and stir into pork mixture. Simmer until pork is cooked. Add drained beans, 1 cup of the cheese, salt and pepper, and simmer a few minutes longer. Turn into large casserole; top with the other cup of cheese and dot with the butter. Bake at 350 degrees for 30 minutes.

Serves 10.

BEEF NOODLE CASSEROLE

1   pound ground beef
2   tablespoons butter
1   clove garlic, minced
1   teaspoon salt
1   teaspoon sugar
¼   teaspoon pepper
1   green pepper, chopped
½   pound mushrooms, sliced
2   cans (8 ounce) tomato sauce
1   package (7 ounce) flat noodles
1   bunch green onions with tops
1   package (8 ounce) cream cheese
1   cup sour cream
½   cup Parmesan cheese

Cook beef in butter until well crumbled. Add garlic, salt, sugar, pepper, green pepper, mushrooms and tomato sauce. Cook over low heat for 20 minutes. Cook noodles according to directions on package. Drain. Slice onions and tops; mix with cream cheese and sour cream. After meat sauce and noodles have cooled, grease a 2-quart casserole and alternate layers of noodles, cheese mixture and meat sauce. Repeat. Sprinkle top with Parmesan cheese. Bake at 350 degrees for 15 or 20 minutes or until cheese is bubbly.

Sauces

MOLASSES BARBECUE SAUCE

1   can (6 ounce) tomato paste
½   cup catsup
½   cup water
¼   cup molasses
1   teaspoon prepared mustard
2   tablespoons butter or margarine
1   tablespoon Worcestershire sauce
1   garlic clove, minced
1   tablespoon chopped onion
1   bay leaf
¼   cup wine vinegar

Mix well. Let come to a boil and boil for 5 minutes. Use to baste meat.

Yields about 2½ cups.

• C A T S U P •

Catsup, catchup, or ketchup? There are as many theories on the origin of the name as there are spellings for the familiar tomato sauce once made from either fruits or vegetables. It may be derived from the Javanese *katjap,* a very sweet soy sauce, or from the Chinese *kê-tsiap,* a brine for pickled fish. Catsup was the preferred spelling at the turn of the century. "Ketchup," today's most common spelling, was a food processor's spelling of the word.

BARBECUE SAUCE

14   ounces catsup
3   cups water
3   cups vinegar
1   cup brown sugar
1   cup white sugar
1   large onion
1   clove garlic
5   whole cloves
10   (or more) whole allspice
2½   teaspoons dry mustard
1   bay leaf
½   cup butter or margarine
     Salt, pepper, cayenne and Tabasco, to taste

Combine first 12 ingredients. Cook down to ⅔ amount. Add salt, black pepper, cayenne and Tabasco to taste. Keeps well.

Yields 1 gallon sauce.

NOTE: *This sauce was always made in large quantities for use at the Snedden's beautiful farm near Broken Arrow, Oklahoma. The barbecue pit was immense — large enough to cook a quarter of a steer or several dozen chickens at a time.*

Desserts, Rolls & Pancakes

BOURBON BALLS

60   vanilla wafers, rolled thin (about 9 ounces)
2   tablespoons cocoa
3   tablespoons dark corn syrup
12   tablespoons bourbon
1   cup nuts, chopped fine
1   cup figs, ground
1¼   cups powdered sugar

Mix all ingredients thoroughly. Roll into balls and then into powdered sugar. Store in tin boxes.

FIG PUDDING WITH HARD SAUCE

PUDDING:

½ pound figs, chopped fine
1 cup suet
2⅓ cups stale bread crumbs
½ cup milk
1 cup sugar
¾ teaspoon salt
1 teaspoon vanilla

Combine ingredients and steam in buttered and lightly sugared 1½-quart mold for 3 hours. Serve with brandied hard sauce to taste.

HARD SAUCE:

1 cup powdered sugar, or more
½ cup butter
Brandy

Cream butter and sugar. Add brandy to flavor. Stand up like whipped butter.

Serves 6.

CHOCOLATE ICEBOX PIE

¾ pound sweet chocolate
3 tablespoons sugar
2 tablespoons butter
3 tablespoons cold coffee
6 eggs, separated
1 teaspoon vanilla

Place chocolate, sugar, butter and coffee in top of double boiler. When thoroughly blended, remove from heat and add well-beaten egg yolks. Then fold in stiffly beaten egg whites. Add vanilla. Pour into individual baked tart shells or one 10-inch baked pie crust. Chill for several hours. Serve with whipped cream.

PEACH COBBLER

Pastry
8 (to 10) ripe peaches
1 cup sugar
1½ tablespoons flour
Nutmeg to taste

Butter sides and bottom of an 8-inch baking dish and line with pastry, fitting pastry carefully into dish. Peel and slice peaches. Blend sugar with flour and nutmeg and add to peaches. Fill 3-quart casserole with peaches; dot generously with butter. Roll out top crust and sprinkle with 1 tablespoon sugar; roll sugar into crust lightly and place on top of peaches. Make a few slashes in top of crust and bake at 400 degrees for 30 or 40 minutes or until done.
Serve warm with thick sweet or sour cream.

Serves 6.

CLEORA'S GRAHAM CRACKER APPLE PUDDING

2 tablespoons butter or margarine
6 tart apples, chopped coarsely
1¼ cups graham cracker crumbs
1 cup pecans, chopped very fine
1½ cups sugar
1 teaspoon nutmeg

Butter an 8-inch baking dish with butter or margarine. Put ½ of apples in bottom of dish. Mix graham cracker crumbs, pecans, sugar and nutmeg. Sprinkle ½ of crumb mixture over apples. Add second layer of apples. Top with balance of crumb mixture over apples. Make 5 or 6 cuts through mixture to bottom of baking dish with spoon. Cover and bake at 325 degrees for 1 hour. Uncover and bake 15 minutes longer. Serve warm with plain or whipped cream.

Serves 6 to 8.

STRAWBERRY BAVARIAN

1   quart hulled strawberries
1   cup sugar
1   envelope gelatin
¼   cup cold water
3   tablespoons boiling water
1   tablespoon lemon juice
2   cups heavy cream, whipped

Crush the berries and add sugar. Let stand for half an hour at room temperature. Soak gelatin in cold water until soft, then dissolve it in the boiling water. Stir gelatin into the strawberries. Add lemon juice.

Chill the mixture and, when it is about to set, add the whipped cream. Pour the mixture into a wet mold. Chill until firm. Unmold and garnish with whipped cream and whole strawberries. Serve with any additional sauce desired.

Serves 8.

SAUCE SUGGESTION: *Vanilla sauce flavored with Kirsch, a cherry-flavored brandy.*

CLEORA'S BRAZIL NUT PUDDING

1   cup dates
1   cup boiling water
1½ tablespoons butter
1   teaspoon soda
1   egg, lightly beaten
1   cup sugar
¾   cup flour
1½ cups soft bread crumbs
¼   teaspoon salt
1   cup Brazil nuts, chopped fine
½   teaspoon nutmeg
½   teaspoon cinnamon

Pour boiling water over dates, butter and soda. Set aside to cool. Beat egg and sugar until light. Add date mixture to egg and sugar. Add flour, bread crumbs and salt. Stir in chopped Brazil nuts and spices. Pour into a 1-quart mold or 6 small molds which have been greased and sprinkled with sugar. Steam 1½ hours or until done.

SAUCE:

2   egg yolks, beaten until light
1½ cups powdered sugar
¾   pint heavy cream, whipped
    Brandy

Beat egg yolks until light. Beat in sugar and add whipped cream gradually to egg mixture until all is folded in. Add brandy to taste.

Serves 6.

CAKE-CRUMB PUDDING

3   eggs, separated
½   cup sugar
¼   teaspoon salt
½   teaspoon vanilla
½   teaspoon almond extract
1   cup fine cake crumbs
2   cups milk, scalded
    Raspberry jam
1   teaspoon sugar

Beat egg yolks; add ¼ cup of sugar, salt and extracts and beat until light. Add cake crumbs. Add scalded milk; mix thoroughly. Pour into buttered 3-quart baking dish. Set in pan of hot water and bake at 325 degrees for 1½ hours or until custard is firm.

Remove from oven and spread thick layer of raspberry jam over top. Beat egg whites with remaining sugar until stiff. Spread meringue over top of pudding. Sprinkle lightly with 1 teaspoon granulated sugar. Return to oven and bake for 10 minutes or until brown. Serve warm or cold.

CLEORA'S GRAHAM CRACKER TORTE

5   eggs, separated
1½ cups sugar
1¼ cups graham cracker crumbs
1   cup ground pecan meats
¼   teaspoon salt
¼   teaspoon baking powder
1   teaspoon vanilla

Beat egg yolks until thick and lemon colored. Add 1 cup of the sugar gradually. Add crumbs, nuts, salt and baking powder mixture. Beat egg whites until stiff but not dry; beat in remaining ½ cup sugar. Mix by folding meringue into first mixture. Add vanilla.

Cut brown paper to fit 3-quart Pyrex oblong baking dish. Grease paper well. Pour batter into dish and bake at 275 degrees for 1 hour or until torte tests done with toothpick. Cool thoroughly.

To remove from baking dish: slide a long spatula between the paper and the torte. Place torte on a serving dish. Cover with sliced sweetened strawberries and whipped cream, sliced sweetened fresh peaches and whipped cream, or sweetened raspberries and a scoop of vanilla ice cream.

• G R A H A M •
Flour

The Reverend Sylvester W. Graham was a mid-19th-century Presbyterian preacher from Connecticut who campaigned against white breads and for bread made from unbolted (unsifted) whole wheat flour. The flour that bears his name is a coarse-ground, steel-cut flour containing more bran than regular whole wheat flour. It is a basic ingredient in that typically American "biscuit" — the graham cracker.

Serves 12 to 14.

NOTE: *Many interesting desserts can be made using torte as base.*

EDITOR'S NOTE: *Baker's parchment, available in rolls at specialty stores, can be used instead of the brown paper.*

PLUM PUDDING

1   loaf stale white bread (1 pound)
2   cups scalded milk
2   cups sugar
1   pound suet
¼   pound *each* candied red and green cherries, pineapple, citron and candied orange peel
1   package (8 ounce) dates
½   pound dark raisins
½   pound light raisins
2   cups all-purpose flour
1   teaspoon *each* salt, cloves, nutmeg, cinnamon and mace
½   teaspoon soda
2   teaspoons baking powder
½   cup molasses
½   cup wine
¼   cup lemon juice
4   eggs, separated
2   cups broken pecans

Soak bread and sugar in milk. Chop suet and fruits; dredge with flour mixed with salt, spices, soda and baking powder. Set aside. Add molasses, wine, lemon juice and egg yolks to bread. Stir in fruit and pecans. Place the egg whites on a platter and whip until stiff. Fold them lightly into the batter. Fill 4 well-greased 1-quart molds ¾ full and steam 3 hours or until done. Remove puddings from molds before they are cold. Keep in a cool place or refrigerator. Serve with hard sauce.

Yields 4 puddings, 8 to 10 servings each.

ALMOND RING WITH FROZEN STRAWBERRIES

4   egg whites
1   cup sugar
½   cup zwiebach crumbs
1½ cups blanched almonds
½   teaspoon almond extract
1   package (10 ounce) frozen strawberries
¼   cup sugar

Put the blanched almonds through meat grinder. Beat egg whites to a stiff froth and fold into them first a tablespoon of sugar, then a tablespoon of chopped almonds until all are used. Grease a ring mold carefully with Crisco. Mix the finely rolled zwiebach with the remaining sugar and line the mold with them. Put in the almond mixture. Sprinkle remaining crumbs over the top. Bake at 325 degrees for 30 to 40 minutes. Turn upside down on serving platter. Serve cold with frozen strawberries, crushed and sweetened a little, in the ring.

Birdseye and Frozen

• F O O D •

Clarence Birdseye first encountered frozen fish on a fur-trading trip to Labrador in 1915. Impressed by the quality of the defrosted fish, he began experiments with quick-frozen haddock which resulted in the development of a successful freezing method. General Foods bought Birdseye's process, introducing a full line of frozen fruits, vegetables and fish in Springfield, Massachusetts in 1930.

ENGLISH FRUIT TRIFLE

    Sponge cake, cut in pieces
1   cup strawberry jelly
    Grated lemon rind from 1 lemon
½   pint cooking sherry (1 cup)
3   tablespoons brandy
    Fresh fruit in season (1 pint of strawberries, for example)
12 (to 18) crushed macaroons
1   pint thick egg custard
    Whipped cream
    Slivered almonds

Place half of sponge cake in bottom of a 3-quart glass bowl. Coat with strawberry jelly and grated lemon rind. Soak with sherry and brandy. Cover with layer of fruit and crushed macaroons. Coat with custard and allow to set. Repeat the above procedure. Top with fresh whipped cream and slivered almonds.

Serves 6 to 8.

PINEAPPLE SOUFFLÉ

¼   cup butter or margarine
¼   cup flour
3   eggs, separated
⅓   cup sugar
1   cup milk, scalded
1   cup crushed pineapple
⅛   teaspoon nutmeg
¼   teaspoon vanilla
    Whipped cream

Melt butter or margarine; add flour and blend thoroughly. Add scalded milk gradually, stirring constantly; then add pineapple. Beat egg yolks slightly; mix with sugar and add to the mixture. Cook until thickened, being careful not to let the mixture boil. Cool slightly; add flavorings and fold in egg whites beaten until stiff. Bake at 300 degrees for 45 minutes. Serve hot with whipped cream.

AMBROSIA APPLE PIE

1   unbaked 9-inch pie crust
1½   cups quick cooking oats
1½   cups water
½   teaspoon salt
1¾   cups sugar
4   tablespoons flour
½   teaspoon cinnamon
4   large, tart cooking apples

Line a 9-inch pie tin with crust. Cook oats, salt and water for 5 mintues. Rub through a sieve and reserve ½ cup of strained oats. Mix oats with 1 cup sugar and flour. Pour this mixture on top of crust in pie tin.

Pare and slice apples into medium thick slices. Add ¼ cup water; cover and let apples cook over low fire for 10 mintues. Drain off all the juice. Arrange apple slices on top of oatmeal mixture. Sprinkle with ¾ cup sugar with cinnamon added. Dot generously with butter and bake at 450 degrees for 50 minutes or until done.

Cool thoroughly and serve with favorite cheese.

Serves 6 to 8.

PECAN CANDY

3   cups brown sugar
3   tablespoons dark Karo syrup
1   cup milk
¼   teaspoon cream of tartar
3   tablespoons butter
3   cups pecans
     Pinch of salt

Boil sugar, Karo and milk to soft ball stage (238 degrees on a candy thermometer). Add butter, cream of tartar and salt. When butter melts, remove from fire. Beat until mixture begins to thicken. Mix in nuts and drop from spoon on oiled paper.

GLAZED PEACHES WITH ALMONDS

Peach halves
Brown sugar
Butter
Chopped almonds
Orange liqueur

Coat large peach halves with brown sugar, butter, chopped almonds and an orange liqueur. Then brown lightly under broiler.

NOTE: *You may use a table-top broiler.*

WALNUT CAKE

1½   cups butter
2   cups sugar
6   eggs, separated
¾   cup milk
¼   cup brandy
1   teaspoon vanilla
3½   cups sifted flour
½   teaspoon salt
2   cups coarsely chopped walnuts
1   teaspoon cream of tartar
     Confectioner's sugar

Cream butter and sugar until smooth. Mix in egg yolks, lightly beaten. Mix milk with brandy and vanilla. Stir flour alternately with liquids. Add walnuts to the batter. Beat egg whites until foamy; add cream of tartar and beat whites until they hold definite peaks. Fold meringue into batter gently but thoroughly. Pour mixture into a 10-inch tube pan, oiled, lined with brown paper and oiled again. Bake at 275 degrees for 2½ to 3 hours or until it tests done. Cool cake completely. Peel off paper carefully. Sprinkle top with sifted confectioner's sugar.

• THE ICEBOX •

Ice cut from the frozen lakes of the northern states was shipped all over the country and throughout the world during most of the 19th century and well into the 20th. The first practical automatic refrigerators for home use went on sale in 1918 but they were not common until the 1930s. As late as the early 1940s, cookbooks still contained instructions on the use and care of "ice refrigerators."

ICEBOX ROLLS

1   cake yeast
½   cup warm water
1   cup milk
1   teaspoon salt
½   cup sugar
⅔   cup shortening
2   eggs
1   cup mashed potatoes
5   (to 6) cups flour

Dissolve yeast in warm water. Set aside. Scald milk, leaving it in the saucepan. Add salt, sugar and shortening. Cool. Beat eggs; add potatoes, milk and yeast mixture. Beat flour into egg mixture, 1 cup at a time — more if needed to make a stiff dough. Let rise until double in size (about 2 hours). Divide dough to make 2 or 3 loaves or into rolls. Let rise 1 to 1½ hours until double in size. Bake at 250 degrees for 10 minutes. Increase heat to 300 degrees and bake 40 to 45 minutes. Turn oven off; let stay 10 to 15 minutes.

Yields 2 or 3 loaves or 2 to 3 dozen rolls.

NOTE: *You can put the dough in the refrigerator and it will keep for 2 to 3 days.*

FEATHER-LIGHT CORNMEAL PANCAKES

1   cup all-purpose flour
1   teaspoon salt
1   teaspoon sugar
2   teaspoons baking powder
½   teaspoon soda
1¼   cups sour milk
1   egg
¼   cup melted shortening
1   tablespoon light molasses
½   cup yellow cornmeal

Sift first 5 ingredients together. Combine egg, milk, shortening and molasses. Add sifted dry ingredients and cornmeal; stir just until well blended. Bake on ungreased griddle. Serve with melted butter and your favorite syrup or honey.

Pickles

BREAD AND BUTTER PICKLES

1   gallon medium-sized cucumbers
8   small white onions, sliced
1   green pepper, cut in narrow strips
1   sweet red pepper, cut in narrow strips
½   cup coarse-medium salt
        Cracked ice
5   cups sugar
1½   teaspoons tumeric
½   teaspoon ground cloves
2   tablespoons mustard seed
2   teaspoons celery seed
5   cups vinegar

Slice cucumbers in thin rounds. Add sliced onions and peppers cut in narrow strips. Add salt; cover with cracked ice; mix thoroughly. Let stand 3 hours. Drain. Combine remaining ingredients; pour over cucumber mixture. Bring to a boil; seal in sterilized jars.

· F O R T I E S ·

The Forties

Dips, Spreads & Salads

MEXICAN COLE SLAW
HOWARD WHITEHILL

2   cups mayonnaise
¾   cup sweet gherkin pickle juice
1   teaspoon salt
½   teaspoon pepper
1   large head firm white cabbage, grated fine
2   large carrots, grated fine
1   large onion, grated fine

Mix mayonnaise, pickle juice, salt and pepper; blend well and pour over grated vegetables. Let stand 2 or more hours (overnight is best) before serving.

Serves 6.

NOTE: *This slaw stays crunchy as long as it lasts. Mr. Whitehill brought this recipe from Mexico.*

ARTICHOKE DIP

2   slices crumbled bacon
1   can (15 ounce) artichokes, drained and chopped
½   cup mayonnaise
1   tablespoon onion, chopped
1   tablespoon lemon juice
    Salt and red pepper to taste

Fry bacon until crisp; cool and crumble fine. Mix with artichokes, mayonnaise and other ingredients. Chill. Serve with mild crackers or raw vegetables.

Yields about 1½ cups.

OLD ENGLISH SPREAD

1   jar (3 ounce) pimento cream cheese
½   cup sweet pickle relish
½   cup grated sharp cheese
2   tablespoons chopped pimentos

Mix until creamy. Serve with thin rye bread fingers. If spread is served as dunk, add generous amount of chopped parsley.

Yields about 1½ cups.

COTTAGE CHEESE SPREAD

1   cup cottage cheese
1   tablespoon olive oil
1   tablespoon finely chopped parsley
2   tablespoons cream
1   teaspoon grated onion
10 stuffed olives, chopped fine

Mix all ingredients together. Chill 4 hours. Serve with Italian bread sticks.

BLEU CREAM HOUSE SPECIAL

1   package (3 ounce) cream cheese
½   cup crumbled bleu cheese
½   cup mayonnaise
1   tablespoon Worcestershire sauce
    Capers

Combine ingredients in mixing bowl. Mash and beat until mixture is quite smooth. Sprinkle capers on top. Serve with crackers.

Yields about 1⅓ cups.

• M A Y O N N A I S E •

Mayonnaise was first made in the 1880s by a French chef. This indispensable emulsion of egg yolks and oil has been called "mayonnaise," "mahonnaise" and "magnonaise." One view holds that "mayonnaise" comes from *moyeu,* a very old French word for egg yolk. Cookbooks at the turn of the century contain directions for making mayonnaise which was first bottled commercially in 1913.

AVOCADO AND YOGURT SALAD DRESSING

1   very ripe avocado, peeled, pitted and cubed
1   cup plain yogurt
⅓   cup *each* diced onion and diced green pepper
¼   cup mayonnaise
1   teaspoon dill weed
½   teaspoon lemon juice
¼   teaspoon *each* sugar and minced garlic
    Salt and white pepper to taste

Put all ingredients in blender and blend until it is smooth.

Yields 2½ cups.

Breakfast & Supper Breads

WAFFLES WITH HONEY BUTTER

WAFFLES:

    2   cups all-purpose flour
    1½   teaspoons salt
    2   teaspoons sugar
    4   tablespoons melted shortening
    4   eggs, separated
    1¾   cups milk

Sift dry ingredients into bowl. Add milk, egg yolks and melted shortening. Beat thoroughly. Fold in stiffly beaten egg white. Let set 10 minutes and meanwhile heat waffle iron to good heat, but not to burning point. With a pastry brush, brush both sides of waffle iron (only to bake first waffle, unless iron is new and unseasoned. In this case grease slightly before each waffle is baked). Serve with honey butter.

HONEY BUTTER:

    1   cup honey
    1½   cups softened butter

Stir honey into butter until it is creamy. Spread enough honey butter on hot waffle to fill all the holes.

Yields about 12 waffles.

FRENCH DROPS

    1   cup water
    3   tablespoons sugar
    1   teaspoon grated orange rind
    ¼   cup butter
    ⅛   teaspoon salt
    1   cup flour
    3   eggs

Place water, sugar, orange rind, butter and salt in a saucepan, and bring to boiling point. Add flour all at once and cook for a minute or 2, stirring constantly until mixture leaves sides of pan. Turn into a bowl and cool slightly. Add eggs, one at a time, and beat with a rotary beater or electric mixer until mixture is smooth. Drop from a teaspoon into hot fat (365 degrees). Balls will brown and then crack. Turn and brown on all sides about 3 to 4 minutes in all. Drain on absorbent paper. Cool. Roll in powdered sugar or granulated sugar.

Yields 3 dozen.

GARLIC BREAD WITH PARMESAN CHEESE

    ½   cup butter or margarine
    1   long loaf French bread
    1   (or 2) peeled cloves garlic
    ½   cup grated Parmesan cheese
         Paprika

Allow butter to stand at room temperature until soft. Add 1 or 2 cloves garlic, crushed slightly. Let mixture stand at room temperature for 1 hour or longer for flavor to permeate butter. Remove garlic. Slice bread diagonally into thick slices, being careful not to sever them completely.

Spread garlic butter generously between slices and over the top of bread. Sprinkle loaf with salt, then grated Parmesan cheese. Dash with paprika and bake at 350 degrees for 15 or 20 minutes. Serve whole, letting guests break off pieces as desired.

ORANGE MUFFINS

2   cups sifted flour
2   tablespoons baking powder
1   teaspoon salt
3   tablespoons melted butter
1½ teaspoons grated orange rind
    Scant ½ cup seedless raisins
1   egg, well beaten
1   cup milk

Sift flour, baking powder, and salt. Add the liquid mixture all at once to the dry ingredients, stirring just enough to moisten the flour. Do not beat the batter. Pour batter into well-greased muffin pans, filling them ⅔ full and bake the muffins in a 350 degree oven for 20 to 25 minutes, or until they test done.

Yields 12 muffins.

Soups, Sauces & One-Dish Meals

ENCHILADAS DE ACAPULCO

12 chiles anchos (dried very dark red chiles)
6   chiles tepines (very tiny red chiles)
1   clove garlic
1   teaspoon oregano
1   teaspoon salt
¼   teaspoon black pepper
¼   teaspoon cumin (optional)
½   teaspoon ground coriander
3   large onions
1½ pounds lean veal or chicken
2   tablespoons margarine or olive oil
1   large can tomato purée
1   small can ripe olives, pitted
¼   pound blanched almonds
½   pound Parmesan (grated) cheese
24 tortillas
1   pint sour cream

Remove the seeds from chiles and scald in hot water until tender. Save the water. Run the chiles through finest grinder blade and then run through Foley mill to remove all skin particles possible.

Now finely chop 3 tablespoons of onion and sauté with garlic in margarine or olive oil. Add the chiles mixture, the water from the chiles and the spices. Simmer slowly for several minutes until the flavors are well mixed.

Cool and put in the refrigerator overnight. In the meanwhile the meat should have been simmering gently until tender. When ready and cooled, chop into small pieces, and into this, chop the pitted olives and the blanched almonds and return to broth in which the meat was cooked. Cool and refrigerate.

Grate the cheese and place in a jar; the extra drying time will help it. Leave the so far untouched onions in a handy place; wash the dishes and go to bed.

Next day, put about ⅓ of the sauce back into a deep broad heavy pan; heat thoroughly. Finely chop rest of the onion. Place the bowls with the meat, the grated cheese, the onion and the stack of tortillas in a handy place

Put on a large chef's apron. One at a time dip the tortillas into slowly simmering sauce until soaked and heated. Take out gently and lay on a large plate. Into each tortilla, roll a reasonable amount of the chopped meat, chopped olive and blanched chopped almonds mixture and a teaspoon of the finely chopped onion.

Carefully stack the enchiladas, folded side down, on a large platter. Sprinkle each layer with a little more onion and a generous portion of grated cheese. Over entire platter of enchiladas, sprinkle more onion and cheese and another ⅓ of sauce well heated.

Serve from the platter with a wide spoon that will not permit the rolls to break apart. The rest of the sauce (thoroughly heated), together with a generous bowl of sour cream, should be placed upon the table for handy reference. Serve with Mexican refried beans, a tomato and lettuce salad or guacamole, beer, burgandy, or black coffee — very good!

Serves 8 to 10.

CLEORA'S BEEF STEW

1   aitchbone, weighing 5 pounds
4   cups potatoes, cut thick
2   cups carrots, cut in 1-inch cubes
1   cup onions, thinly sliced
1   cup red wine
¼   cup flour for thickening
    Salt and pepper
2   cans (10½ ounce) bouillon
    Water

Soak vegetables in the red wine for about 4 hours until wine has permeated vegetables. Wipe meat, remove from the bone; cut in 2-inch cubes; sprinkle with salt and pepper and dredge with flour. Cut some of the fat in small pieces and fry out in frying pan. Add meat, stirring constantly so that the surface might be quickly seared. When well browned, remove to kettle. Put wine from vegetables and bouillon in the kettle and let simmer for about 3 hours until meat is tender. (It may be necessary to add a little more red wine.) Before the last hour of cooking, add carrots and onion. Cook potatoes separately and add them to the stew at the last minute. (This way, potatoes do not become mealy.) Remove bones and skim fat; thicken with the flour mixed with ¼ cup cold water. Cook 5 minutes.

Serves 8 generously.

DRESDEN SAUCE

1   cup sour cream
1   teaspoon Dijon mustard
1½ teaspoons horseradish
     Salt to taste

Mix ingredients until well blended; cover and refrigerate until needed.

Yields 1 cup sauce.

NOTE: *This creamy horseradish sauce can be served with a standing rib roast or a fondue and with fish, corned beef or sliced meat.*

CREAM OF SPINACH SOUP

3   cups well-seasoned chicken broth
1   onion, sliced 1-inch thick
2   cups cooked spinach (leaves only), rubbed through coarse sieve or Foley mill
1   cup heavy cream
2   tablespoons butter
2   teaspoons brown sugar
½   clove garlic, crushed
    Dash of nutmeg
    Salt to taste
    Whipped cream
    Paprika

Let chicken broth and onion come to boil. Simmer for 5 minutes. Remove onion. Add other ingredients and heat to the boiling point but do not let boil. Serve at once with a dab of whipped cream dusted with paprika on top.

Serves 6.

The

• A I T C H B O N E •

As with other things, the way in which beef is cut has changed over the years. A meatcutter's diagram in a 1900 cookbook shows the rump section divided diagonally in two. The upper section is labeled rump, but between it and the round is the "aitchbone, good for stews and pot roasts."

JOE'S MUSHROOM SAUCE
JOSEPH THOMAS

4   slices bacon
2   medium-sized onions, chopped fine
1   rib celery, chopped fine
2   large tomatoes, seeded and chopped fine
3   tablespoons clarified butter
½   pound fresh mushrooms
1   small clove garlic, crushed
1   tablespoon molasses
1   tablespoon catsup
3   tablespoons chili sauce
1   tablespoon Worcestershire sauce
3   tablespoons sherry
    Salt and pepper to taste

Cut bacon in small strips crosswise and sauté slightly. Drain, cool and chop fine. Set aside. Sauté onions, celery and tomatoes in 3 tablespoons clarified butter until tender but not brown. Add mushrooms, garlic and molasses and simmer 15 minutes. Add catsup, chili sauce, and Worcestershire sauce. Correct seasoning for salt and cracked pepper to taste. Add sherry. Serve with steak, chops or dry rice.

Yields about 2½ pints.

NOTE: *My brother Joe never forgot Mother's cooking lessons and gave me this recipe when I visited him and his family in New York City in 1946.*

Desserts

RUM PUDDING

CRUST:

2   cups ginger snaps, made into crumbs
½   cup sugar
½   cup melted butter or margarine

Mix ginger snap crumbs, sugar and melted butter or margarine together and pat into a 9-inch spring-form cake pan. Chill.

FILLING:

1   tablespoon unflavored gelatin
4   tablespoons cold water
2   cups milk
4   egg yolks
½   cup sugar
1¼   teaspoons cornstarch
1½   squares melted chocolate
1   teaspoon vanilla
4   egg whites
½   cup sugar
¼   teaspoon cream of tartar
4   tablespoons rum (more if you like)

To make the filling, soak gelatin in cold water; set aside. Scald milk. Combine sugar and cornstarch. Beat egg yolks. Add sugar and cornstarch to egg yolks. Add scalded milk slowly. Cook in double boiler until custard coats spoon. Take out 1 cup custard. To this, add melted chocolate and vanilla. Mix well and cool. Pour into chilled crust. Stir gelatin into remaining custard. Let cool but not stiffen.

Make a stiff meringue of egg whites, sugar, cream of tartar and rum. Fold into remaining custard. When chocolate mixture has set, cover with rum custard.

TOPPING:

1   cup heavy cream
2   tablespoons powdered sugar
    Grated semi-sweet chocolate or chocolate shot

Mix topping ingredients and spread over rum custard Sprinkle generously with grated chocolate or chocolate shot. Place in refrigerator for at least 4 hours (overnight is not too long). Makes a light and delicious dessert.

Serves 8 to 10.

The Electric
• M I X E R •

The beating of egg whites and cake batters was, until the invention of the electric mixer, one of a cook's most arduous tasks. In 1915, the Hobart Corporation brought out its first restaurant-size mixer and home mixers bearing the name Kitchen Aid were introduced in 1919. They were sold door-to-door and were not available in stores until several years later.

PECAN CAKE

1 pound all-purpose flour
1 pound white raisins
½ pound candied pineapple
½ pound candied cherries (red & green)
1 pound pecans, broken in pieces
1 pound butter
1 pound sugar
6 egg yolks, beaten
1 teaspoon soda dissolved in ⅓ cup hot white wine
3 tablespoons lemon extract
6 egg whites

Cream butter and sugar. Add beaten egg yolks; mix well. Add half of flour to fruit and nuts (cut fruits in chunky pieces, except raisins). Add remaining flour alternately with wine and soda mixture. Add fruit mixture to creamed ingredients and mix well. Add lemon extract. Mix well. Fold in egg whites which have been beaten until softly stiff (not dry). Bake at 275 degrees in a 10-inch tube pan which has been well greased with 2 layers of greased brown paper lining the bottom. Bake about 2 hours. If smaller loaf pans are used, bake for less time.

Serves 10.

BLACK WALNUT COOKIES

½ cup butter or margarine
1 cup sugar
1½ tablespoons milk
3 ounces melted chocolate
1¼ cups sifted all-purpose flour
½ teaspoon baking powder
2 eggs
1½ cups walnuts
1 teaspoon vanilla

Cream butter or margarine until light; beat in eggs, vanilla and slightly cooled chocolate. Mix chopped nuts with flour and baking powder. Stir into above mixture. Add milk. Chill for one hour then drop on greased baking sheet. Bake at 350 degrees for 10 minutes.

Yields 2½ to 3 dozen cookies.

DATE NUT CAKE

1 cup flour, sifted 3 times
½ teaspoon salt
2 teaspoons baking powder
1½ cups pecans, cut coarsely if large, whole halves if small
5 eggs, separated
1 cup sugar
1 teaspoon vanilla
1½ pounds pitted dates, cut coarsely

Add ½ cup of flour, salt and baking powder to pecans. Beat egg yolks with sugar until light; add vanilla. Blend in remaining flour until well mixed. Stir in floured nuts and dates. Beat egg whites until stiff. Fold into batter until well mixed. Pour into greased loaf pan lined with well-greased brown paper in bottom. Bake at 325 degrees for 1 hour. Let cake get cold before slicing.

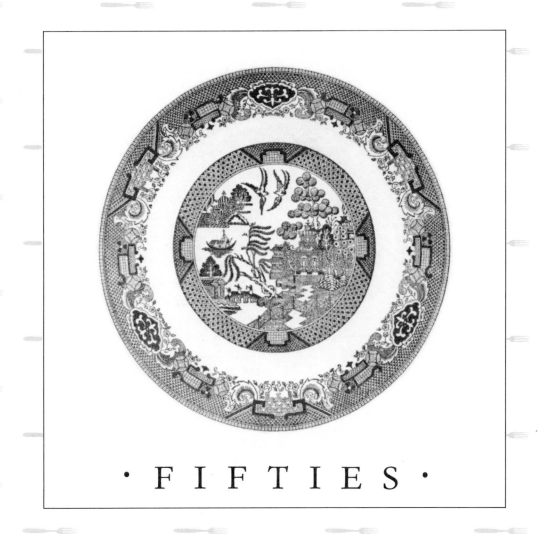

· F I F T I E S ·

The Fifties

Bohemian Sweet Rolls
(Kolacky)

1¼ cups scalded milk
1   cup melted butter
1   cup sugar
1   teaspoon salt
2   packages yeast, dissolved in ¼ cup lukewarm
     water
3¼ cups flour
4   eggs, well beaten
     Eggwash of 1 beaten egg and melted butter

Combine dissolved yeast with cooled milk, butter, sugar and salt. Stir in 3 cups flour, beaten eggs and beat the dough thoroughly. Add 3 to 4 more tablespoons flour to make a dough that is kneadable but not too firm. Knead the dough in a lightly floured bowl until it is smooth and satiny. Put in a buttered bowl; cover it and let it rise until it is doubled in bulk. Turn the dough out on a board and shape it into balls 1½ inches in diameter. Set the balls on an oiled baking sheet; make a depression in the center of each and brush the tops with 1 beaten egg. Fill the depression with prune filling. Cover the rolls and let them rise until they are double in bulk. Bake the kolacky at 375 degrees for 15 to 20 minutes. Brush the tops with melted butter and sprinkle them with confectioner's sugar.

Prune Filling:

2   pounds prunes, cooked and pitted
     Sugar to taste
1   teaspoon cinnamon
¼   teaspoon cloves
     Dash of nutmeg
     Prune juice or lemon juice

Put prunes through a food chopper. Sweeten with sugar. Add spices. Filling should have the consistency of thick applesauce. If it is a little dry, add some of the prune juice or lemon juice (for a tart flavor).

NOTE: *As a day-old pastry, Kolacky can be warmed up again and sprinkled with a little more confectioner's sugar and they taste as though they were just baked.*

SOUR CREAM PANCAKES

2 eggs, separated
2 tablespoons sugar
¾ teaspoon salt
1 cup cottage cheese, drained
1 cup sifted all-purpose flour
½ teaspoon baking soda
1 cup dairy sour cream
¼ cup melted butter, cooled

Beat egg yolks, sugar and salt together until thick and light colored. Add cottage cheese and beat until well blended. Add a mixture of sour cream and butter alternately with flour and baking soda, adding half of each at a time. Allow batter to stand 10 minutes. Beat egg whites until stiff, but not dry, peaks are formed. Fold into batter. Drop by tablespoonfuls to make dollar-sized pancakes on a greased griddle. Bake until lightly browned on one side; turn and brown other side. Keep warm until all the batter is used. Serve pancakes hot with jelly and dairy sour cream. Sprinkle with powdered sugar if desired.

Serves 4.

Instant
• S O U P   M I X •

In 1939 the Thomas J. Lipton Company marketed Lipton's Noodle Soup, the first dry soup mix. By 1942, there were over 65 brands of dry soup mix available, largely due to a shortage of tin during the war. By 1948, the war was over, tin was plentiful again, and only two companies were selling dry soups. Lipton was one of the two, and in 1952 the company brought out the soup that became a seasoning in its own right — Lipton's Onion Soup Mix.

ONION BREAD

2 packages yeast, dissolved in ½ cup warm water
2 tablespoons shortening
3 tablespoons sugar
2 teaspoons salt
1 package onion soup mix
1½ cups hot water
5½ cups sifted all-purpose flour

In a large bowl, mix shortening, sugar, salt, onion soup mix, and hot water. Cool to lukewarm. Add softened yeast. Gradually stir in flour to form stiff dough. Let rise in warm place (85 to 90 degrees) until light and doubled in bulk. Punch down and let rise again for ½ hour. Form into loaves. Let rise until double in bulk (about 1 hour). Bake at 375 degrees for 35 to 40 minutes.

Yields 2 loaves.

Casseroles & Entrees

STUFFED HAM

12 (to 14) pound ham with bone
¼ cup cooking oil
½ cup day-old cubed buttermilk cornbread
½ cup minced water chestnuts
½ cup sliced ripe olives
1½ tablespoons ground sage
1½ tablespoons ground dill weed
1 clove of garlic minced
½ cup chopped parsley
½ cup chopped celery
½ cup red cooking wine
1 teaspoon basil
1½ pounds pecans, ground fine
1 apple chopped coarse
cheesecloth
whole cloves

Have butcher bone ham. Trim excess meat from around bone and set aside.

Heat cooking oil in skillet and add cornbread, water chestnuts, olives, sage, dill weed, garlic, parsley, celery, basil and excess meat from ham bone. Sauté for about 20 minutes or until ingredients are well blended.

Pack sautéed ingredients into the cavity left when bone was removed from the ham, wrap ham in cheesecloth and tie to secure. Place stuffed ham in covered roasting pan, add wine and chopped apple and enough liquid to parboil the ham (about 1½ cups). Let liquid come to slow simmer until tender (about 3 hours).

Remove ham from broth and let cool completely. Then glaze and decorate with cloves.

GLAZE FOR BAKED HAM

1 cup brown sugar
¼ cup flour
1 teaspoon dry mustard
¼ cup maple syrup
3 tablespoons liquor in which ham has been cooked

If regular smoked ham is used, cook ham with bone in. Cook slowly for 4 hours on top of stove. Let cool in water. Remove from liquid. Skin ham and remove a good portion of fat. Score ham diagonally. Combine ingredients for glaze and spread over ham. Bake at 350 degrees for 45 minutes or until brown and glazed.

If precooked tenderized ham is used, bake in shallow pan at 325 degrees for 15 minutes per pound. If a meat thermometer is used, insert in thickest part of ham. Remove when thermometer reads 120 degrees.

Yields about 1½ cups.

SWEET POTATO CASSEROLE

6 large sweet potatoes, boiled and skinned
2 tablespoons butter
1 cup chopped pecans
1½ cups brown sugar
2 eggs, well beaten
4 ounces rum
Miniature marshmallows

Mash and whip potatoes. Add other ingredients except marshmallows. Place in buttered casserole. Bake in 350 degree oven 30 minutes. Then top with marshmallows. Return to oven and bake until marshmallows brown. Serve hot.

Serves 6.

CURRIED CHICKEN

1   young hen, about 3 pounds
2   tablespoons chicken fat
1   large onion, chopped
3   cups chicken broth (cook down broth from
    simmering chicken)
1   tablespoon red currant jelly
1   tablespoon curry powder
    Grated rind of ½ orange
    Juice of ½ lemon
½   cup sherry
½   cup rich milk
2   heaping tablespoons flour
1   apple, chopped

CONDIMENTS:

    Chopped celery
    Hard-cooked eggs put through sieve
    Toasted grated coconut
    Crisp crumbled bacon
    Chopped toasted almonds or peanuts
    Chutney and fried bananas

Simmer hen until tender. Cool and cut into bit-size pieces. Put chicken fat in pot. Cook onion until tender but not brown. Add chicken broth, jelly and other ingredients, except flour, milk and chicken. Stir milk into flour and stir into hot broth. Add chicken by folding in gently. Heat a few minutes longer. Serve over dry rice with condiments arranged in separate bowls.

Serves 6.

NOTE: *Curried chicken and pear salad with cream cheese balls in pits, or any favorite salad, and a light dessert make a good buffet or Sunday night supper.*

• C O N D E N S E D •
Soup

The first condensed soup was marketed under the Campbell label in 1897. The flavor was tomato and the idea was the brainchild of Dr. J. T. Dorrance. By 1913 the Campbell line included 21 soups, some of which are no longer made. The much used "sauce" soup, cream of mushroom, made its debut in 1934. Recipes using condensed soup as an ingredient became popular as a time-saving device during and after World War II, when "Rosie the Riveter" joined the work force.

ALBACORE TUNA CASSEROLE

1   package (7 ounce) elbow macaroni
1   tablespoon butter or margarine
2   tablespoons chopped onion
1   can (10½ ounce) cream of mushroom soup
½   cup water
½   cup American cheese, grated
1   can (6½ ounce) albacore tuna, flaked
2   tablespoons sliced pimentos
1   tablespoon chopped parsley

Prepare macaroni according to package directions. Preheat a 10-inch skillet, uncovered, over medium heat for two minutes. Sauté onion in butter for about 5 minutes. Add soup, water, cheese, tuna and pimento. Stir until cheese melts. Add macaroni and heat, uncovered, for 5 minutes. Reduce heat to simmer to keep warm for serving. Garnish with parsley.

Serves 4 to 6.

Aluminum

• F O I L •

Aluminum foil was used in commercial food packaging as early as 1912 but executives at Reynolds Metals testing the material for home use were spurred on by an incident that occurred 20 years later. One of the vice-presidents of Reynolds was roused from a Thanksgiving nap by his frantic wife, who could not find her turkey roasting pan. He hastened to the company lab for some test foil and the foil-wrapped turkey was cooked to a turn. Although the Depression and World War II delayed the advent of Reynolds Wrap, it was eventually marketed in 1947.

CORN CHOWDER

6   slices bacon, diced
½   cup finely chopped onion
2   cups diced raw potato
1½   cups water
2   teaspoons salt
⅛   teaspoon pepper
2   cups cream-style corn
2   tablespoons margarine, melted
2   tablespoons flour
3   cups milk
     Parsley, shredded cheese or corn chips

Fry bacon until crisp. Remove bacon. Sauté onion in 2 tablespoons bacon drippings until transparent but not brown. Cook potatoes in the water with salt and sautéed bacon in covered pan until potatoes are tender. Add corn. In large saucepan blend margarine and flour; stir in milk and cook until slightly thickened. Add corn mixture. Sprinkle parsley, shredded cheese or chips over top.

Serves 6.

EAST-WEST LAMB

1   leg of lamb
2   garlic cloves, cut into slivers
½   teaspoon *each* rosemary, sage and thyme
2   cups dry white wine
1   cup soy sauce

Trim roast, wipe with damp cloth. Make several slits all over; insert garlic slivers and rosemary in slits. Rub lamb with thyme and sage. Combine wine with soy sauce and pour over lamb. Allow to stand several hours or overnight in refrigerator basting frequently with marinade. Roast at 350 degrees continuing to baste occasionally. Cook approximately 30 minutes per pound (can be cooked all day at 250 degrees). Meat is done when it registers 175 degrees on meat thermometer.

OYSTER LOAF

2   dozen oysters
     Deep fat for frying
½   cup heavy cream
     Pepper and salt to taste
     Dash of Tabasco
1   loaf French bread
     Butter

Remove oysters from their liquor, saving the liquor to use later on the oyster loaf. Fry oysters in hot fat; drain on absorbent paper. Cut off top of bread and scoop out inside. Toast ⅓ of the removed bread and butter it generously; then crumble it. Put freshly fried oysters in a bowl; pour over them the cream; add toasted bread crumbs and the seasonings, and fill the hollowed loaf with the mixture. Replace the top crust and bake at 350 degrees for 20 minutes, basting frequently with oyster liquor. Slice and serve hot with dill pickles.

Serves 4 to 6.

VEAL CHOPS FRANÇAISE

1   egg
2   tablespoons milk
1   teaspoon salt
   Few grains pepper
½   teaspoon dry mustard
6   veal chops
1   cup dry cracker or rusk crumbs
4   tablespoons fat
1   clove garlic
½   cup dry white wine
1   can (10½ ounce) condensed mushroom soup

Beat egg with milk, salt, pepper and dry mustard. Dip chops in the crumbs, then into the egg mixture and again into the crumbs.

Melt fat in a heavy skillet, add the garlic and cook over medium heat until golden brown. Take out the garlic. Then sauté or fry chops on each side until a rich lovely brown. Mix the mushroom soup with wine, pour over chops, cover tightly and cook over very low heat on top of the stove for 45 minutes or until meat is tender when pierced with a fork.

Serves 6.

CRUSTED HAM LOAF

2   pounds ground cooked ham
1   pound ground lean pork
1   cup fine dry bread crumbs
2   eggs, slightly beaten
1   cup milk
   Pepper
½   cup brown sugar, mixed with 1 teaspoon dry mustard
   Ground cloves

Mix ham and fresh pork together; combine with bread crumbs and season with pepper. Add eggs and milk. Pack into loaf pan. Mix brown sugar and mustard and sprinkle on top. Lightly sprinkle with cloves. Bake at 325 degrees for 2 hours.

Serves 6 to 8.

GREEN BEAN CASSEROLE

3   packages (10 ounce) frozen French style green beans, thawed
1   pound mushrooms, sliced
1   medium onion, sliced
½   cup butter
¼   cup flour
2   cups warm milk
1   cup light cream
½   teaspoon Tabasco
2   teaspoons soy sauce
½   teaspoon pepper
1½   cups toasted slivered almonds

Sauté mushrooms and onion in butter. Add flour, milk and cream. When sauce is thickened, add Tabasco, soy sauce, pepper and cheese. Blend until cheese is melted. Add thawed beans. Pour into 3-quart casserole; sprinkle with toasted almonds. Bake in 375 degree oven 35 minutes.

Serves 8 to 10.

Salads, Sauces & Pickles

LETTUCE WEDGES WITH OPTIONAL DRESSINGS

Iceberg lettuce cut into wedges (as many as needed)
4 cups mayonnaise
1 cup chili sauce
¼ cup capers

TOPPINGS FOR DRESSINGS:

Finely chopped cooked egg whites
Chopped green onion
Chopped cooked egg yolks
Chopped pimento
Black caviar (lumpfish), or Beluga, whichever your expensive taste calls for

In a decorative bowl that will hold 5 cups salad dressing, mix the mayonnaise, chili sauce and capers. Make five wedge-shaped marks across the top of the dressing and place one of the toppings in each wedge-shaped space.

NOTE: *This salad is especially good for formal dinners or buffets. When ready, the hostess can mix with pride the beautiful dressing to be spooned over lettuce wedges.*

Yields 5 cups.

BING CHERRY SALAD

2 packages (regular size) cherry Jello
1 Number 2 can Bing cherries, dark and sweet
2 regular (6 ounce) Cokes
1 cup nuts, chopped fine

Drain cherries. Dissolve Jello in hot cherry juice. Cool. Pour in Coke; let set like jelly; fold in cherries and nuts. Pour in individual molds.

Serves 6 to 8.

CUCUMBER SAUCE

12 large cucumbers
6 onions
½ cup salt
3 sweet red peppers
1 cup sugar
1 tablespoon mustard seed
1 tablespoon celery seed
Vinegar

Grind vegetables. Add salt and let stand one hour. Drain. Add celery seed, mustard seed, sugar and enough vinegar to cover. Boil 15 minutes. Pour into sterilized jars. Seal.

Yields 6 pints.

Jerusalem

• A R T I C H O K E S •

Jerusalem artichokes are the knobby, starchless tubers of a native American sunflower. The French explorers who carried them back to the Old World noticed a similarity in flavor to the familiar globe artichoke. The new plant was called *girasole* ("turning to the sun") in Italy and the word evolved in time to "Jerusalem."

YELLOW SQUASH PICKLES

10 (to 12) unpeeled young yellow squash, each about 10 inches long
3 very large onions
1 gallon water
1 cup salt
5 short cups vinegar (4 cups plus 6 tablespoons)
2 cups granulated sugar
½ cup brown sugar
5 tablespoons whole mustard seed
2 tablespoons celery seed
1 teaspoon turmeric

Cut squash and onions in very thin slices. Put the vegetables in a brine made of water and salt. Soak in a large enameled kettle for 12 to 18 hours. Drain the squash and onions for about 1 hour but do not wash them.

In the same kettle, combine remaining ingredients. Boil this mixture for 5 minutes. Add the drained squash mixture and simmer the pickles for 30 minutes. Bring the mixture to a boil, pack in hot sterilized jars and seal.

Yields a little more than 4½ quarts.

JERUSALEM ARTICHOKE AND CAULIFLOWER PICKLES
LOUISE MACK

3 quarts Jerusalem artichokes
4 large onions
6 green peppers
1 large cauliflower
1 gallon water
1 pint salt

Slice or chop artichokes and onions. Cut peppers fine and break cauliflower into flowerets. Mix all together and cover with salt and water. Let stand 24 hours. Pour into colander and drain well.

SAUCE:

1 cup flour
6 tablespoons dry mustard
1 tablespoon tumeric
4 cups sugar
2 quarts vinegar

For the sauce, mix all dry ingredients and add enough vinegar to make a paste. Heat remaining vinegar and pour over mustard mixture. Return to stove and boil until it thickens, stirring constantly. Add vegetables; bring to boil and seal in jars while hot.

Yields 8 to 10 pints.

CLEORA'S CREAM PIE WITH CHERRY TOPPING

1½ pints half-and-half
6 tablespoons cornstarch
¾ cup sugar
3 egg yolks
¼ teaspoon salt
1 baked 9-inch pie shell

Remove ¼ cup half-and-half and heat remainder in a double boiler over hot water. Sift cornstarch and sugar together. Mix ¼ cup half-and-half with cornstarch and sugar; add egg yolks and salt. Add sugar mixture to half-and-half in double boiler stirring constantly until thick and smooth. Remove from fire. Add almond extract and cool.
Pour into pie shell. Cool.

TOPPING:

1 can (16 ounce) cherry pie filling
¼ teaspoon almond extract
¼ cup sugar
2 (or 3) drops red food coloring
Whipped cream (optional)

Combine cherry pie filling with almond extract, sugar and food coloring and spread over top. Chill 2 or 3 hours. Cover with whipped cream if desired.

Serves 6 to 8.

COCONUT CHESS PIE

2 cups sugar
2 cups water
1½ teaspoons vanilla
8 egg yolks
1½ cups shredded coconut
1 unbaked pie crust

Cook sugar and water to medium syrup. Add ½ cup butter while syrup is cooking. Remove from heat. Add vanilla, well-beaten egg yolks and coconut. Pour in unbaked crust and bake 35 to 45 minutes at 350 degrees or until custard is set and tests clean on knife inserted in center.

ORANGE CREAM SAUCE
MONA FARREN

2 egg yolks
½ cup sugar
 Juice and grated rind of 1 orange
1 cup heavy cream, whipped
1 teaspoon lemon juice
1 can (11 ounce) Mandarin oranges, drained

Mix all ingredients except cream. Cook over *low* heat until thickened (about 5 minutes after it reaches boiling point). Chill; add whipped cream. Fold in Mandarin oranges. Serve over angel food cake. Delicious!

• C A K E   M I X E S •

Cake mixes were first introduced in the 1930s. During the 1940s, sales of "cake in a box" increased as more and more women joined the wartime labor force. By the war's end the food industry recognized that cake mixes were here to stay. Pillsbury came out with a white cake mix in 1947, and chocolate fudge cake followed a year later.

· SIXTIES ·

The Sixties

Appetizers & Salads

EGGS STUFFED WITH ANCHOVY AND OLIVE

6   hard-cooked eggs, halved lengthwise
1   cup pitted black olives
3   anchovy fillets
3   teaspoons capers
2   teaspoons olive oil
1   garlic clove

In a blender food processor fitted with steel blade, purée all the ingredients. Chill the purée for 30 minutes. Fill the reserved halves with the purée, mounding it.

Yields 12 stuffed eggs.

NOTE: *Cut a thin slice from the bottom of each egg so they will stand upright.*

ROQUEFORT STUFFED SHRIMP

24 large cooked shrimp
1   package (3 ounce) cream cheese
1   ounce Roquefort or bleu cheese
½   teaspoon prepared mustard
    Dash garlic salt
1   cup finely chopped parsley

Split shrimp part way down vein side; remove intestine. Mix cheese, mustard and garlic salt. Blend thoroughly. With pastry tube, stuff shrimp. Roll cheese stuffed side in parsley. Chill and serve on bed of shredded lettuce. Broil left over shrimp.

Serves 4 to 6.

CHINESE BARBECUED BABY DRUMSTICKS

3 pounds chicken wings
⅓ cup soy sauce
3 tablespoons sugar
3 tablespoons brown sugar
3 tablespoons vinegar
1 teaspoon ground ginger
2 cloves garlic, crushed
½ cup strong chichen broth
Fresh ground pepper

Separate each wing into 3 pieces. Discard the tips. Marinate the wings in the other ingredients, well mixed, for about 2 hours, turning if necessary so that all pieces are covered. Place on a rack and bake uncovered at 350 degrees for an hour or a little longer. Turn once and baste 2 or 3 times with the marinade.

If you have a baster, keep the marinade in the pan. Baste from there; it makes a thicker glaze. But be careful it does not burn.

Serve with Chinese hot mustard.

CHINESE HOT MUSTARD:

Add boiling water to the best quality dry mustard, just enough to make a thin paste.

NOTE: *Both little joints are delicious, but quite different. The whole disjointed chicken may be cooked this way too, also cubes of beef and pork on skewers.*

TOMATO-MOZZARELLA SALAD

Fresh lettuce leaves
4 large ripe tomatoes, sliced ¼-inch thick
2 packages (8 ounce) mozzarella cheese, finely sliced
1 red onion, sliced into fine rings
1 can flat anchovies, well drained

Arrange lettuce leaves on a round, flat salad plate. Arrange tomatoes over lettuce. Cut cheese in strips and pile on tomatoes. Pile onion rings over tomatoes. Arrange anchovies over onions.

DRESSING:

5 tablespoons olive oil
1½ tablespoons red wine vinegar
1 large clove garlic, peeled and minced
2 tablespoons fresh basil, minced
1 tablespoon parsley, minced
Salt and fresh ground pepper

Shake dressing ingredients until well blended and dribble over salad.

Serves 6 to 8.

COLD STUFFED TOMATOES

1 tomato per guest
Scrambled eggs seasoned with dry mustard and onion
Mayonnaise
Lettuce leaves

Dip each tomato in boiling water and remove skin. At the stalk end, hollow out the interior in a neat, round hole, removing all the core and leaving a space.

Fill the holes with cold scrambled eggs to within half an inch of the top. Fill remaining space with mayonnaise, being careful it does not run down sides. Serve each tomato on a crisp lettuce leaf.

MARINATED VEGETABLES

1   bunch broccoli
1   head cauliflower
1   pound fresh mushrooms
1   pound fresh asparagus
1   small bottle pimento olives (optional)
1   cup vinegar
1   teaspoon pepper
1   tablespoon sugar (I like more)
1   tablespoon dill weed
1   teaspoon salt
1   teaspoon minced garlic
1½ cups vegetable oil

Break broccoli, cauliflower and asparagus in bite-size lengths. Peel tough outer skin off vegetables. Cut asparagus in 2-inch lengths, using all the tender stalk. Place in bowl. Mix remaining ingredients and pour over vegetables. Marinate 24 hours. Stir occasionally. Drain.

Serves 4.

NOTE: *Can also be used as finger salad for buffet dinner.*

EGGS POACHED IN BEER

Beer
Eggs
Buttered toast

Pour beer into egg poacher or skillet. Heat slowly. Add salt to taste and proceed same as when poaching eggs in water. Remove eggs to thin slices of buttered toast. Pour melted butter over eggs and serve with crisp bacon.

CUCUMBERS IN SOUR CREAM

1   medium cucumber, unpeeled
1   teaspoon salt
½   cup sour cream
1   tablespoon vinegar
1   (or 2) drops Tabasco sauce
2   tablespoons snipped chives or onion
1   teaspoon dill seed
    Dash of pepper

Cut cucumber in very thin slices and sprinkle with salt. Let stand 30 minutes. Drain thoroughly. Combine remaining ingredients. Pour over cucumber slices and stir gently. Chill 30 minutes before serving.

Serves 4 to 6.

CHOPPED LIVER APPETIZER

1   pound calf's liver (preferably in one piece — do not season)
6   green onions
4   tablespoons rendered chicken fat or butter

Bake calf's liver at 325 degrees until your meat thermometer reads 150 degrees (about 30 minutes). *Do not season.* Cool and remove skin and veins from liver; chop meat with a sharp knife (do not grind it in food chopper). Mince green onions; cook until wilted in 2 tablespoons rendered chicken fat or butter and mix with the liver. Chill. Just before serving, combine with another 2 tablespoons rendered chicken fat or butter and season with salt.

Yields about 1½ cups.

NOTE: *Served on lettuce and accompanied by thinly sliced rye or pumpernickel bread, this makes a delicious first course.*

• T A B O U L E H •

In the 1930s tabouleh was brought to Oklahoma by Lebanese and Syrian immigrants, a number of whom opened restaurants or delicatessens where the salad was sold as a specialty item. Fifty years later it is a standard item in restaurant salad bars and bulghur, the sun-parched wheat used to make tabouleh, is widely available in supermarkets.

STAY-CRISP SLAW

8   cups shredded cabbage (use knife)
2   carrots, shredded
1   green pepper, cut in very thin strips
½   cup chopped onion
¾   cup cold water
1   envelope unflavored gelatin
⅔   cup sugar
⅔   cup vinegar
2   teaspoons celery seeds
1½ teaspoons salt
¼   teaspoon pepper
⅔   cup salad oil

Mix vegetables; sprinkle with ½ cup of the cold water. Chill. Soften gelatin in other ¼ cup cold water. Mix sugar, vinegar, celery seeds, salt and pepper in saucepan; bring to boil. Stir in softened gelatin. Cool until slightly thickened. Beat well. Gradually beat in salad oil. Drain vegetables; pour dressing over top and mix lightly until coated. May be served immediately or stored in refrigerator.

Serves 8.

LEBANESE TABOULEH SALAD
JANET ELSON

1   cup bulghur wheat (medium grind)
1½   cups chopped green onions (green part too)
1½   cups chopped parsley
1   cup chopped mint leaves
2   large tomatoes, cut in ½-inch wedges

DRESSING:

⅔   cup lemon juice
⅔   cup olive oil
2   teaspoons salt, or to taste

Wash bulghur three times. Soak wheat in ½ cup water for two hours or until water is absorbed and wheat is tender. Add onions, parsley, mint and tomatoes. Mix dressing ingredients and stir into salad. Refrigerate after two hours.

TOMATO-ORANGE ASPIC

1   envelope unflavored gelatin
1   cup orange juice
¾   cup condensed tomato soup
     Dash cayenne
¼   teaspoon salt
¾   cup diced celery
     Lettuce
     Mayonnaise
¼   cup chopped parsley

Soak gelatin in ½ cup orange juice for 5 minutes. Set over hot water and stir until dissolved. Then combine with remaining orange juice. Add tomato soup and seasonings and celery and blend. Rinse a 1-quart mold or individual molds in cold water and pour in aspic. Unmold on bed of lettuce. Garnish with mayonnaise and parsley.

Serves 6.

PICKLED SHRIMP AND PEPPERS

1   pound cooked medium Gulf shrimp
1⅔ cups white vinegar
1⅓ cups sugar
⅔   cup lemon juice
1   tablespoon pickling spices
1   teaspoon celery salt
4   dashes liquid hot pepper sauce
4   whole cloves
3   small white onions, sliced thin
1   small green pepper, cut in 1-inch squares
1   small red pepper, cut in 1-inch squares

In a saucepan, combine vinegar, sugar, lemon juice, pickling spices, salt, celery salt, hot pepper sauce and cloves. Heat until sugar dissolves, stirring constantly. Chill. Arrange layers of onion, peppers and shrimp in a glass serving dish. Pour vinegar mixture over shrimp. Cover and chill overnight to develop flavor.

Yields 15 to 20 appetizer servings, depending on number of shrimp per pound.

The Food
• P R O C E S S O R •

An American entrepreneur named Carl Sontheimer is generally regarded as the father of the food processor. In the late 1960s he tried selling his idea to every large kitchen appliance manufacturer in America but was turned down by all of them. Undaunted, he took his proposal to France, where the first food processor, the Cuisinart, was produced in 1972.

Rolls, Breads & Muffins

BRAN CORNBREAD

½   cup shortening
½   cup sugar
2   eggs, well beaten
1   cup all-purpose flour
½   cup yellow cornmeal
3   teaspoons baking powder
½   teaspoon salt
1½ cups bran cereal

Cream shortening and sugar. Add eggs. Add bran to milk and let stand 5 minutes. Sift together flour, cornmeal, baking powder and salt. Add to creamed mixture. Mix bran in thoroughly, then flour and cornmeal. Bake in square 8-inch pan in 400 degree oven 20 to 30 minutes until done. Serve with butter.

ROLLED OATS MUFFINS

1½ cups rolled oats
¾   cup sifted all-purpose flour
4   teaspoons baking powder
2   tablespoons shortening
¼   cup sugar
1   egg
1   teaspoon salt
1   cup milk

Cream shortening with sugar and add beaten egg. Mix and sift baking powder, flour and salt together. Add rolled oats to creamed mixture; then add milk alternately with sifted dry ingredients. Beat just enough to mix well. Spoon into greased muffin tins and bake 20 minutes at 375 degrees.

Yields about 12.

OATMEAL ROLLS

2   cups scalded milk
1   cup rolled oats
1   package active dry yeast, dissolved in ⅓ cup warm water
⅔   cup brown sugar
3   tablespoons shortening, melted
1   egg
2   teaspoons salt
5   (to 6) cups flour

Pour scalded milk over rolled oats; cool to lukewarm. Add yeast which has been dissolved in water, brown sugar, melted shortening, egg and salt. Beat in about 3 cups flour, enough to make sponge. Let rise about 1 hour. Add between 2 and 3 cups flour to make soft dough. Knead until smooth. Let rise until double in bulk. Roll out to ½-inch thickness. Cut and shape rolls. Let rise until double. Bake at 375 degrees for 20 or 25 minutes.

Yields about 3 dozen rolls.

JOHNNY CAKE

1   cup yellow cornmeal
1   cup flour
3   teaspoons baking powder
½   cup sugar
3   tablespoons melted shortening
2   egg yolks
1   cup milk
2   egg whites, stiffly beaten

Sift dry ingredients; add milk, beaten egg yolks and melted shortening. Fold in beaten egg whites. Bake in an 8-inch square, well-greased pan at 350 degrees for 20 minutes.

Serves 4 to 6.

Egg Dishes

BAKED EGGS IN MAPLE TOAST CUPLETS

6   slices fresh bread
2   tablespoons butter or margarine
2   tablespoons maple-blended syrup or buttered syrup
3   slices crisp bacon, crumbled
6   eggs
    Salt and pepper

Butter six 2¾-inch wells of muffin pan. (Measure wells across top.) With rolling pin lightly press out each slice of bread. Preheat oven to 400 degrees. In a small skillet combine butter and syrup; heat, stirring to blend. Brush bread slices with syrup on one side. Carefully press bread slice, brushed side up, into each muffin well. Sprinkle crumbled crisp bacon into each cuplet. Carefully break 1 egg into each cuplet; sprinkle with salt and pepper. Cover with sheet of foil; bake 20 minutes or to desired doneness. To serve, carefully remove each cuplet from muffin well to a warm place.

Serves 6.

Journey

• C A K E •

Johnny cake, whose name evolved from "journey cake," is an old form of corn bread. It was quickly baked, sometimes without leavening, and was sturdy enough to carry on a circuit rider's rounds. One version, fisherman's johnny cake, was spread on a flat board and placed nearly upright before an open fire for baking.

CHILLED CHEESE SOUFFLÉS

½ cup grated Parmesan cheese
½ cup grated Gruyere cheese
½ teaspoon Dijon-style mustard
   Salt, pepper and cayenne to taste
1 envelope unflavored gelatin
1 cup plus 2 tablespoons chicken stock or consommé
2 tablespoons tarragon vinegar
1½ cups heavy cream, whipped
3 tablespoons fine, dry bread crumbs, browned in butter

Tie wax paper around the tops of 6 ramekins or individual soufflé dishes to make a collar about 1 inch high. In a bowl combine Parmesan, Gruyere, mustard, salt, pepper and cayenne. Soften gelatin in 2 tablespoons stock and mix it with 1 cup hot stock until the gelatin is dissolved. Stir in tarragon vinegar and the cheese mixture. Chill until it is syrupy. Whip it until it is frothy and fold in whipped cream. Fill the prepared dishes with the soufflé mixture, letting it come above the rims. Chill the soufflés until they are set. To serve the soufflés remove the wax paper collars. Stud the sides of each soufflé with thinly sliced stuffed olives, and sprinkle the tops with bread crumbs.

Serves 6.

POACHED EGG AND EGGPLANT

Poached eggs
Slices of fried eggplant
Hollandaise sauce
Bacon, crumbled

For each person, place a poached egg on a slice of fried eggplant. Top with a generous tablespoon of Hollandaise sauce and dust with bacon crumbs. Serve this egg dish in individual ramekins and you are on the road to success. Serve in a charming dish with a cover and you advance even further.

Yields 1 serving per person.

NOTE: *You may substitute a slice of fried tomato for the eggplant.*

CREOLE EGG CASSEROLE

8 tablespoons butter or margarine, divided
3 tablespoons all-purpose flour
1 cup milk
1 cup chopped celery
1 cup chopped onion
1 cup chopped green pepper
1 can (28 ounces) tomatoes
1 teaspoon salt
¼ teaspoon pepper
6 hard-cooked eggs, sliced
   Buttered bread crumbs

To make white sauce, melt 3 tablespoons butter in saucepan. Gradually add flour, stirring constantly. Gradually add milk; stirring constantly, cook until thick.

Melt 5 tablespoons butter in skillet; sauté celery, onion and green pepper until tender. Add tomatoes, salt and pepper; cook over medium heat until thick. Add to white sauce, mixing well. Place a layer of eggs in lightly greased 2-quart casserole; pour half of creamed mixture over eggs. Repeat layers. Sprinkle with bread crumbs. Bake at 350 degrees for 20 to 30 minutes.

Serves 6.

CARAWAY CHEESE OMELET

4   egg yolks
4   egg whites, stiffly beaten
½   teaspoon salt
    Dash of ground black pepper
¼   cup milk
1   tablespoon butter
½   cup shredded Cheddar cheese
2   slices bacon, cooked and crumbled
½   teaspoon caraway seed
    Parsley garnish

Beat egg yolks until light. Add salt, pepper and milk. Fold into egg whites. Turn into butter melted in a hot 9-inch frying pan or omelet pan. Cook over low heat until omelet puffs up and is golden brown on bottom (about 3 to 5 minutes). (Peek underneath by lifting edge of omelet with a spatula.) Sprinkle cheese, crumbled bacon and caraway seed on omelet and quickly place in a 350 degree oven for 10 to 15 minutes longer or until top springs back when pressed with finger.

Make 1-inch cuts at opposite sides of omelet and crease with back of knife. Fold on the crease by slipping spatula under half the omelet and lifting. Slide onto platter; arrange broiled link sausages around omelet and garnish with parsley. Serve at once.

Serves 4.

NOTE: *Caraway seeds can flavor more than rye bread or sauerkraut. The tangy seasoning has an affinity for eggs in any form. It improves chilled tomato juice cocktails and can be blended into cream cheese or cottage cheese, as well as other cheeses to add zest.*

If you haven't done much experimenting with the spice, try adding about ½ teaspoon of it to your next cheese omelet. Serve it with sausage for a late Sunday breakfast or evening supper.

Entrees

HUNGARIAN LENTIL SOUP
WENIFRED COWAN

3   pounds brisket of beef or rump, with bone
1   lamb's neck
1   piece smoked meat (end of smoked tongue), about ½ pound
3   quarts water
2   bay leaves
2   cups lentils
2   onions with skins
½   rib celery
    Salt and pepper to taste
3   cloves garlic, minced
1   teaspoon thyme
3   (or 4) carrots
1   potato with skin
1   can (16 ounce) tomatoes
½   pound Kosher salami, cut into strips
½   pound fresh or dried mushrooms, sliced
3   knockwurst, cut into thin rounds
1   cup chopped parsley

Cook first thirteen ingredients until meat, lentils and vegetables are soft and tender. Remove meat and skim fat off top of soup. Put vegetables through sieve (reserving a few carrots to give color). Cook slowly about 2 hours.

Add tomatoes, salami, mushrooms and knockwurst to strained vegetables. Simmer for another hour, then add parsley. (Some of the lentils can be sieved.) Reserved carrots can be sliced or chopped and added to finished soup.

Serve with green salad, dessert, a bottle of good red wine and dark pumpernickel bread.

Serves 12 to 14.

Chicken Tetrazzini
with Cheddar and Mushroom Sauce
Cordelia Jenkins

2	pounds whole chicken breasts, split
3	pounds chicken legs and thighs
3	celery tops
3	parsley sprigs
2	medium carrots, pared and sliced
1	onion, quartered
2	teaspoons salt
10	whole peppercorns
1	bay leaf
3	cups water

Place chicken in 6-quart kettle with 3 cups water, celery, parsley, carrots, onion, salt, peppercorns and bay leaf. Bring to boiling and simmer, covered, 1 hour or until chicken is tender.

Remove chicken from stock to bowl; set aside. Strain stock; return to kettle. Bring to a boil; boil gently, uncovered, until reduced to 2 cups (about 30 minutes). Remove chicken meat from bones in large pieces — there should be about 6 cups.

SAUCE:

¾	cup butter, chicken fat or margarine
¾	cup all-purpose flour
3	teaspoons salt
⅛	teaspoon nutmeg
	Dash cayenne
1	quart milk
4	egg yolks
1	cup heavy cream
½	cup dry sherry
1	pound thin spaghetti
2	cans (6 ounce) whole mushrooms, drained
1	pound sharp Cheddar cheese, grated (4 cups)

To make the sauce, melt fat in large saucepan. Remove from heat. Stir in flour, salt, nutmeg and cayenne until smooth. Gradually stir in milk and the 2 cups stock; bring to a boil, stirring constantly. Boil gently, stirring constantly, 2 minutes or until slightly thickened.

In small bowl, beat egg yolks with cream. Gently beat in a little of the hot mixture. Return to sauce pan. Cook over low heat, stirring constantly until sauce is hot. Do not let it boil. Remove from heat. Add sherry.

Cook spaghetti as package label directs; drain. Return spaghetti to kettle. Add two cups sauce and toss until well blended. Remove another 2 cups sauce and refrigerate, covered. To remaining sauce, add cut up chicken and the mushrooms.

Divide spaghetti into two 12x8x2-inch baking dishes, arranging around edges. Spoon half of chicken mixture into center of each. Sprinkle 2 cups cheese over spaghetti in each dish. Cover with foil; refrigerate. About 1 hour before serving, preheat oven to 350 degrees. Bake, covered, 30 minutes or until piping hot. Just before serving, reheat reserved sauce and spoon over spaghetti in baking dishes.

Serves 12 generously.

• B U T T E R •

Butter was first produced by machine in large quantities at a creamery in Orange County, New York in 1850, the same year the centrifugal cream separator was invented. In 1921 the Minnesota dairy farmers' cooperative, which was to become the Land O'Lakes Company, began marketing butter in paper-wrapped sticks and one-pound packages for home use.

CABBAGE ROLLS
MARK WIEDENMANN

FILLING:

2   pounds ground beef
1   cup cooked rice
2   cloves garlic, minced
2   small onions, chopped
1   tablespoon salt
½   tablespoon pepper
¾   cup water
2   small heads cabbage (cut hearts out)
1   can (29 ounce) sauerkraut

Mix meat together with rice, garlic, onions, salt and pepper. Bring water to boil and put in whole cabbage. Remove when leaves look wilted but have not lost their color (about 3 minutes). Separate cabbage leaves, selecting 16 large leaves. Place a mound of filling in center of each leaf, fold sides over and roll up.

SAUCE:

1   can (32 ounce) tomato juice
2   cans (8 ounce) tomato sauce
2   cans (16 ounce) whole tomatoes
2   tablespoons salt
    Juice of 2 lemons
1   teaspoon pepper
1   cup cider vinegar
1½ cups honey
2   (or 3) cloves garlic, minced
1   cup brown sugar
2   onions, diced

To make the sauce, put all ingredients in large pot and let simmer. Put cabbage rolls in roaster. Cover with sauerkraut. Pour sauce over all. Put in 350 degree oven covered for 2 hours. Continue cooking uncovered for 1 hour or longer.

Serves 6 to 8.

POLENTA WITH MEAT SAUCE

1   teaspoon salt
1   cup yellow or white cornmeal
1½   cups cold water
2½   cups boiling water

Mix cornmeal, cold water and salt to smooth paste. Stir into boiling water in the top of a double boiler. Cook over low heat, stirring constantly until it bubbles. Set the pan over boiling water and cook the polenta, covered, stirring it occasionally, for 35 to 40 minutes or until it has the consistency of a thick, smooth purée. Pour the polenta into a 9-inch square pan and chill it. Cut the polenta into squares, arrange them on a buttered baking sheet and bake them at 350 degrees for 25 to 30 minutes, until they are heated through.

MEAT SAUCE:

1   onion, chopped, sautéed in
1   tablespoon olive oil
¼   pound ground beef
¼   pound mushrooms, trimmed and chopped
⅓   cup red wine
1   can (6 ounce) tomato paste
1   garlic clove, chopped
¼   teaspoon dried basil
     Salt and pepper to taste
     Enough water or stock to make thin sauce

To make the meat sauce, sauté onion in olive oil until it is golden. Stir in ground beef and mushrooms and cook mixture for about 15 minutes or until meat loses its red color. Add red wine and cook mixture a few minutes longer. Stir in tomato paste, garlic, salt, pepper, basil and stock or water. Cook sauce, uncovered, 25 to 30 minutes, stirring it occasionally. Serve over polenta.

Serves 8 to 10.

PEPPERED RIB EYE OF BEEF ROAST

5 (to 6) pounds boneless rib eye of beef roast
½ teaspoon garlic powder
¼ cup coarsely cracked black pepper
¼ teaspoon ground cardamon seed
1 tablespoon tomato paste
1 teaspoon paprika
1 cup soy sauce
¾ cup vinegar

Sprinkle garlic powder over roast. Combine pepper and cardamon; rub all over beef and press with heel of hand. Place in shallow baking pan; pour mixture of remaining ingredients over roast. Refrigerate overnight, spooning marinade over meat occasionally. Remove meat from marinade and let stand at room temperature 1 hour. Save marinade. Wrap meat in foil and place in shallow pan. Roast at 300 degrees for 2 hours (for medium rare). Open foil; ladle out and reserve drippings. Brown roast uncovered at 350 degrees while preparing au jus.

AU JUS:

1 cup reserved drippings
1 cup water
1½ tablespoons cornstarch dissolved in ¼ cup cold water

To prepare au jus, strain drippings. Skim off excess fat. Add 1 cup water. Bring to a boil, adding a little of marinade if desired. To thicken, stir in cornstarch and water.

Serves 8 to 10.

HE-MAN BARBECUED STEAK

3 pounds sirloin steak (1½ to 2 inches thick)
1 can (12 ounce) beer
½ cup chili sauce or catsup
½ cup salad oil
2 tablespoons soy sauce
1 tablespoon prepared mustard
1½ teaspoons Tabasco
1 medium onion, chopped
2 cloves garlic, pressed or minced
½ teaspoon salt
½ teaspoon freshly ground pepper
⅛ teaspoon liquid smoke

Combine all ingredients except steak. Simmer for a few minutes. Brush both sides of steak with hot sauce; grill steak 4 inches from medium hot coals 10 to 15 minutes. Turn. Baste with extra sauce and broil 8 to 10 minutes (second side takes less time). Serve with remaining sauce.

Serves 6 to 8.

NOTE: *Good with a green salad and crusty rolls with fruit for dessert.*

ROAST SQUAB STUFFED WITH WILD RICE

1½ cups wild rice
2 tablespoons finely chopped parsley
½ cup finely chopped celery
¼ cup chopped onion
1 medium size apple, chopped
3 cups water
1 teaspoon salt
½ teaspoon pepper
8 squabs
½ cup butter or margarine, melted
½ cup sauterne

Wash rice thoroughly, then place in a large pan with parsley, celery, onion, apple, water and 1 teaspoon of the salt. Cover and boil 30 minutes. Drain. When rice is cool enough to handle, stuff squabs with mixture. Truss. Season melted butter with salt and pepper and roll squab in the butter. Place squabs, breast up, on a rack in a roaster. Pour wine over. Cover pan; then bake at 350 degrees for 30 minutes. Increase heat to 400 degrees and continue cooking for 30 minutes. Remove cover and, basting occasionally, bake for 15 minutes longer to brown. Use drippings for gravy.

CURRIED LOBSTER SCRAMBLE

6 eggs
¼ cup light cream
½ teaspoon onion salt
2 tablespoons butter or margarine
½ teaspoon curry powder or to taste
2 cups well-drained lobster meat
4 slices white bread
  Catsup
  Watercress or parsley

About 20 minutes before serving, lightly beat eggs with cream and onion salt. In skillet, over low heat, melt butter or margarine; stir in curry powder and lobster meat; heat. Toast bread; cut in halves. Meanwhile pour egg mixture into skillet and toss with lobster while eggs cook to desired doneness. Spread catsup on toast halves, then heap curried lobster on them. Garnish with watercress or parsley.

Serves 4.

VARIATION: *Substitute 2 cans (6½ ounce) King crabmeat, well drained, or 2 packages (6-ounce) frozen King crabmeat, thawed and well drained, for lobster.*

GOURMET FLOUNDER

1¼ pounds flounder fillets (4 pieces)
1 teaspoon salt
¼ teaspoon seasoned pepper
1 tablespoon dill weed
⅓ cup milk

Preheat oven to 350 degrees. Sprinkle fillets with salt, seasoned pepper and dill weed. Lay side by side in 12x8x2-inch baking dish; pour on milk, then bake 25 minutes.

Let flounder cool in milk. With wide spatula remove drained fillets to serving platter. Refrigerate at least 3 hours.

SOUR CREAM SAUCE:

½ cup sour cream
2 tablespoons lemon juice
½ teaspoon sugar
½ teaspoon salt
⅛ teaspoon white pepper
2 tablespoons snipped chives
1 tablespoon dill weed
½ cup finely chopped cucumber

In a small bowl combine sour cream, lemon juice, sugar, salt, white pepper, chives, dill weed and cucumber. Refrigerate. About 5 minutes before serving, place heaping tablespoon sour cream sauce in center of each flounder fillet. Pass remaining sauce. Garnish platter with fresh dill sprigs.

Serves 4.

SCALLOPED OYSTERS

1¼ stick butter (10 tablespoons)
1   cup celery (inner stalks), chopped very fine
4   ounces saltine crackers finely crumbled by
     hand
2   ounces (4 tablespoons) Worcestershire sauce
5   drops (no more) Tabasco
     Salt and pepper
1   quart fresh shucked oysters, tightly packed
     (do not drain)
     Paprika

Grease casserole lightly with butter. Simmer celery 15 minutes in barely enough water to keep from burning.

Melt butter. Put ⅓ of cracker crumbs in a 1-quart casserole and add in layers, ½ of oysters, ½ of celery, ½ of condiments, and ⅓ of butter. Repeat these layers. Put final ⅓ of cracker crumbs on top. Cover with final ⅓ of butter; sprinkle with paprika. Bake in preheated oven at 350 degrees for 45 minutes.

Serves 6.

NOTE: *One stack from a pound box of saltines will be enough for this recipe.*

Worcestershire

• S A U C E •

The ancient Phoenicians prepared a condiment similar to the modern Worcestershire sauce. It was also used by the Romans and came to England by way of India. A governor of Bengal asked Lea and Perrin to prepare the sauce from his personal recipe, but he was not happy with the way it turned out. The recipe, which contained 100 ingredients, was filed away and rediscovered years later when Lea and Perrin introduced its famous Worcestershire sauce.

ARKANSAS SHRIMP BAKE

1   pound Gulf shrimp, peeled and deveined
1   cup chopped onion
1   cup sliced celery
⅓   cup margarine
1   can (16 ounce) tomato wedges, undrained
3   cups cooked rice
1   teaspoon dill weed or oregano
4   ounces crumbled Feta cheese
½   cup sliced black olives

Cook onions and celery in margarine until tender. Add tomato wedges and heat. Stir in rice, dill weed, half of the shrimp, cheese and olives. Spoon into shallow casserole and top with remaining shrimp, cheese and olives. Bake at 350 degrees for 25 minutes or until shrimp is cooked.

Serves 6.

KING CRAB CAKES

2   tablespoons minced shallots or green onion
1   tablespoon butter
1   pound King crab meat
1   cup mashed potatoes
1   beaten egg
½   teaspoon salt
     Lemon wedges
     Watercress

Cook onion or shallots in butter; combine with crab meat, beaten egg, mashed potatoes and salt. Form into 8 oval cakes, dust very lightly with flour and sauté in butter or margarine until lightly brown on both sides. Serve garnished with lemon wedges and sprigs of watercress.

Yields 8 servings.

KING CRAB WITH OKRA
CHARLES ROSS

1   pound cut okra
½   onion, chopped
½   green pepper, chopped
1   clove garlic
2   cups canned tomatoes
3   cups water
1   pound mushrooms, sliced
2   tablespoons flour
1   pound raw shrimp, cleaned and deveined
1   pound lump crab or King crabmeat
4   tablespoons vegetable oil
1   teaspoon paprika
     Bay leaf, basil and chili powder, and salt and pepper to taste

Sauté vegetables until well heated. Add canned tomatoes and water. Cook over low heat until okra loses the ropiness. Add other seasonings. Add shrimp and crabmeat. Cook until shrimp is done (about 10 minutes). To thicken slightly, make a thin paste of flour and cold water, and add. Serve over dry rice.

CHINESE CRAB

2   medium onions
3   stalks celery
2   medium carrots
4   green onions, tops and all
3   tablespoons salad oil or olive oil
3   tablespoons butter
3   tablespoons chili sauce
1   tablespoon soy sauce
2   cups crabmeat
4   eggs

Put crabmeat in top of double boiler to heat. Cut onions, celery and carrots lengthwise into thin strips 1½ inches long. Slice green onions into rings. Sauté in oil and butter until lightly browned and barely tender. Stir carefully to avoid breaking the vegetables. Add chili sauce, soy sauce, salt and pepper to taste. Add crabmeat. Beat eggs slightly and stir into mixture. Continue stiring at intervals until eggs are set. Serve immediately.

Serves 4.

NOTE: *The secret here is to follow the "stir fry" method of Chinese cooking. Then you won't overcook the vegetables.*

SALMON TIMBALES

4   slices white bread
¼   cup milk
2   tablespoons butter
1   medium onion, finely chopped
1   pound red salmon
3   eggs
½   teaspoon salt
½   teaspoon tarragon

Soak bread in milk. Heat butter. Add onion to butter and cook until limp. Add salmon, seasonings, bread and beaten eggs. Bake in greased timbales or casserole at 350 degrees for 30 minutes.

SAUCE:

2   tablespoons butter
2   tablespoons flour
1   cup scalded milk
1   cup grated Cheddar cheese

Make sauce by blending butter and flour, then adding milk and cheese. Serve over salmon.

Serves 6.

Vegetable Dishes

GREEN BEANS CASSEROLE

2   tablespoons butter or margarine
½   cup sliced onion
2   tablespoons minced parsley
2   tablespoons flour
1   cup sour cream
½   teaspoon grated lemon peel
1   teaspoon salt
¼   teaspoon pepper
5   cups frozen French style green beans (cook first and drain)
½   cup grated cheese
½   cup buttered bread crumbs

Sauté onion and parsley in butter until tender but not brown. Add flour, sour cream, lemon peel, salt and pepper. Add well drained beans. Mix well. Pour in casserole. Sprinkle cheese on top; then bread crumbs. Bake 30 minutes at 350 degrees.

Serves 6 to 8.

CREAMY CARROT RING WITH PEAS

2   tablespoons butter or margarine
4   tablespoons flour
¾   cup milk
4   egg yolks
2   cups hot, mashed, cooked carrots
1   cup soft bread crumbs
1   teaspoon salt
¼   cup sugar
4   egg whites, stiffly beaten

For the ring, melt butter in top of double boiler; add flour and blend. Add milk and slightly beaten egg yolks and cook until thickened. Add carrots, crumbs, salt and sugar. Blend. Fold in stiffly-beaten egg whites, and turn into a well-greased 10-inch ring mold. Bake at 350 degrees or until firm. Turn carrot ring out on chop plate.

FILLING:

2½   cups frozen peas
1   teaspoon sugar
1   clove garlic, crushed
2   teaspoons butter

Fill with peas cooked in very little water, drained and seasoned with sugar, garlic and butter.

Serves 8.

FARMER'S CHOP SUEY

2   cups cottage cheese
2   cups sour cream
1   teaspoon salt
1   cup unpeeled cucumbers
2   cups torn lettuce
3   green onions with tops, chopped
½   cup sliced radishes
½   cup sliced green pepper
½   cup celery, thinly sliced
2   eggs, hard-cooked, quartered
1   pint cherry tomatoes, halved

Mix cottage cheese, sour cream and salt. Chill 1 hour. Cut cucumbers in half, if large; salt and chill. Drain. Line salad bowl with lettuce; fill with cottage cheese mixture. Arrange cucumbers, onions, radishes, green pepper, celery, eggs and tomatoes on top. Toss all together.

Serves 8.

STUFFED ZUCCHINI

1   pound cooked, flaked fish or crabmeat
3   cloves garlic, crushed
⅔   cup olive oil
1   cup seasoned, dry bread crumbs
1   cup chopped parsley
½   teaspoon pepper
4   medium zucchini (about 8 inches long)
¼   cup chopped onion
¾   cup tomato purée
⅔   cup chicken broth
1   teaspoon salt
½   teaspoon liquid hot pepper sauce

Cook garlic in ⅓ cup olive oil for 2 or 3 minutes. Add bread crumbs and stir until brown. Remove from heat and add parsley, pepper and flaked fish. Set aside. Cut zucchini in half lengthwise. Scoop out centers and reserve. Chop reserved centers of zucchini and sauté in ⅓ cup olive oil with chopped onion. Add tomato purée, chicken broth and liquid hot pepper sauce. Simmer for 15 minutes. Pour tomato sauce into rectangular baking dish. Stuff fish into the centers of zucchini. Arrange in tomato sauce. Bake at 375 degrees until tender — about 30 minutes.

Serves 6 to 8.

EGGPLANT NIÇOISE

1   eggplant, cut in half, lengthwise
2   tomatoes, chopped
    Onions, finely chopped
    Shallots, finely chopped
    Garlic, finely chopped
2   green peppers, finely chopped
    Butter and oil
    Bread crumbs

Remove seeds from eggplant making a hollow space. Cook other vegetables in butter and oil over low fire until tender. Then stuff eggplant halves with the mixture. Cook them under broiler for a while, then put bread crumbs and a little butter on top and broil for 10 minutes or until brown.

Serves from 2 to 4 people, depending on the size of eggplant and whether or not the dish is a separate course or merely served as a vegetable.

Desserts

LEMON MOUSSE AND BLUEBERRIES
MARY ANN JACOBS

1   quart blueberries
1   cup sugar
5   eggs, separated
    Juice of 2 lemons (about ¼ cup)
2   tablespoons grated rind
1   cup heavy cream

Wash blueberries and remove stems. Pour berries into a glass serving bowl and sprinkle with ¼ cup sugar.

In top of a double boiler, beat egg yolks and remaining sugar to a lemon color. Add the lemon juice and rind and cook over simmering water, whisking constantly until it coats a heavy spoon. Do not let it come to boil. Immediately remove from heat and cool. Beat egg whites until stiff but not dry and fold into lemon mixture. Chill. Fold in whipped cream. Just before serving, pour over berries.

Serves 8.

White Chocolate Mousse in Baked Almond Cups with Strawberry Sauce
Joe Pacetti

Mousse:

1   quart heavy cream
1   pound sugar
1   cup water
1   cup egg whites
2   pounds white chocolate, cut into small cubes

Whip the cream until stiff and refrigerate. Heat the sugar and water until mixture reaches 250 degrees on a candy thermometer. Meanwhile, beat the egg whites until they form soft peaks and then add the hot mixture in a slow, steady stream and blend for 3 minutes with an electric mixer. Add the chocolate and continue beating for another minute.

Remove whipped cream from refrigerator and stir into chocolate mixture. Chill.

Strawberry Sauce:

4   pints fresh strawberries
4   (to 6) tablespoons sugar (to taste)
2   tablespoons Kirsch

Crush strawberries in a food processor (or mash them) until they are quite fine. Stir in sugar and Kirsch.

Baked Almond Cups

4   eggs
1   cup sugar
1   cup granulated or sliced almonds
¼   cup all-purpose flour

Mix ingredients in mixing bowl until mixture is just porous, not smooth (don't overmix batter — almond pieces should be visible.)

Grease large cookie sheet with butter and spread 3 inch dollops of batter on pan. Spread each mound out with back of spoon so it is less than ¼ inch thick

and about 4 to 5 inches in diameter. Bake in preheated 400 degree oven for 8 to 10 minutes until batter looks brown around the edges.

Gently lift each rounded piece off pan while still warm. Place in small soup cups (about 4 inches in diameter). Mold crust so it makes a cup, overlapping edges slightly. Let cool, remove from cups.

Pour strawberry sauce on dessert plate and top with molded cup filled with mousse. Garnish with 3 fresh blueberries.

Serves 10.

Note: *This recipe was given to the Mansion on Turtle Creek in Dallas. If you haven't been to the Mansion on Turtle Creek, you haven't been to Dallas.*

Almond Tarts

1   cup butter
1   cup sour cream
2   egg yolks
2   cups flour

Cream butter and mix with sour cream and egg yolks. Blend in flour and roll into small balls. Place in refrigerator until cold. Press dough into tiny muffin tins about 1 inch in diameter.

Meringue:

2   egg whites, stiffly beaten
½   cup sugar, divided
½   teaspoon almond extract
1½ cups almonds, ground fine

Make meringue of beaten egg whites and ¼ cup sugar and almond extract. Work remaining ¼ cup sugar with almonds. Combine mixtures and fill muffin tins which have been lined with pastry. Add a half teaspoon of your favorite jam on top for variation and bake at 325 degrees for 15 minutes.

INDIVIDUAL BAKED ALASKAS

6   dessert cake shells or slices of sponge cake
1½   pints ice cream
6   egg whites
¾   cup sugar
⅛   teaspoon cream of tartar
     Grated coconut
     Chopped nuts

Place the dessert shells on a piece of brown paper on a thick board. If using cake slices, hollow out a place in the center of each. Freeze the cake.

Cover each piece of cake with ½ cup of ice cream, leaving a half inch edge of cake uncovered. Freeze.

Beat the egg whites with the cream of tartar until stiff then gradually beat in the sugar. Cover the ice cream with meringue and sprinkle with coconut and nuts. Bake in a 500 degree oven or place under the broiler for 4 to 5 minutes until nicely browned. Slide off paper onto chilled serving plates and serve immediately.

ENGLISH ROLLED COOKIES

1   scant cup flour
1   teaspoon ginger
½   cup molasses
½   cup butter
⅔   cup sugar
1   cup nuts, finely chopped

Sift flour with ginger. Heat molasses to boiling point. Add butter, sugar; then, stirring constantly add flour. Drop small amounts from top of spoon on an inverted cookie sheet with sides (jelly roll pan). Sprinkle with nuts and bake at 300 degrees for 15 minutes. Cool slightly. Remove from pan with spatula and roll over handle of wooden spoon to form a hollow tube. Remove from handle and cool.

Yields about 4 dozen.

ONE-HUNDRED-DOLLAR CAKE

1   cup butter
2½   cups sugar
5   egg yolks
4   tablespoons cocoa
1   teaspoon soda
2   tablespoons baking powder
     Pinch of salt
3   cups flour
5   tablespoons strong coffee
1   teaspoon vanilla
1   cup buttermilk
5   egg whites, stiffly beaten

Cream butter and sugar. Add egg yolks one at a time, beating well after each one. Add cocoa. Sift together soda, baking powder, salt and flour. Add coffee and vanilla to buttermilk. Mix flour and liquids alternately to creamed mixture. Add stiffly beaten egg whites by folding in gently. Spray two 9-inch layer cake pans with non-stick spray. Line bottoms with wax paper and spray paper. Bake at 350 degrees for 30 minutes or until cake tests done. Turn out on racks and ice.

Icing:

1   pound powdered sugar
2   teaspoons cocoa
½   cup butter
1   egg yolk
5   tablespoons strong coffee
3   teaspoons vanilla

To make icing, sift sugar and cocoa in a large bowl. Mix with butter and egg yolk. Add coffee and vanilla. Beat until creamy. Spread between layers and on top and sides of cake.

NOTE: *This is a very good cake. The name speaks for itself.*

GREEK HONEY-CHEESE CAKE

PASTRY DOUGH:

1 cup flour
¼ cup sugar
1 teaspoon grated lemon rind
½ cup butter, softened
1 egg

For pastry, sift together flour and sugar; add lemon rind. Blend in butter and egg. Wrap in waxed paper and chill while making filling. When ready, roll ⅛-inch thick and press onto bottom and sides of spring form pan; trim edges.

FILLING:

3 cups small-curd cottage cheese
¼ cup flour
¼ cup sugar
½ cup honey
¼ teaspoon salt
1 teaspoon vanilla
1 teaspoon grated lemon rind
½ cup currants
4 egg yolks, well beaten
4 egg whites, stiffly beaten

For the filling, mix cottage cheese, flour, sugar, honey, salt, vanilla, lemon rind, currants and egg yolks until well blended; fold into egg whites. Pour mixture into prepared pan; spread evenly.

TOPPING:

½ cup blanched, slivered almonds
¼ cup sugar
1 teaspoon cinnamon

For the topping, mix almonds, sugar and cinnamon; sprinkle over filling.
Bake at 350 degrees for 1 hour; then turn off heat, open door and let cool in oven. Refrigerate several hours or overnight. To serve, remove cake from pan and place on platter.

GLAZE:

1 cup sour cream
1 tablespoon honey
Lemon slices

For the glaze, blend sour cream and honey; fill center of cake. Garnish with lemon slices.
This cake can be stored in refrigerator several days.

Serves 9 to 10.

APRICOT PIE

Flaky pie dough
1 can (29 ounce) halved apricots
3 teaspoons cornstarch
¼ cup sugar
1½ cups syrup drained from fruit
¼ teaspoon nutmeg
2 tablespoons soft butter
Egg wash (1 egg yolk, beaten with 2 tablespoons milk)

Line 9-inch pie tin with flaky pie dough. Brush slightly with melted butter and set in refrigerator to chill. Roll out top crust. Cut strips for lattice top: make strips wide enough to lie around edge of pie.
Drain apricots, reserving syrup. Fill bottom crust with apricots, placing them close together, leaving little or no space between. Sift cornstarch with sugar; add syrup from fruit, nutmeg and soft butter. Pour over fruit. Lattice with strips. Brush a little egg wash over top crust. Bake at 375 degrees for 35 to 45 minutes until pie is golden brown.

Serves 8.

Italian Cheese Cake

⅔ cup butter
2 cups flour
½ teaspoon salt
2 tablespoons dry sherry

For the cake: cut butter into flour and salt and gradually add sherry and enough cold water until the mixture holds together and cleans the bowl. Roll out the dough ⅓-inch thick and line a 10-inch buttered pie plate.

Cut the remaining pastry into strips ½-inch wide for a lattice topping.

Filling:

4 eggs
⅓ cup sugar
1 teaspoon vanilla
1½ pounds ricotta (a creamy cottage cheese) run through a fine sieve
¼ pound toasted almonds, chopped
    Confectioner's sugar

For the filling: beat eggs and sugar until foamy. Stir in vanilla. Add cheese to this mixture and beat until well blended and smooth. Pour this filling into prepared cake shell and sprinkle almonds over filling.

Place lattice strips of pastry over the top, pinching edges firmly together. Cut enough strips to go around edge of crust and press down firmly. Bake at 350 degrees for 45 minutes, or until filling is firm and the pastry is a golden brown. Remove from the oven and cool. Sprinkle with confectioner's sugar before serving.

Serves 6 to 8.

German Chocolate Cake

1 package (4 ounce) Baker's German Sweet Chocolate
½ cup boiling coffee
2 cups sugar
1 cup butter or margarine
4 egg yolks
1 teaspoon vanilla
2½ cups sifted cake flour
1 teaspoon baking soda
½ teaspoon salt
½ cup buttermilk
4 egg whites, stiffly beaten

To make the cake, melt chocolate in hot coffee. Cool. Cream butter or margarine and sugar until fluffy. Add yolks, one at a time, beating well after each. Blend in vanilla and chocolate. Sift flour with soda and salt; add alternately with buttermilk to chocolate mixture, beating after each addition until smooth. Fold in beaten egg whites. Pour into three 8- or 9-inch layer pans, lined on bottoms with greased wax paper. Bake at 350 degrees for 30 to 40 mintues. Cool. Frost tops only.

Coconut-Pecan Frosting:

1 cup evaporated milk
1 cup sugar
3 egg yolks, slightly beaten
½ cup butter or margarine
1 teaspoon vanilla
1⅓ cups shredded coconut
1 cup chopped pecans

To make the frosting, combine milk, sugar, egg yolks, butter and vanilla. Cook over medium heat until thickened (about 12 minutes). Add coconut and pecans. Cool until thick enough to spread. Beat occasionally.

Yields 2½ cups frosting.

PECAN DATE COOKIES
CORDELIA JENKINS

70	pitted dates
70	pecan halves
¼	cup butter
¾	cup brown sugar
1	egg
½	cup sour cream
1½	cups flour
¼	teaspoon salt
½	teaspoon soda
½	teaspoon baking powder

Stuff 1 pecan half in each date. Cream butter and sugar; beat in egg and sour cream. Sift flour with salt, soda and baking powder and add to first mixture. Dip dates one at a time until covered with cookie batter. Place on greased cookie sheet. Bake at 350 degrees for 10 minutes or until done.

ICING:

½	cup butter
3	cups powdered sugar
3	tablespoons water
1	teaspoon vanilla

For the icing, let butter brown over medium heat. Add sugar, water and vanilla; blend well. Ice cookies while warm.

Yields 70 cookies.

• B U T T E R M I L K •

Before the widespread production of machine-made butter in the 1920s, the churn and dasher were household necessities. The liquid remaining after butter was churned was known as sweet buttermilk. Freshly formed butter was washed several times in cold water to remove all traces of the buttermilk lest it turn sour. Modern cultured buttermilk is a different product altogether as it is made by fermentation using bacterial cultures. Controls determine whether buttermilk, sour cream, yogurt or cheese will be the end result. Liquid butter is sometimes added to commercial buttermilk to give it a "freshly churned" appearance.

BANANA CAKE
JANET ELSON

½	cup butter
1½	cups sugar
4	eggs, separated
1	cup mashed bananas
¼	cup buttermilk
1½	cups flour
2	teaspoons baking powder
¼	teaspoon salt
1	cup chopped pecans
1	teaspoon soda, dissolved in
2	teaspoons water
1	teaspoon vanilla

For cake, cream butter and sugar; add egg yolks, slightly beaten and beat until light. Add mashed bananas and buttermilk; mix well. Add vanilla.

Sift flour, salt and baking powder 3 times. Add 1 cup pecans to flour. Add flour and pecans to butter mixture. Beat well. Add soda. Beat egg whites; fold into batter. Grease and flour two 9-inch pans. Divide batter. Bake at 350 degrees for 25 or 30 minutes.

ICING:

2   cups powdered sugar
3   tablespoons soft butter
2   tablespoons cream
1   teaspoon rum

Spread icing between layers and on top of cake.

Serves 8.

LIQUEUR SOUFFLÉ

4   tablespoons butter
4   tablespoons flour
1½ cups light cream
⅓   cup sugar
5   egg yolks
½   cup brandy or fruit cordial, divided
10 ladyfingers
6   egg whites

Melt butter in a saucepan. Add flour and mix to a smooth paste. Gradually add cream, stirring constantly until the boiling point is reached. Add sugar and cook over a low heat for 4 minutes, stirring frequently. Let cool for 5 minutes. Beat egg yolks in a bowl. Gradually add cream, beating constantly. Add half the brandy. Cool for 10 minutes. Preheat oven to 350 degrees. Soak ladyfingers in remaining brandy. Beat egg whites until stiff, but not dry, and fold into cream mixture. Butter a 2-quart soufflé dish and dust lightly with sugar. Pour half the soufflé mixture into it. Drain the ladyfingers and arrange them in dish. Cover with remaining soufflé mixture. Bake at 350 degrees for 30 minutes. Serve at once.

Serves 6 to 8.

NOTE: *A soufflé must be served and eaten as soon as it is ready. A delay of a few minutes is enough to allow the soufflé to fall. Have your guests wait for the soufflé because it will not wait for them.*

CLEORA'S APRICOT MERINGUE PIE

5   tablespoons cornstarch
1½ cups sugar
1½ cups boiling water
1   tablespoon lemon juice
1   cup dried apricots, cooked and strained
    through coarse sieve
3   egg yolks, beaten
1   tablespoon butter
    Pinch salt

Sift sugar and cornstarch together. Blend well, stir into boiling water and cook until thick and clear, stirring constantly. Add lemon juice, sieved apricots, butter, beaten egg yolks and salt to cornstarch mixture. Cook in double boiler 10 minutes. Cool and pour into baked 9-inch pie shell.

MERINGUE:

4   egg whites
9   tablespoons sugar

Make meringue of egg whites beaten until stiff. Add 8 tablespoons sugar, 2 tablespoons at a time, beating continuously until meringue is stiff and shiny. Spread over pie; sprinkle top with 1 tablespoon sugar and bake 15 minutes at 325 degrees until golden brown.

Yields 1 large and delicious pie.

EGGNOG RING

24 plain lady fingers (split)
8   large egg yolks
¾   cup bourbon
2   teaspoons vanilla
8   large egg whites
1   cup sugar
2½ teaspoons unflavored gelatin, soaked 5 minutes in cold water
1   pint whipping cream
8   almond macaroons, broken in pieces
1   can (16 ounce) Queen Anne cherries, drained
¾   cup toasted, slivered almonds, coarsely chopped

Lightly butter sides of mold and place lady fingers around sides, standing up. Set aside.

Beat egg yolks until light and thick. Add bourbon and vanilla. Mix thoroughly and strain into meringue made with egg whites and sugar. Dissolve gelatin by heating over low fire. Cool slightly and add to egg mixture. Pour in a 3-quart spring-form mold and place in refrigerator several hours until firm. Overnight is all right.

When ready to serve, unmold on serving plate. Meanwhile, mix macaroons, cherries and almonds. Fold into slightly sweetened whipped cream. Fill ring and serve.

Serves 12 or more.

CREAM CHEESE PASTRY

24 small shells
1   package (3 ounce) cream cheese, softened
1   cup all-purpose flour
½   cup butter

Combine cream cheese and butter. Blend well until smooth. Add flour, mixing well. Refrigerate dough 1 hour; then shape into 24 balls. Put each ball in a greased miniature muffin tin, shaping into a shell. Bake at 350 degrees for 15 minutes before filling.

ALMOND MACAROON PIE
JENNY ELLIOTT

½   cup fine saltine cracker crumbs (10 to 12 crackers)
⅔   cup chopped pecans
3   egg whites
1   cup sugar
½   teaspoon baking powder
¼   teaspoon salt
1   teaspoon almond extract
1   cup whipping cream, whipped and sweetened

Combine cracker crumbs and pecans; set aside. Beat egg whites until stiff. Combine sugar and baking powder; fold into egg whites. Fold in cracker crumbs and pecans, salt and almond extract. Pour into lightly greased 9-inch pie pan and bake in 325 degree oven for 20 to 30 minutes. Increase heat to 425 degrees for the last few minutes of baking time. Several hours before serving, spread top of pie with sweetened whipped cream.

LEMON ANGEL PIE

MERINGUE CRUST:

4 egg whites
¼ teaspoon cream of tartar
¾ cup sugar

For the crust: beat egg whites until frothy. Add cream of tartar; beat until soft peaks are formed. Add sugar gradually, beating until stiff peaks are formed. Spread over bottoms and sides of a buttered 9-inch pie pan. Bake at 275 degrees for 1 hour. Set aside to cool.

LEMON FILLING:

4 egg yolks
½ cup sugar
3 tablespoons lemon juice
1 teaspoon grated lemon rind
1 cup whipping cream

For the filling: in the top of a double boiler beat egg yolks; add sugar, lemon juice and lemon rind. Cook over boiling water until thickened, stirring constantly. Remove from heat and allow to cool. Whip cream until stiff. Fold half of the whipped cream into cooled lemon custard, blending gently. Pour into cooled meringue crust. Sweeten remaining whipped cream and spread over filling. Pie may be frozen if desired.

Serves 6 to 8.

RUM PUDDING
CORDELIA JENKINS

2 large eggs, separated
½ cup sugar
6 tablespoons rum
1 tablespoon gelatin, soaked in ¼ cup cold milk and dissolved in ¼ cup hot milk
1 teaspoon vanilla
1 pint heavy cream, whipped
   Lady fingers

Beat yolks with ¼ cup sugar. Add rum. Beat whites until stiff and beat in remaining sugar to make meringue. Add dissolved gelatin mixture and fold vanilla and whipped cream into meringue. Line 1-quart mold with lady fingers. Pour in rum filling, pack in salt and ice and freeze for 3 hours or overnight.

Serves 6.

NOTE: *Packing a dessert in salt and ice instead of putting it in the freezer makes it softer.*

• T H E   B L E N D E R •

Electric blenders for home use were first marketed by a number of companies at the close of World War II. In 1946, John Oster introduced a blender intended for home use. It was not an overnight success. However, as it became more widely used in restaurants and clubs to mix drinks, its popularity in the home grew accordingly.

Pickles & Relishes

FRENCH PICKLES

6   pounds cucumbers, sliced thin
½   cup pickling salt
1   quart vinegar
4½ cups sugar
3   pounds white onions
3   teaspoons celery seed
3   teaspoons white mustard seed
7   tablespoons olive oil

Mix cucumbers well with canning salt and soak overnight. Next morning, press out all salt water. Boil vinegar and sugar five minutes. Add remaining ingredients, except for olive oil, when mixture comes to a boil; let boil five minutes more. Take off fire. When boiling stops, add olive oil. Pack in sterilized jars and seal.

Yields about 6 pints.

NOTE: *Do not soak onions in salt.*

• C H U T N E Y •

The word "chutney" is derived from the Hindi *chatni* and refers to a sweet and/or spicy condiment made from fruits or herbs, usually mixed with spices, onions, garlic, vinegar and lemon or lime juice. Indian chutneys range from sweet to fiery and can be roughly divided into two groups — those bottled as preserves, and fresh chutneys made daily in Indian households.

MANGO CHUTNEY

1   quart apple cider vinegar
7   cups brown sugar
2   packages (15 ounce) seedless raisins
10 cloves garlic, chopped fine
1½ cups chopped onions
3   tablespoons salt
1½ tablespoons red sweet pepper
¾   cup root ginger, crushed fine or grated
10 cups mangoes, cut and peeled

Cook all ingredients, except mangoes in a kettle slowly for 40 minutes. Then add mangoes and cook until thick. Seal in sterilized jars.

Yields about 3½ quarts.

NOTE: *Peaches may be substituted.*

BEET AND HORSERADISH RELISH

2   quarts boiled beets, chopped fine
2   quarts white cabbage, finely grated
1   teaspoon celery seed (optional)
1   cup horseradish
2   cups sugar
2   teaspoons salt
    Freshly ground pepper to taste
¾   cup vinegar

Mix all ingredients together thoroughly. Let stand in refrigerator 1 or 2 hours before serving.

Yields 4½ to 5 pints.

NOTE: *This relish is good to the last spoonful and is particularly good with ham, fresh pork and poultry.*

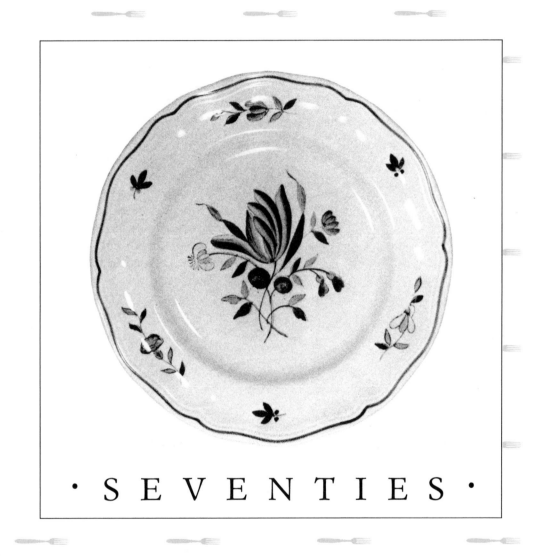

· S E V E N T I E S ·

The Seventies

DUCKLING PÂTÉ

1   duckling (4 to 5 pounds)
1   cup chopped mushrooms
12 ounces cream cheese
5   ounces toasted chopped almonds
2   tablespoons grated onion
1   teaspoon Kitchen Bouquet
1   teaspoon Worcestershire sauce
½   teaspoon Tabasco sauce
1   cup sour cream

Cut duckling in quarters and stew with giblets until done. Cool in broth. Take meat from bone. Discard bones. Put meat and giblets twice through food chopper; it should yield about 4 cups of meat. Blend mushrooms, cream cheese, almonds, and onion seasonings. Then blend into meat with sour cream. Stir carefully until well mixed. Pour into small casserole and chill. Serve as spread on Melba toast rounds as canapes. Keeps well in refrigerator.

Serves 8.

LIPTAUER

2   packages (8 ounce) cream cheese
¼   cup (½ cube) sweet butter
2   tablespoons heavy cream

Whip until fluffy and form in a mound on a decorative dish. Surround with small dishes of chopped onion, chopped anchovy fillets, capers and chopped chives. Also have a large bowl of radish roses on hand as well as some thinly sliced rye bread.

Yields 3 cups of spread.

HOT MUSHROOM DIP

1 pound fresh mushrooms
1 large clove garlic, crushed
2 tablespoons butter or margarine
2 tablespoons olive oil
1 small onion, peeled and grated
⅛ teaspoon dry mustard
½ teaspoon soy sauce
⅛ teaspoon paprika
   Salt and pepper to taste
1 tablespoon flour
1 cup sour cream
1 package (3 ounce) cream cheese
1 jigger brandy
1 jigger sherry

Wash but do not peel mushrooms. Place in wooden bowl with garlic and chop very fine. Heat oil and butter in heavy skillet. Add onion and let cook a short time. Add mushrooms. Cook three minutes, stirring constantly. Add seasonings, flour and sour cream (mixed to a paste). Then add cream cheese, brandy and sherry. Stir until thickened and well heated. Pour into chafing dish. Serve with Melba toast.

Serves 8.

CAMEMBERT EN CROÛTE

½ cup flour
2 ounces cream cheese
   Dash of salt
½ stick butter or margarine
1 can (6 ounce) camembert
1 egg yolk
2 teaspoons water

Blend flour, cream cheese and butter. Work together to make crust. Mold into ball and chill about 3 hours. Roll pastry to about 8 inch circle and ⅛ inch thick. Place cheese in center of circle of pastry. Gather pastry, pleating as you turn. Give a slight twist and pinch off excess. Press down to top of cheese. Roll balance of pastry and cut leaves or whatever you think pretty. Roll trimmings left into tiny rope and lay around top of croute. Refrigerate 1 hour. Mix egg yolk and water together. Wash croute with this mixture. Place on cooky sheet and bake at 450 degrees 20 minutes. Serve at once. Let guests serve themselves.

SOUR CREAM SPINACH SALAD
DAISY PORTERFIELD

2 heads Bibb lettuce
2 large heads Iceberg lettuce
2 pounds fresh spinach
2 bunches green onions, sliced thin
2 pounds bacon, cooked until crisp and crumbled
½ cup sour cream
1 pint cottage cheese
¼ cup sugar
3 tablespoons vinegar
2 teaspoons horseradish
½ teaspoon dry mustard
¼ teaspoon salt
1 cup pecan pieces (optional)

Wash and dry spinach and lettuce. Tear into bite-size pieces. Add green onions, ½ of bacon and nuts, if used. Blend sour cream, cottage cheese, sugar, vinegar, mustard, salt and horseradish. Blend well and toss carefully with greens. Sprinkle balance of bacon over salad.

Serves 6 to 8.

Avocado and Red Pepper Salad

Dressing:

2 tablespoons red wine vinegar
¼ cup olive oil or salad oil
1 teaspoon sugar
1 tablespoon lemon juice
1 clove garlic, minced or pressed
2 tablespoons finely chopped shallots or green onions
2 tablespoons chopped fresh mint or crumbled dry mint
 Salt and pepper

Salad:

2 cups thinly-sliced cucumber
1 large avocado, peeled, pitted and sliced
1 large red sweet pepper, seeded and sliced
 Crisp lettuce leaves
2 hard-cooked eggs, sliced

Pour vinegar into a small bowl. Using a wire whip, beat vinegar while slowly adding the oil so mixture thickens slightly. Add the sugar, lemon juice, garlic, shallots or green onions, mint and salt and pepper. Whip until blended and sugar is dissolved. Cover and set aside several hours to blend flavors. Just before serving, combine cucumber, avocado, and red pepper. Stir dressing, pour over vegetables and toss gently, but thoroughly. Lift cut vegetable mixture and arrange in a shallow, lettuce-lined salad bowl. Top with eggs.

Serves 4.

Watercress and Potato Salad

2½ pounds (3 or 4 large) potatoes
3 cups watercress leaves
3 hard-cooked eggs, chopped
1 cup sliced, unpeeled radishes
¼ cup minced onion
⅔ cup olive oil
⅓ cup vinegar
 Salt and pepper to taste

Cook potatoes until just tender. Cool, peel and dice. Mix with watercress leaves, eggs, radishes and onion. Dress with olive oil, vinegar and salt and pepper.

Serves 6.

Avocado-Stuffed Red Peppers

2 large avocados
¼ cup lemon juice
1 tablespoon olive oil or salad oil
1 clove garlic, minced or pressed
½ cup finely-chopped, mild, white onion
2 tablespoons capers, drained
4 medium red sweet peppers
 Shredded iceberg lettuce
2 hard-cooked eggs, finely chopped

Peel and pit avocado. With a fork, mash flesh well. Stir in lemon juice, oil, garlic, onion, capers and salt and pepper to taste. Cover and chill as long as 4 hours. Meanwhile, slice tops off of peppers about 1 inch below stem. Set tops aside. Remove seeds from pepper shells. Then cut 5 or 6 slits down pepper sides, almost to the bottom, forming a petal-like effect. To serve, arrange pepper shells on 4 individual salad plates lined with shredded lettuce. Spoon avocado mixture evenly into peppers. Then sprinkle with chopped egg. Top with stem end of pepper or place it alongside.

Serves 4.

BACON AND EGG SALAD

½   pound bacon, crisp
½   cup bacon fat
2   large heads romaine lettuce, broken in pieces
½   cup chopped green onions
6   hard-cooked eggs, sliced
     A few sprigs fresh tarragon (optional)
¼   cup wine vinegar
     Salt and freshly ground pepper to taste

Crumble bacon; set aside. Put romaine in a chilled salad bowl. Add onions, eggs and tarragon. To serve, sprinkle with bacon and dress with hot bacon fat, wine vinegar and salt and pepper.

Serves 6.

NOTE: *I like to serve this salad with Hot Cheese Biscuits, which can be made by simply adding Cheddar cheese to your favorite biscuit dough.*

TOMATO SOUP SALAD

1   can (10 ounce) tomato soup
1   envelope unflavored gelatin
¼   cup cold water
3   packages (3 ounce) cream cheese
1   cup mayonnaise
1½   cups chopped celery
½   cup sliced stuffed olives
1   cup chopped nuts (optional)

Heat soup to boiling point. Add gelatin which has been softened in cold water. Add cream cheese and beat until smooth. Let cool until slightly thickened. Then add mayonnaise, celery, stuffed olives and nuts, if desired. Pour into individual molds or one larger mold. Chill until firm.

Yields 6 to 8 servings.

SALADE NIÇOISE

1   package (9 ounce) frozen whole green beans
1   can (2 ounce) anchovy fillets
      Milk
3   medium tomatoes
1½   teaspoons salt
½   head Iceberg lettuce
½   cup thinly sliced cucumbers
4   hard-cooked eggs, quartered lengthwise
      Pitted ripe olives

DRESSING:

¼   teaspoon freshly ground black pepper
1   teaspoon sugar
½   teaspoon prepared mustard
1   small clove garlic, crushed
½   cup olive oil
3   tablespoons lemon juice

About 20 minutes before serving:
    Cook green beans 1 minute less than label directs; then refrigerate at once. Soak anchovy fillets in a little milk to remove saltiness. Skin tomatoes by letting them stand in boiling water 8 to 10 seconds and peeling, then cut into ¼-inch slices and sprinkle with 1 teaspoon salt. Tear lettuce into bite-size pieces, wash, drain.
    Prepare French dressing by combining pepper, sugar, mustard, garlic and ½ teaspoon salt in a small bowl; then add oil and lemon juice and mix well.
    Put lettuce in salad bowl. Over it, sprinkle a few teaspoons of dressing; then layer cucumber slices, quartered eggs, tomato slices, green beans and dressing until all used up, having green beans on top. Over green beans, lay anchovy fillets lattice-wise, then decorate with ripe olives.

Serves 6 or 8.

NOTE: *This is a delightful first course.*

SPINACH SALAD
MARY SEGER

1   pound fresh spinach
1   large head lettuce
½   pound mushrooms, sliced
½   pound bacon, crumbled
1   bunch green onions, chopped
2   hard-cooked eggs, sliced

DRESSING:

½   cup mayonnaise
2   tablespoons Dusseldorfer mustard
¼   cup lemon juice
½   cup peanut oil
1   tablespoon tarragon vinegar
⅛   teaspoon sugar

Wash and drain greens until dry. Tear into bite-size pieces. In a large bowl, mix mushrooms, bacon, and onions with greens. Mix mayonnaise, mustard, lemon juice, vinegar, oil and sugar. Shake well and blend into greens. Toss lightly, but thoroughly. Decorate with sliced hard-cooked eggs.

Serves 6.

• C E V I C H E •

Ceviche (also spelled *seviche)* may have originated in Polynesia and is served throughout Latin America. It is made with cubes of raw fish marinated in lime or lemon juice. The citric acid in the juice "cooks" the fish, turning it white and changing its texture so that it is indistinguishable from fish cooked over heat.

CRANBERRY MOLD
MAE MORRISON

2   pounds cranberries, ground
2   cups sugar
1   package *each* strawberry and cherry gelatin
2   cups boiling water
1   cup coarsely chopped pecans
1   cup seeded red grapes

Heat cranberries and sugar until sugar is dissolved. Do not boil. Dissolve gelatin in boiling water. Cool. Add grapes, pecans and cranberries to gelatin. Pour in molds. Refrigerate overnight until set. Serve with poultry, fresh pork or ham.

CEVICHE

1   pound fresh fish fillets, skinned
1   cup fresh lime juice (juice from 8 to 10 limes)
1   large onion, finely chopped
2   medium tomatoes, chopped
30 pitted green Spanish olives
⅛   teaspoon ground cumin
20 capers
¼   cup olive oil
    Salt to taste
    Pepper to taste
1   tablespoon parsley, chopped
1   teaspoon oregano

Dice fillets into dime-size pieces and place in a glass bowl. Cover pieces with lime juice and marinate for 4 to 5 hours in refrigerator. Drain pieces and blot off excess lime juice. Combine pieces with remaining ingredients and mix well in a glass bowl. Cover and refrigerate mixture until cold, then serve as a salad or hors d'oeuvre.

Serves 24.

ORANGE, ONION AND AVOCADO SALAD

3   California oranges
3   large, sweet onions
    French dressing
1   large avocado
    Lemon juice
    Watercress or endive

Slice oranges and onions rather thin. Arrange in a flat, shallow dish; pour any good French dressing over mixture. Cover and let stand in refrigerator at least 8 hours, tossing once or twice so that every part of the fruit comes in contact with the dressing.

When ready to serve, peel and slice avocado, drop the slices into lemon juice for a moment, and then arrange alternate slices of avocado, oranges and onions on a bed of crisp watercress or endive. Dress with the French dressing marinade.

Serves 6.

NOTE: *It is the long marinating period which brings out the delightful flavor of this unusual combination.*

MOLDED GRAPEFRUIT AND AVOCADO SALAD

2½   tablespoons unflavored gelatin
1   cup grapefruit juice
1   cup sugar
1   cup boiling water
3   tablespoons lemon juice
3   cups grapefruit sections
½   (to 1) cup slivered almonds
2   ripe avocados, cut in squares (optional)

Let gelatin soak in grapefruit juice 5 minutes. Dissolve gelatin and grapefruit juice in boiling water and add sugar to mixture. Add lemon juice. Let set in a pan of ice water, stirring often, until mixture begins to set. Add grapefruit sections, avocado and almonds. Pour in ring mold or in individual molds. Unmold on lettuce leaves. Top with poppy seed dressing or mayonnaise, into which has been added a little sour or whipped cream.

Serves 12 to 15.

POTATO SALAD

1   medium onion
3   cups boiling water
1¾   teaspoons salt, divided
6   medium potatoes, peeled and sliced
6   hard-cooked eggs, halved
1   cup sweet pickle cubes or relish
1   cup finely chopped celery
¾   cup mayonnaise
2   tablespoons sweet pickle juice

Cut 2 slices from onion; place in boiling water. Finely chop remaining onion; set aside. Add 1 teaspoon salt and potatoes to boiling water; cover and simmer 10 minutes or until done. Drain and cool. Separate yolks and whites of eggs. Finely chop whites; combine with pickles, celery and chopped onion. Mash yolks; blend in mayonnaise, pickle juice and remaining ¾ teaspoon salt, blending well. Combine yolk mixture with egg white mixture. Cube potatoes; blend into egg mixture. Cover and refrigerate several hours.

Yields 10 to 12 servings.

CHICKEN SALAD IN CONSOMMÉ RING

1 envelope unflavored gelatin
¼ cup cold water
2 cans (10½ ounce) condensed chicken broth
1 tablespoon horseradish
1 medium cucumber, chopped fine

Soak gelatin in cold water 5 minutes. Heat chicken broth to boiling. Add gelatin and horseradish. Cool. Chill until syrupy. Add cucumber. Pour in ring mold. Chill until firm. Unmold on bed of lettuce. Fill with chicken salad.

CHICKEN SALAD:

2 cups chicken, cut in bite-size chunks
   Seasoned salt to taste
1 cup celery, coarsely chopped
¼ cup ripe olives, sliced
1 cup diced avocado
   Enough mayonnaise to blend well

For chicken salad, combine ingredients and blend well. Serve with baked pear halves.

BAKED PEAR HALVES:

6 large pears
1 cup water
½ cup sugar
2 tablespoons lemon juice

Peel and core pears. Place in a Pyrex baking dish. Add water, sugar and lemon juice. Cover with foil and bake at 350 degrees for 20 to 30 minutes, basting often. Serve warm.

Serves 12.

TEXAS GREEN BEAN SALAD

2 cans (20 ounce) whole green beans
1 tablespoon vegetable oil
1 tablespoon vinegar
1 small onion, grated
   Salt and pepper to taste
1 cup sour cream
1 teaspoon horseradish
1 teaspoon lemon juice
½ cup mayonnaise
¼ teaspoon dry mustard
1 small onion, sliced
1 cup frozen baby lima beans, cooked and drained

Marinate green beans overnight in oil, vinegar, onion, salt and pepper. Add remaining ingredients the next day and let stand in refrigerator until ready to serve.

Serves 10.

JELLIED TUNA

2 egg yolks
1 teaspoon salt
1 teaspoon dry mustard
   Few grains cayenne
1½ tablespoons butter
¾ cup milk
2 tablespoons vinegar or lemon juice
1 tablespoon unflavored gelatin, softened in
¼ cup cold water
1 can (7 ounce) Albacore tuna, flaked

Beat eggs in top of double boiler; add salt, dry mustard, butter, cayenne, milk, and vinegar or lemon juice. Cook over hot water, stirring constantly until thickened. Dissolve gelatin in cold water. Add gelatin and flaked tuna to egg mixture. Mix thoroughly. Turn into wet mold or loaf pan. Turn out onto bed of lettuce.

MINTED GRAPE SALAD

1   package lemon gelatin
1   cup melted mint jelly
1   envelope unflavored gelatin
¼   cup cold water
6   tablespoons lemon juice
1   pound seedless grapes
     Lettuce leaves
     Watercress
     Oil
     Lemon juice

Make lemon gelatin as label directs, adding ¼ cup less water than called for. Add mint jelly and stir. Sprinkle unflavored gelatin in cold water to soften; place over low heat and stir until gelatin is dissolved. Remove from heat and stir into lemon-mint jelly mixture. Add lemon juice. Refrigerate until stiff enough to mound when dropped from a spoon. When gelatin mixture mounds, fold in grapes. Turn into 5½-cup ring mold and refrigerate until firm enough to unmold. At serving time, dip mold into warm water (not hot) to depth of gelatin. Loosen around edge with tip of paring knife. Place serving dish on top of mold and turn upside down. Shake, holding serving dish tightly to the mold. Lift off mold. Garnish with lettuce; then fill center with watercress which has been dipped in a seasoned dressing of oil and lemon.

Serves 6.

Soups & Stews

CORDON BLEU TOMATO SOUP
MARY ANN JACOBS

1   tablespoon arrowroot
2   tablespoons cold water
2   tablespoons butter
2   onions, sliced thin
2   tablespoons flour seasoned with paprika
5   cups chicken broth
2   pounds tomatoes (fresh or canned)
     Bouquet garni composed of parsley stems, celery tops, chives and dill
     Peel of 1 lemon
5   whole cloves
1   teaspoon tomato paste
1   cup burgundy
     Salt and freshly ground pepper
     Freshly chopped parsley for garnish

Mix together arrowroot and cold water. Set aside. Melt butter in a deep pan and sauté onions very slowly until soft. Remove from fire and stir in flour and paprika. Return to stove, bring to a boil and cook for a minute or two. Add chicken broth, tomatoes (peeled, quartered and coarsely chopped if fresh), herbs, lemon peel, cloves and tomato paste. Simmer, covered, over low heat for 45 minutes. Strain and return to stove. In a small separate pan, warm the burgundy, ignite and burn off the alcohol. Add to soup. Season with salt and pepper, tasting carefully as both broth and wine will give a salty taste. Bring soup to a boil and add arrowroot mixture to thicken slightly. Simmer for a few minutes more. Serve in hot bowls and sprinkle with parsley.

Serves 6.

BOOKBINDERS SOUP
MARY ANN JACOBS

3   ribs celery, chopped
½   onion, chopped
1   green pepper, chopped
4   tablespoons garlic butter (4 tablespoons
    butter mixed with ¼ teaspoon garlic
    powder)
1   pound, more or less, red snapper
8   ounces tomato juice
8   ounces beef consommé
8   ounces clam juice
2   teaspoons pickling spice, put in a bag
1   teaspoon Maggi sauce
4   teaspoons tomato paste
    Roux (about 1 tablespoon flour and enough
    water to form a paste)
1   tomato, peeled and chopped
    Cream sherry to taste

Sauté all vegetables but tomato in 4 tablespoons garlic butter. Set aside.

Poach fish in water without any seasoning until done. Add 8 ounces water from poaching fish to tomato juice, consommé, clam juice, pickling spice, Maggi sauce and tomato paste. Add liquid to vegetables. Simmer 15 minutes or more. Thicken with a roux of flour and water. Add flaked fish and chopped tomato. Add sherry last.

Serves 6.

NOTE: *This soup freezes well.*

AZOREAN SOUPA

3   (to 4) pounds top or bottom round
1   shin bone
3   sprigs fresh mint
1   pound linguisa or Polish sausage
1   medium onion
1   teaspoon salt
1   heaping teaspoon whole cloves
1   heaping teaspoon whole allspice
2   inches stick cinnamon
1   cup catsup
1   small yellow turnip, peeled and diced
4   medium white potatoes, peeled
1   medium head of cabbage, cut in wedges
1   medium Hubbard squash, unpeeled and cut
    in wedges
1   loaf of Vienna bread, broken in large pieces

Place the mint, meat and shin bone in a large pot or kettle. Add enough water to cover the meat twice. Add the sausage (whole), the onion, salt, spices (tied in cheese cloth) and catsup. Bring to boil and cook over medium heat for 1½ hours. Add turnips, and cook for 1 hour longer. Add whole potatoes and cabbage wedges, and place pieces of squash on top. Continue to cook until squash and potatoes are tender.

To make soupas, put chunks of bread into large serving bowl. Place sprigs of mint on top of bread and ladle liquid from the meat and vegetable mixture over the bread until it is well soaked and softened. Keep the bread mixture warm while dishing out the meat and mixture onto a serving platter.

NOTE: *If you can't get the fresh mint, use mint that you dry yourself. When you can get it fresh, take more than you need. Wash the whole sprigs and put them in a paper bag. Tie the top of the bag tightly and leave it in a warm place. The mint will dry and be ready to use when you need it, and it's much better than the commercial flakes.*

BUTTERNUT SQUASH BISQUE WITH APPLE

1   small butternut squash (about 1 pound),
    unpeeled, cut in half, and seeded
2   tart green apples, peeled, seeded, and
    chopped
1   medium onion, coarsely chopped
    Pinch of marjoram
    Pinch of rosemary
1   quart chicken stock
2   slices white bread, trimmed and cubed
1½ teaspoons salt
¼   teaspoon pepper
2   egg yolks
¼   cup heavy cream

Combine squash halves, chopped apples and onion,
herbs, stock, bread cubes, salt and pepper in a large
heavy saucepan. Bring to a boil and simmer,
uncovered, for about 45 minutes or until vegetables
are soft. Scoop flesh of the squash out, discard the
skin and return the pulp to soup. Purée the soup in
the blender until smooth (probably two blender
loads). Return the puréed soup to the saucepan. In a
small bowl beat the egg yolks and cream together.
Beat in a little of the hot soup. Then stir back into the
saucepan. Heat, but do not boil, and serve
immediately.

Serves 6.

ONION SOUP GRATINÉE WITH CALVADOS

2   medium onions, thinly sliced
2   tablespoons butter
½   teaspoon thyme
4   cups chicken broth
    Salt and pepper to taste
1   ounce Calvados or applejack
8   triangles thinly sliced bread
½   cup Gruyère cheese, grated

Sauté sliced onions in butter in a large saucepan until
they are lightly colored. Add the thyme and chicken
broth. Season with salt and pepper and simmer
covered over medium heat for 20 minutes. Add the
Calvados and pour into oven-proof bowls. Top each
with triangles of bread. Sprinkle with grated cheese
and bake at 450 degrees for 5 to 7 minutes or until
golden brown. Serve immediately.

Serves 4.

BOUILLABAISE

1   cup butter
1   quart boiling water
1   pound fillet of flounder, cut in pieces
10   small clams
1   clove garlic
2   bay leaves
1   teaspoon salt
2   onions, minced fine
     One small, unpeeled lobster, live
1   cup raw shrimp, unpeeled
10   oysters (remove eyes)
     Sprig of parsley
     Pulp of 1 lemon
½   teaspoon powdered saffron
1   cup sherry

Melt butter. Add butter and all the other ingredients,
except sherry, to boiling water. Bring to a boil, reduce
heat and cook covered for 20 minutes. If necessary,
thicken with a little flour. Add sherry and pour into
soup plates or bowls over slices of toasted French
bread.

Serves 4 to 6.

CREOLE BLACK BEAN SOUP

¼ pound fat salt pork, diced
½ pound beef neck or shin, bone in, in pieces
    (beef rib bones, optional)
1 cup chopped onion
1 large carrot, diced
1 large clove garlic, minced
2 cups black beans, soaked in water to cover
    (preferably overnight)
2 large bay leaves
2 whole cloves
¼ teaspoon ground mace
⅛ teaspoon dry mustard
⅛ teaspoon cayenne pepper
    Salt to taste
½ cup dry sherry
1 small lemon, seeded and thinly sliced
1 hard-cooked egg, thinly sliced

Sauté the salt pork and beef lightly, then add the onion, carrot and garlic. Cook, stirring until the onion is limp and slightly colored. Add the beans and the water in which they were soaked, with enough additional water to make 10 cups in all. Add the bay leaves, cloves, mace, mustard and cayenne.

Bring to a boil, then lower heat, cover and cook slowly until the beans are mushy, about 3 to 3½ hours. Remove the bones and whole spice from the soup and discard. Purée the soup in a blender or put through a food mill. Season with salt, then reheat and add the sherry. Garnish with lemon and egg slices.

Serves 10.

OYSTER STEW

½ cup butter
½ teaspoon grated onion
1 pint oysters with liquor
1½ pints milk
½ cup light cream
½ teaspoon salt
    Pepper or paprika to taste
2 tablespoons minced fresh parsley
½ cup dry white wine (optional)

Combine butter and onion in top of double boiler; sauté lightly over direct heat. Add oysters with liquor, milk, cream, salt and pepper or paprika. Place over simmering water until oysters float and liquid is heated thoroughly. Add parsley and wine the last half minute. Serve hot.

Serves 4.

Sauces & Stuffings

DUXELLE (CHOPPED MUSHROOMS)

½ cup butter or margarine
1 pound mushrooms, chopped very fine
2 shallots, chopped very fine
2 cloves garlic, crushed
2 teaspoons salt
1 teaspoon pepper
½ teaspoon tarragon
2 teaspoons lemon juice
2 tablespoons heavy cream
6 tablespoons Madeira wine

Sauté all ingredients except lemon juice, cream and wine until nearly done. Add liquids and continue cooking until all liquids are absorbed and mushrooms are dry.

NOTE: *A good stuffing for pork chops.*

BERCY BUTTER

(SHALLOT BUTTER)

2   teaspoons finely chopped shallots
¼   cup dry white wine
¼   cup butter
2   teaspoons finely chopped parsley

Simmer shallots and white wine in a saucepan until reduced to ¼ original quantity. Cool. Cream butter and parsley. Blend into the wine and shallot mixture. Serve on broiled meats.

Serves 4.

OYSTER STUFFING

3   dozen oysters
½   loaf stale bread
    Liver and gizzard of fowl
1   tablespoon bacon drippings or lard
2   tablespoons butter
3   large onions, chopped fine
1   tablespoon parsley (chopped)
1   tablespoon thyme
    Salt and pepper to taste
1   bay leaf, crumbled

Boil liver and gizzard. Drain oysters and use liquor to moisten stale bread, which should be squeezed afterwards until quite dry. Chop oysters and set aside. Chop liver and gizzard and boil in water. Melt bacon drippings or lard in frying pan. Add onions and fry to golden brown. Add drained liver and gizzard. When they begin to brown, add seasonings, salt and pepper and mix well. Add butter, blending all thoroughly. Add the oysters. Stir and cook for 5 minutes. Remove from fire and stuff fowl.

Yields enough stuffing for a 10-pound turkey.

CORNBREAD DRESSING GIBONEY

¾   cup chopped scallion, including green tops
¼   cup butter
3½ cups cubed, day-old buttermilk cornbread
½   cup chicken stock or broth
1   cup minced celery
½   cup *each* minced parsley, minced water
    chestnuts, pine nuts, toasted or chopped
    pecans, and sliced pitted ripe olives
4   mushrooms, chopped
1½ teaspoons *each* sage and dill weed
½   teaspoon *each* minced garlic and salt

In a skillet, sauté ¾ cup chopped scallion in ¼ cup butter until soft. Combine remaining ingredients except for chicken stock or broth. Stir in chicken stock or broth; bring the liquid to a boil and pour it over the cornbread mixture. Toss the dressing and add salt and pepper to taste.

Yields about 8 cups dressing or enough to stuff 15-pound turkey.

MADEIRA SAUCE

1   can (10½ ounce) beef bouillon
2½ tablespoons cornstarch
½   cup Madeira
2   tablespoons A-1 sauce

Mix cornstarch with ¼ cup cold beef bouillon. Add Madeira and A-1 sauce. Bring remaining bouillon to a simmer, then add Madeira mixture, stirring briskly to insure smoothness. Stir in any drippings from the beef or lamb you will serve the sauce with.

NOTE: *This sauce is good served over Duxelle and meat.*

POULTRY STUFFING WITH WINE

2   tablespoons butter
2   large onions, chopped
1   green pepper, chopped
1   rib celery
1   clove garlic, crushed
1½   cups pecans, chopped
2   pounds lean sausage
1   can (4 ounce) mushrooms, chopped
8   slices stale bread crumbled
1   cup dry sherry

Brown onions slightly in butter. Add green pepper, celery, garlic, nuts and ground meat. Cook slightly; season. Add mushrooms. Add bread which has been slightly moistened with the wine. Juice from mushrooms may be added if it is too dry. Mix well and cook 5 minutes. Remove from fire and stuff fowl.

Yields enough stuffing for a 10-pound turkey.

BRAZIL-NUT DRESSING

1   large onion
1   cup celery, coarsely chopped
½   cup butter or chicken fat
1   cup chicken broth
2   quarts very dry bread cubes
½   teaspoon baking powder
1   teaspoon salt
½   teaspoon pepper
2   eggs, well beaten
1   tablespoon sage
2   cups thinly sliced Brazil nuts

Sauté onion and celery until tender. Add chicken broth and seasonings to bread cubes. Add eggs and Brazil nuts. Rub inside of turkey with oil; stuff lightly and truss for roasting.

Yields enough to stuff a 10-pound turkey.

BRANDIED DILL SAUCE FOR POACHED FISH

⅓   cup mayonnaise
½   cup sour cream
1   tablespoon fresh lemon juice
1   tablespoon tarragon vinegar
1   tablespoon dill weed
2   tablespoons white wine
1   tablespoon brandy
     Salt
     Dash cayenne pepper

Mix thoroughly. Serve over poached or baked salmon.

Yields about 1 cup.

BROWN SAUCE

½   cup beef or veal drippings
1   carrot, diced
1   onion, diced
1   celery heart, diced
½   bay leaf, crumbled
     Pinch of thyme, crumbled
½   cup flour
10   black peppercorns
1   cup tomato sauce
1   clove garlic, minced
6   cups good beef stock

Melt drippings and add vegetables, bay leaf and thyme. When vegetables begin to brown, add flour and stir until flour is brown. Add the remaining ingredients and simmer until mixture is reduced by half, about 2½ hours. Stir occasionally and skim fat which rises to top as it simmers. Strain sauce and use. It should be the consistency of heavy cream.

Yields about 3½ cups.

Barbecue Sauce with Garlic

¼ cup lemon juice
¼ cup melted butter or margarine
1 large clove garlic, minced
1 onion, grated
1 bay leaf
¼ teaspoon thyme
½ teaspoon salt
½ teaspoon celery salt
½ teaspoon coarse black pepper

Mix well. Use as marinade and to baste meat.

Yields about 1 cup.

Sauces for Beef

(1) Spinach Mayonnaise

2 cups mayonnaise
¾ cup blanched spinach, squeezed and coarsely chopped
2 tablespoons minced onion
2 tablespoons snipped chives
3 tablespoons minced sour or sweet pickles, if desired

Blend all ingredients.

Yields about 3 cups.

(2) Curry Cream Sauce for Roasts

2 tablespoons butter
1 tablespoon flour
1 tablespoon curry powder
2 egg yolks
4 tablespoons white wine vinegar
1 tablespoon cold water
1 tablespoon tomato paste
1 cup sour cream
  Salt to taste

In a skillet, cook flour, curry powder and butter over low heat, stirring for 2 minutes. In a bowl, beat egg yolks and vinegar. Remove roux from heat; add water and pour in the yolk mixture, whisking. Cook the sauce over low heat, stirring until it thickens. Remove the pan from the heat; stir in tomato paste and fold in sour cream and salt to taste.

Yields about 1½ cups.

(3) Horseradish Sauce for Roast Beef

¼ cup prepared, grated horseradish
1 teaspoon white wine vinegar
¼ teaspoon salt
1 teaspoon sugar
1 cup mayonnaise
2 tablespoons prepared mustard
½ cup sour cream or ½ cup heavy cream, lightly whipped

Serve the sauce with sliced, cooked roast beef.

Yields 2 cups.

Charlotte's Mustard Sauce

½ cup dry mustard
1 cup brown sugar
2 tablespoons flour
1 cup consommé
1 cup vinegar
3 eggs, well beaten

Mix thoroughly and cook in double boiler until thick.

Yields about 4 cups.

CHICKEN BARBECUE SAUCE

½ cup olive oil
½ cup Rhine wine
¼ cup lemon juice
½ teaspoon dried rosemary
½ cup honey
½ teaspoon Tabasco
1 teaspoon Worcestershire sauce

Combine and beat until well blended. Store in jar.

Yields about 1¾ cups.

SOUR CREAM AND HORSERADISH SAUCE

¼ cup sugar
¼ teaspoon salt
2 teaspoons dry mustard
3 tablespoons vinegar
½ cup sour cream
2 teaspoons horseradish

Blend dry ingredients. Add vinegar, sour cream and horseradish. Keeps well in refrigerator.

Yields about 1 cup.

• PINE NUTS •

Pine nuts are the hard-shelled seeds of a Mediterranean evergreen. They are often toasted before being added to rice or vegetable dishes. They are widely used in Italy and in the Middle East, and are common in the southwestern United States, where they grow well and are known as piñon nuts.

Lamb Dishes

ZUCCHINI STUFFED WITH LAMB AND PINE NUTS
SALLY PELIZZONI

6 medium zucchini
Flour
2 cloves garlic
1 onion, chopped
½ cup pine nuts
½ cup chopped parsley
1 teaspoon oregano
1½ pounds ground lamb
Olive oil
2 eggs, lightly beaten
¼ cup tomato paste
Butter
1 cup lightly whipped cream

Halve the zucchini, scoop out centers and cut centers into cubes, reserving the shells.

Dust zucchini cubes lightly with flour, and sauté them with 1 garlic clove until they are well browned. Set half the browned cubes aside and put half in a bowl with onion, pine nuts, parsley, oregano and 1 minced garlic clove.

Sauté lamb in olive oil. Add lamb to zucchini mixture together with eggs and tomato paste. Fill the zucchini shells with the mixture, top with the reserved cubes and dot with butter.

Bake at 350 degrees for 45 minutes. With the back of a spoon, depress the top of each half and fill with whipped cream. Broil until tops are glazed.

Serves 6.

MUSHROOM STUFFED LAMB

1   leg of lamb, 5 to 6 pounds
¼   cup butter or margarine
½   cup chopped onion
¼   cup chopped celery
1   pound fresh mushrooms, chopped (about 5 cups)
2   cups fresh, whole wheat bread crumbs
½   cup chopped walnuts
1   egg
1½ teaspoons thyme, divided
½   teaspoon salt
¼   teaspoon pepper
    Creme de menthe liqueur (5¾ ounce)

If frozen, thaw lamb in refrigerator overnight. Trim away any excess fat. On a cutting board, hold lamb with round side down and concave side up. Insert a small sharp knife alongside the exposed bone at top. With short strokes, cut along this bone, releasing the meat down to the joint. Begin again from the top and release the meat from the other side of the bone.

With the knife tip, follow the curve of the bone socket and release the meat. Make a slit along the shin bone to free remaining meat from both sides; then lift out bone.

In a medium saucepan, melt butter; sauté onion and celery until golden. Stir in mushrooms; cook 2 minutes. Remove from heat; stir in bread crumbs, walnuts, egg and ½ teaspoon thyme. Spread stuffing over meat and roll up. Tie securely in several places with clean, white string; sprinkle roast with remaining 1 teaspoon thyme, salt and pepper. Place on rack in shallow roasting pan. Insert meat thermometer into thickest part of meat. Roast at 325 degrees for 1½ hours or until meat thermometer registers 140 degrees for rare, 160 degrees for medium and 170 degrees for well done. Remove leg to serving platter; allow to rest 10 minutes before carving. Serve with creme de menthe or mint sauce (see Note).

Serves 6 to 8.

NOTE: *For sauce, instead of creme de menthe liqueur, I substitute one commercial bottle (5¾ ounces) of mint sauce and 1 cup finely chopped fresh mint leaves. By putting mint leaves and mint sauce in blender you get a smooth and delicious sauce or marinade.*

SPICED LAMB SHANKS

4   lamb shanks
1   cup vinegar
1   clove garlic, crushed
2   tablespoons salt
2   tablespoons sugar
1   bay leaf, broken in pieces
½   teaspoon cinnamon
½   teaspoon cloves
¼   teaspoon pepper
1   teaspoon Worcestershire sauce
4   tablespoons fat from stock
4   tablespoons flour
2   cups stock

Put lamb shanks, vinegar and garlic in a large kettle. Cover and marinate at least 4 hours, turning occasionally. Then add salt, sugar, bay leaf, cinnamon, cloves, pepper and Worcestershire sauce. Add enough boiling water to cover meat and cook over slow heat until lamb can be easily pierced with a fork (probably an hour and a half). When meat is cooked, remove from kettle and keep it hot. Strain stock. Skim off fat that rises to the top and place 4 tablespoons fat in heavy skillet. Stir in flour until you have a smooth paste and cook very slowly for 2 minutes. Then add the strained stock gradually and continue cooking until gravy has thickened. Pour over the meat and serve.

Serves four very hungry people, or six with medium appetites.

NOTE: *This is a long cooking job, but worth it.*

LAMB AND VEGETABLE PIE IN MINT CRUST

2 pounds lamb shoulder, cut in 1-inch cubes
1 teaspoon salt
¼ teaspoon pepper
2 tablespoons shortening
1 cup water
1 cup mushrooms, sliced
2 cups peas
6 medium carrots, cut in strips
8 small white onions
1 Mint Crust pie shell

Season cubes of lamb with salt and pepper and brown in skillet with shortening. Add water and mushrooms and simmer 30 minutes. Cook vegetables in boiling water. When done season vegetables and flavor with butter or a sauce. Arrange around edge of Mint Crust pie shell. Remove meat and mushrooms from the skillet. Thicken gravy and pour over meat and mushrooms which can be arranged in the center of the pie with a border of vegetables.

Serves 4 to 6.

NOTE: *A mint sauce may be poured over the carrots or a white sauce over the peas if desired.*

This is a topless pie with vegetables arranged in groups and meat and mushrooms in center. Delicious.

MINT CRUST:

1½ cups flour
1½ teaspoons salt
⅔ cup shortening
¾ cup chopped mint

For pie crust, measure and sift flour and salt together. Cut in shortening until evenly blended. Add chopped mint. If moisture from mint is not sufficient, add a little cold water. Roll out to fit a 9-inch pie tin. Bake at 425 degrees for 10 minutes.

Yields 1 9-inch shell.

CROWN ROAST OF LAMB WITH PILAF

Crown roast of lamb with 20 chops
1 garlic clove
1 teaspoon thyme
   Salt
   Pepper
½ cup dry white wine
½ cup water
3 tablespoons butter or margarine
20 frills for bone ends
   Parsley sprigs

Rub lamb well with garlic, sprinkle with thyme, salt and pepper. Put lamb in pan just large enough to hold it. Remove top and bottom from 46-ounce juice can and place in center of roast to help the roast to brown and keep its shape. Cover bone ends with foil. Place in 400 degree oven for 20 minutes. Reduce heat to 325 degrees and roast the lamb, basting several times for 50 minutes more or to degree of doneness preferred, using meat thermometer — 140 degrees for rare, 160 degrees for medium, and 170 degrees for well done.

Transfer lamb to platter; fill cavity with Rice Pilaf with Pine Nuts (see recipe below) mounding it, and keep hot. Pour off fat from roasting pan; add wine with water and combine with pan drippings. Reduce liquid over high heat by half and season with salt and pepper. Remove from heat and swirl in butter. Strain juices around roast; garnish center of rice with sprig of parsley and garnish platter with parsley bouquets. Replace foil on bone ends with paper frills.

Serves 8.

RICE PILAF WITH PINE NUTS

¼   cup onion, minced
1   clove garlic, minced
¼   cup butter
3   cups long grain rice, uncooked
½   cup golden raisins
5   cups (or more) chicken broth
3   tablespoons butter
2   tablespoons Parmesan cheese, grated
1   cup thinly sliced onions, halved
2   tablespoons butter
½   cup pine nuts
1   cup mushrooms, thinly sliced
2   tablespoons parsley, minced
    Salt and pepper

Sauté minced onion and garlic in butter. Add rice, stirring until well coated. Add raisins and enough chicken broth to cover rice by ¾ inch. Bring to boil over high heat. Transfer to a 350 degree oven and bake covered for 20 to 25 minutes. Transfer to a large bowl, add butter and Parmesan cheese and fluff with fork. Keep hot. Sauté sliced onions in butter and oil. Transfer onions, using a slotted spoon, to a bowl. In the same skillet, sauté pine nuts, tossing them until they are golden. Drain nuts on paper towels. In same skillet, sauté mushrooms, adding more butter if necessary. Combine all ingredients with rice and season pilaf with salt and pepper.

Serves 6 to 8.

LAMB WITH PLUM SAUCE

1   leg of lamb (4 to 5 pounds)
1   can (16 ounce) purple plums
2   tablespoons lemon juice
1   tablespoon soy sauce
1   tablespoon Worcestershire sauce
½   teaspoon dried basil, crushed
1   clove garlic, crushed

Place lamb, fat side up, on rack in shallow roasting pan. Season. Roast at 325 degrees for 2½ to 3 hours or until meat thermometer registers 175 to 180 degrees. Meanwhile, drain plums and reserve ¼ cup syrup. Pit and sieve plums. Combine syrup, plums, lemon juice, Worcestershire, basil and garlic. Baste lamb with sauce 4 times during last hour of roasting. Simmer remaining sauce 5 minutes, and serve with meat.

Serves 8 generously.

Beef, Veal & Pork

CHIPPED BEEF WITH SOUR CREAM
MARCIA WOODS

½   pound chipped beef
1   pint sour cream
½   teaspoon paprika
1   rounded teaspoon flour
½   cup dry white wine
2   heaping tablespoons Parmesan cheese
1   can artichoke hearts, well drained and cut up
1   can (8 ounce) sliced water chestnuts
1   pound sliced mushrooms

Shred and parboil chipped beef. Drain. Heat sour cream with paprika and stir in flour. Pour over chipped beef and cook briefly until thick. Add wine and Parmesan cheese. Cook until consistency of cream sauce. Add water chestnuts, artichokes and mushrooms. Serve on cornbread and sprinkle Parmesan cheese on top.

Serves 6.

SPICY ROAST OF BEEF

FIRST DAY:

Select 10-pound roast of top sirloin, boned. (Eye of round would also be suitable.)

2½ tablespoons salt
1¼ tablespoons coarse black pepper
1 tablespoon dry mustard
1½ tablespoons celery salt
1 teaspoon ground thyme
1 teaspoon ground cloves

Combine salt, pepper, mustard, celery salt, ground thyme, salt and cloves. Mix well and rub thoroughly into beef on all sides. Place beef in a bowl and refrigerate covered overnight.

SECOND DAY:

4 cups red wine vinegar
2¼ cups salad oil
1½ cups catsup

Mix vinegar, salad oil and catsup and pour over beef. Again refrigerate covered overnight.

THIRD DAY:

1¾ cups finely chopped carrots
2 cups finely chopped celery
2 cups finely chopped onion
2 cloves garlic, crushed
2 bay leaves
1 tablespoon dried thyme leaves
¾ pound salt pork, cut in cubes

Four hours before serving, combine carrots, celery, onion, garlic, bay leaves, thyme and ¼ cup water. Place beef on the vegetables and throw away marinade. Surround beef with salt pork. Roast uncovered at 300 degrees for 3 hours. Remove beef to warmed dish and cover with foil. Throw away salt pork.

MADEIRA SAUCE:

1 cup red wine vinegar
20 ounces (2½ cups) beef gravy, made from a mix of your choice
1 cup madeira

Over direct heat, cook vegetables in uncovered roasting pan with vinegar until liquid has evaporated considerably. Place vegetables and remaining liquid into a sauce pan. Stir in beef gravy and bring to a boil. Reduce heat immediately and simmer, covered, but stirring occasionally, for 20 minutes. Press liquid and vegetables through Foley mill or coarse sieve and skim off fat. Stir in madeira and heat gently. Serve beef thinly sliced with Madeira Sauce. Serve leftover beef cold without sauce.

Serves 12 to 14.

HANOVER'S MEAT MARKET'S BARBEQUED BRISKET

4 (to 5) pound brisket of beef
1 can (10½ ounce) condensed beef consommé
1 bottle (5 ounce) soy sauce
¼ cup lemon juice
    Garlic to taste
1 tablespon liquid smoke
½ cup barbecue sauce

Combine consommé, soy sauce, lemon juice, garlic and liquid smoke. Pour over brisket and marinate overnight. Bake covered 250 degrees for 3 hours for 4 pound brisket. Remove and pour barbecue sauce over brisket. Increase temperature to 350 degrees and bake another hour. Let rest 30 minutes. Slice across grain into thin slices.

Yields 16 to 20 servings.

NOTE: *This is good served on Kaiser rolls with cole slaw, a relish tray and hot apple pie.*

Beef Stroganoff

2   pounds beef tenderloin
½   cup butter or margarine, divided
4   medium onions, thinly sliced
1½ pounds mushrooms, thinly sliced
2   tablespoons tomato paste
1½ teaspoons salt
½   teaspoon pepper
½   cup dry sherry
1   ounce brandy
1   pint sour cream
2   tablespoons flour

Slice steak at angle into very thin strips. Melt ½ of butter in large skillet; sauté tenderloin slices over high heat only 1 minute on each side. Remove beef slices and keep warm. Add onions; sauté 10 minutes over medium heat. Remove onions. In remaining butter, sauté mushrooms 5 minutes over medium heat. Return beef and onions to skillet. Add tomato paste and seasonings. Cook over low heat 20 minutes. Mix sour cream with 2 tablespoons flour. Blend thoroughly and stir into meat mixture to thicken. Cook until gravy is thick. Serve over rice or Poppy Seed Noodles.

Serves 6

Poppy Seed Noodles:

Boil 12 ounces fine noodles in large pot of salted water for 12 minutes. Drain, butter and sprinkle with 2 tablespoons poppy seeds. Turn gently and sprinkle with 2 tablespoons finely chopped parsley. Serve immediately.

Serves 6.

Veal Kidneys with Mushrooms

4   veal kidneys
    Salt and pepper
3   tablespoons butter
½   pound medium-to-large mushrooms,
    quartered
1   tablespoon chopped shallots
½   cup Madeira
1   cup brown sauce
¼   cup brandy
1   teaspoon parsley
1   teaspoon tarragon
1   teaspoon chervil
½   teaspoon chopped chives

Remove membranes and tubes from kidneys. Trim surplus fat and reserve. Cut kidneys into thin slices and season with salt and pepper. Melt enough kidney fat to cover the bottom of a shallow skillet. Add kidneys and cook over high heat for 5 or 6 minutes. Drain kidneys in a colander.

Discard fat, but do not wash the pan. Melt 2 tablespoons butter in the pan and cook mushrooms until tender. Add shallots. Cook for 2 minutes longer. Add Madeira, brown sauce and brandy. Bring mixture to a boil and add parsley, tarragon, chervil and chives. Add 1 tablespoon butter. Return kidneys to sauce and keep them warm in a chafing dish. Do not let sauce boil.

Serves 4.

Note: *To make brown sauce, stir 2 tablespoons flour in 3 tablespoons of melted butter over heat until flour is brown. Add 1 cup milk, slowly, stirring constantly, until sauce is of desired consistency.*

Veal Saumoné

1	5-pound loin or rump of veal
2	teaspoons saltpeter
4	onions, sliced thin
½	lemon, sliced
4	cups white wine vinegar
	Bouquet garni composed of 8 juniper berries, 4 sprigs of parsley, 4 whole cloves, 2 bay leaves, 1 sprig fresh tarragon, and a pinch of thyme
2½	quarts water
3	cups dry white wine
8	peppercorns
	Salt
¾	cup fresh chives

Have the butcher flatten the veal. Rub the veal with saltpeter and roll it up jelly-roll fashion. Tie the roll with string. Line the bottom of a large flame-proof casserole or kettle with onions and lemon. Add vinegar and bouquet garni. Marinate the veal in the mixture for 3 or 4 days, turning it once every day. Add water, wine, peppercorns and salt to taste. Simmer veal over very low heat for 3 hours. Cool veal in stock. Chill thoroughly. Remove string and arrange veal on a chilled platter. Spread chives over veal and garnish the platter with sliced French bread and parsley sprigs. Serve the veal cut in thin slices. The veal may be served on bread slices with Shallot Mayonnaise or as an hors d'oeuvre on lettuce leaves.

Serves 8.

Shallot Mayonnaise

6	(to 8 shallots) finely chopped
¼	teaspoon salt
4	tablespoons bread crumbs
1	cup mayonnaise

Pound shallots and salt with a mortar. Soak bread crumbs in a little warm water; press them to drain. Blend bread crumbs thoroughly with shallot paste. Blend mixture with mayonnaise.

Roast Beef Hash

1	ounce butter
4	slices bacon, diced
1½	medium onions
½	cup carrots
½	cup celery
½	cup green pepper
½	cup sweet red pepper
1	pound diced potatoes
1¼	pounds cooked roast beef
1	teaspoon Maggi seasoning
1	teaspoon Worcestershire sauce
1	teaspoon soy sauce
	Pinch of marjoram
	Pinch of sage
1	diced garlic clove
1¾	cups brown gravy
	Cornstarch

Dice all vegetables and roast beef in half-inch cubes. Sauté bacon and onions in butter until onion is soft brown. In a large roast pan add carrots, celery, peppers, potatoes, roast beef, gravy and all remaining seasonings. Simmer until carrots are half cooked. Add potatoes and simmer until potatoes are done. Thicken with cornstarch dissolved in cold water until desired consistency is reached.

Yields 2 quarts.

Note: *Serve for a buffet brunch.*

VEAL PROVOLONE

8   veal cutlets, pounded and scored
2   tablespoons melted butter or margarine
1   can (10½ ounce) condensed tomato soup, undiluted
¼   cup chili sauce
½   teaspoon salt
1   tablespoon Worcestershire sauce
½   teaspoon minced garlic
⅛   teaspoon oregano
⅛   teaspoon coarsely-ground pepper
2   bay leaves
1   teaspoon dried chives
8   slices provolone or mozzarella cheese

Brown cutlets in butter. Remove and set aside. Blend soup, chili sauce and seasonings into pan drippings. Return meat to sauce and spoon sauce over meat. Simmer over low heat for 25 minutes. Place slices of cheese on each cutlet and continue cooking 2 to 3 minutes more or until cheese melts.

Serves 8.

PIQUANT PICCATA VEAL SCALLOPS

4   veal scallops
    Flour
    Salt and pepper
6   tablespoons butter
2   tablespoons olive oil
3   tablespoons lemon juice
2   tablespoons chopped parsley
½   of 8 ounce package green spinach noodles, cooked

Dust scallops with flour, salt and pepper. In a large skillet heat 4 tablespoons butter and olive oil over medium heat until bubbly. Quickly brown scallops in skillet about 2 minutes on each side; remove to warm plate and cover. Add lemon juice and parsley to skillet; remove from heat and swirl in remaining butter. Arrange scallops over noodles. Pour butter sauce over all. Garnish with lemon sauce and additional parsley.

Serves 4.

NOTE: *Serve with tomato salad, tossed with olive oil, vinegar and basil, crunchy bread sticks and chilled white wine.*

CARIBBEAN HOT GINGER SPARERIBS

2   pounds meaty pork ribs, cut into individual ribs
¼   cup brown sugar
¼   cup dry sherry
2   tablespoons vinegar
2   tablespoons soy sauce
1   teaspoon salt
½   teaspoon ground ginger
1   can (14 ounce) crushed pineapple with juice
1   teaspoon Tabasco
¼   cup shredded coconut

Blanch ribs in simmering, salted water for 30 minutes. Drain. In saucepan, combine brown sugar, sherry, vinegar, soy sauce, salt and ginger. Bring to a boil. Add coconut and crushed pineapple with juice; simmer 5 minutes. Remove from heat. Add pepper sauce. Arrange ribs on baking sheet. Brush each rib with sauce. Broil 10 minutes. Turn and broil 8 minutes longer or until done, brushing frequently with sauce to keep ribs moist. Serve hot. If desired, serve with additional pepper sauce.

Serves 4.

CLEORA'S SHALLOT-BROILED PORTERHOUSE

4 Porterhouse or sirloin steaks
2 teaspoons minced shallots
½ teaspoon salt
¼ teaspoon celery salt
¼ teaspoon black pepper
½ cup butter
¼ cup water
1 tablespoon tarragon vinegar
1 tablespoon lemon juice
1 teaspoon meat or vegetable extract
1 teaspoon prepared horseradish

Have steaks sliced 2 inches thick. Blend minced shallots, salt, celery salt and pepper in small bowl. Rub seasoned mixture into both sides of steak. Place steak 3 inches below heat on preheated broiler rack. Broil 5 minutes on one side, then 5 minutes on other side or until steak is cooked to desired degree of doneness. Meanwhile, melt butter in small saucepan over medium flame; add water, tarragon vinegar, lemon juice, meat extract and prepared horseradish. Simmer gently 5 minutes. Pour piping hot sauce over sizzling steak. Serve with baked potatoes and a tossed salad. Allow ½ pound steak or more for each person.

Serves 4 generously.

Poultry

CORNISH HENS STUFFED WITH NOODLES

1 pair veal sweetbreads
1 cup water
1 tablespoon lemon juice
3 teaspoons salt
1½ teaspoons coarse pepper
2 cloves garlic, minced
½ pound butter
1 cup chopped mushrooms
1 large onion, chopped
2 cups fine egg noodles, boiled
1 cup cream
¾ cup Madeira
6 Cornish hens with giblets

Wash the sweetbreads in cold water. Place in a kettle with water and lemon juice. Bring to a boil and cook over low heat for 10 minutes. Drain. Cover with cold water and set aside for 20 minutes. Drain. Remove the membranes and cut sweetbreads in small pieces. Mix 2 teaspoons of salt, 1 teaspoon pepper and the garlic to a paste. Rub into the Cornish hens. Parboil giblets 30 minutes. Cool and grind in a food chopper. Melt half the butter in a frying pan. Add the mushrooms and onion and sauté for 5 mintues, stirring frequently. Add coarsely chopped noodles, giblets, sweetbreads, cream, Madeira and remaining salt and pepper. Mix carefully. Split Cornish hens down the back and remove the backbone. Stuff with the mixture and fasten openings with skewers or with thread. Brown the birds on all sides. Roast breast up in 375 degree oven for 45 minutes. Then reduce heat to 350 degrees and continue baking 20 to 25 minutes or until tender. Baste frequently.

Serves 6.

CHICKEN JUNIPER

1   broiler-fryer (4 to 5 pounds), cut in serving
    pieces, skin removed
½   cup dry sherry
½   cup honey
½   cup flour
½   cup butter or margarine
1½ cups gin
½   cup chopped parsley
½   cup chopped onion
½   teaspoon tarragon
2   tablespoons arrowroot or cornstarch
1   cup cream
    Salt
    Sesame seeds

Rub chicken pieces with sherry, then honey or dip
them in each. Dust lightly with flour and brown in
butter. Arrange in buttered baking dish; pour gin over
and sprinkle with parsley, onion and tarragon. Bake at
350 degrees for 1 hour. Remove chicken, keeping
warm. To thicken sauce, blend arrowroot or
cornstarch with about ½ cup liquid from the pan.
Return to pan; add cream; cook, stirring until
thickened. Salt to taste. Serve sauce over chicken and
sprinkle liberally with sesame seeds.

Serves 4 or 5.

ROAST DUCKLING WITH BING CHERRIES

5   (to 6) pound Long Island duckling
2   teaspoons salt
½   teaspoon pepper
1   cup white wine

Clean the duck carefully. Combine salt and pepper
and rub into the duck. If possible, season the duck a
day ahead of time. Roast in a 475 degree oven for 20
minutes. Drain the fat thoroughly. Pour the wine over
the duck and reduce the oven heat to 350 degrees.

Continue roasting for an additional 1½ hours or until
tender. Meanwhile prepare sauce as follows:

SAUCE:

2   tablespoons sugar
2   tablespoons vinegar
1   tablespoon butter
2   tablespoons flour
1   cup stock, or 1 cup boiling water and 1
    bouillon cube
½   cup orange juice
3   tablespoons grated orange rind
2   tablespoons lemon juice
1   tablespoon lemon rind
1   can (20 ounce) Bing cherries
2   tablespoons brandy

Place the sugar and vinegar in a saucepan and cook
over low heat, stirring occasionally, until the sauce
becomes dark brown in color. In a separate saucepan,
melt the butter; add the flour, and make smooth
paste. Gradually add the stock, stirring constantly
until the boiling point is reached. Cook over very low
heat for 10 minutes, stirring occasionally. Add the
orange juice and rind, lemon juice and rind, 1 cup of
cherry juice and the brandy, stirring constantly while
adding these ingredients. Add the sugar and vinegar
mixture, stirring constantly. Add ¼ cup of pan
drippings to the sauce, but first be sure to skim off all
the fat. Cook for 15 minutes over low heat; then add
the whole cherries but do not add any additional
juice from the can. Allow the sauce to simmer while
carving the duck. Pour a little of the sauce on top of
the pieces of duck and serve the remainder in a sauce
boat.

NOTE: *One duck will serve 6 with rather small
portions. If you are planning an elaborate meal with
many courses, one duck may be sufficient. However, if
the duck course constitutes the main part of the meal,
it will be necessary to roast 2 or 3 smaller ducks. There
is sufficient sauce in the recipe to accompany 2 ducks.*

BROILED CHICKEN WITH HERBS

3   broilers, halved
1½ teaspoons salt
½   teaspoon pepper
1   cup butter, softened
1   tablespoon finely chopped parsley
½   teaspoon marjoram
½   teaspoon chives
½   teaspoon sage
1   teaspoon finely chopped mint
¼   teaspoon fennel seeds or ½ teaspoon oil of
     fennel
¼   teaspoon ground nutmeg
½   teaspoon ground cinnamon
1   cup orange juice

Clean and cut broilers in half; wipe with damp cloth; season with salt and pepper. Blend butter with herbs and spices; rub over inside and outside of broilers. Broil until golden brown, 10 to 15 minutes. Place in roaster; add orange juice and juice from broiler pan. Cover and bake at 375 degrees for about 45 minutes, basting frequently.

Serves 6.

ALMOND CHICKEN BAKE

1   frying chicken, cut up
2   cups water
½   cup chopped celery
1   tablespoon instant minced onion
1½ teaspoons salt
1   can (4 ounce) mushrooms (sliced)
¼   cup butter or margarine
¼   cup all-purpose flour
1   cup light cream or milk
1   cup chicken stock
¼   teaspoon *each* pepper, dill weed and dry
     mustard
½   cup slivered almonds, toasted
2   tablespoons dry sherry

In a pot slowly cook chicken, water, celery, onion, salt and liquid from mushrooms about 30 minutes or until tender. Cool chicken and remove skin and bones, leaving meat in large pieces (about two cups). Melt butter and stir in flour, then cream, 1 cup stock from chicken, pepper, dill weed and dry mustard. Cook and stir until mixture boils and is thickened. Stir in chicken, mushrooms, almonds and sherry. Turn into shallow 1-quart baking dish. Bake at 350 degrees for 30 minutes until bubbly.

Yields 4 or 5 servings.

NOTE: *This dish can be covered with a pastry crust. Flute crust and prick before baking, and bake at 400 degrees for 25 to 30 minutes until golden brown.*

ROAST CAPON WITH ROSEMARY

6   pound capon
     Salt
3   sprays rosemary
1   tablespoon soft butter

Sprinkle the inside of capon with salt. Tuck in rosemary and truss the bird with soft cord. Rub the skin with soft butter; sprinkle with salt and set the bird on a rack in a roasting pan. Roast the capon in a 425 degree oven for 15 minutes to brown the skin. Reduce the temperature to 325 degrees and roast the bird, basting frequently with the pan drippings, for 1 hour and 30 to 45 minutes or until drumstick is tender when pressed and moves easily in the socket. Let the capon stand at room temperature for 10 to 15 minutes before carving.

Fish & Seafood

SHRIMP DE JONGHE

1   pound Gulf shrimp, peeled and deveined
1   cup toasted, dry bread crumbs
¼   cup chopped green onions and tops
¼   cup chopped parsley
2   cloves garlic, chopped
¾   cup crushed tarragon
¼   teaspoon nutmeg
¼   teaspoon salt
     Dash of pepper
¼   cup melted margarine
¼   cup sherry

Combine crumbs, onions, parsley and seasonings. Add margarine and sherry and mix thoroughly. Add shrimp to crumb mixture and toss lightly. Place in well-greased casserole and cover with aluminum foil. Bake at 350 degrees for 45 minutes or until shrimp is done and crumbs are lightly browned. Remove foil during last 15 minutes of cooking.

Yields 6 servings.

SHRIMP AND SCALLOP NEWBURG

1   pound fresh cleaned shrimp
¾   pound scallops
6   tablespoons butter or margarine
3   tablespoons flour
¾   teaspoon paprika
½   teaspoon salt
¼   teaspoon nutmeg
2½   cups light cream
½   cup milk
3   egg yolks

Split shrimp in half lengthwise (if large in 4 pieces). Parboil in small amount of water about 2 minutes. Drain. Melt butter in top of double boiler. Drop in shrimp and scallops. Sauté a few minutes over direct heat. Sprinkle flour and seasonings over it. Stir until blended. Gradually add cream and milk. Cook until it thickens, stirring constantly. Then place over hot water. Add egg yolks, one at a time, stirring constantly. One or two tablespoons sherry may be added at last minute also. Serve with very thin buttered toast.

Serves 6.

SPAGHETTI AND OYSTERS

24   oysters, shucked
     Liquor from oysters
     Water
½   cup butter
¼   cup flour
1   cup chopped scallions
½   cup minced parsley
1   tablespoon Worcestershire sauce
     Salt and pepper to taste
1   pound cooked spaghetti

Add enough water to liquor to make 1 quart. Transfer the liquid to a sauce pan. Bring to a simmer. Add oysters and cook for 3 minutes or until the edges curl. Transfer oysters with a slotted spoon to a dish and set aside, covered with a buttered sheet of waxed paper. Reserve the liquid.

In a heavy saucepan, melt butter; add flour and cook the roux over low heat, stirring, for 3 minutes. Remove the pan from heat; add the reserved liquid in a stream, whisking, and cook the sauce over high heat for 10 minutes, stirring occasionally. Reduce heat to moderate and add scallions, parsley, Worcestershire sauce, salt and pepper. Simmer for 15 minutes. Add the oysters and simmer 1 minute or until they are heated through. Serve the sauce over spaghetti.

Serves 4.

TROUT AMANDINE

2 pounds Gulf trout fillets or other fresh fillets
¼ cup flour
1 teaspoon seasoned salt
1 teaspoon paprika
¼ cup melted butter or margarine
¼ cup sliced almonds
2 tablespoons lemon juice
4 (to 5) drops liquid hot pepper sauce
1 tablespoon chopped parsley

Cut fillets into 6 portions. Combine flour, seasoned salt and paprika. Roll portions in flour mixture and place in a single layer, skin side down, in a well-greased baking dish. Drizzle 2 tablespoons melted butter over portions. Broil about 4 inches from heat source for 10 to 15 minutes or until fish flakes easily when tested with a fork. While fish is broiling, sauté almonds in remaining butter until golden brown, stirring constantly. Remove from heat and mix in lemon juice, hot pepper sauce and parsley. Pour over portions and serve at once.

Serves 4 to 5.

• B L A C K - E Y E D •

Peas and Good Luck

"Eat peas with the kings and cherries with the beggars," an old saying goes. The black-eyed pea, which came to America from Africa via the West Indies, is the pea of choice for New Years Day feasting, especially in the southern United States where eating black-eyed peas on New Years Day has long been considered essential to insure good fortune in the coming year. Apparently, the idea is that a humble start will invite richer fare throughout the year.

Baked Dishes & Casseroles, Rice & Pasta

BLACK EYED PEAS CREOLE

2 strips bacon
1 cup onion, chopped
1 cup bell pepper, chopped
1 cup celery, chopped
1 can (20-ounce) tomatoes
1 tablespoon sugar
1 large bay leaf
½ teaspoon basil
   Salt and fresh ground pepper to taste
2 packages (10 ounce) frozen black-eyed peas

Fry bacon until crisp; remove from fat and drain. Brown onion, green pepper and celery in fat. Add crumbled bacon and tomatoes, sugar, bay leaf, basil, salt and pepper. Simmer 5 minutes. Add frozen black-eyed peas to mixture. Cook slowly for 1½ to 2 hours, adding water when needed.

Serves 8.

CHEESE STRATA

6 slices white bread
1 cup coarsely grated, sharp Cheddar cheese
1 small onion, minced
1 tablespoon parsley, minced
1 tablespoon butter
2 eggs
1 cup milk
½ teaspoon *each* Dijon-style mustard and Worcestershire sauce
   Pepper to taste

Trim the crusts from bread slices. Arrange 3 of the slices into a buttered 1-quart augratin dish; distribute cheese on the bread and top with remaining slices. In a skillet, sauté onion and parsley in butter until onion is softened. In a bowl, whisk together eggs and milk, mustard, Worcestershire sauce and pepper. Pour the custard over the bread and chill the dish, covered, for 1 hour. Bake the dish uncovered in a pre-heated 350 degree oven for 50 minutes or until it is puffed and golden.

Serves 3.

BRAZILIAN CASSEROLE WITH BANANAS

½ cup olive oil
1 large onion, finely chopped
4 cloves garlic, coarsely chopped
2 pounds lean ground beef
6 ribs celery, chopped fine
2 green peppers, chopped fine
20 (to 30) sprigs parsley
2 cans (1 pound) Italian plum tomatoes
6 eggs
    Salt and pepper
1½ cups dry red wine
1 teaspoon red pepper flakes or to taste

Sauté onion and garlic in oil until tender. Take care not to let garlic burn. Combine meat, celery, peppers, parsley, tomatoes and eggs. Mix well with hands; season with salt and pepper. Add to casserole; cook until meat loses red color, then cook 15 minutes. Add 1 cup of the wine and cook another 15 minutes. Stir in remaining wine and red pepper flakes and cook, stirring occasionally, 1 hour longer (a total of 1½ hours). By this time most of liquid will have been absorbed. If not, increase heat to speed evaporation. Serve with fresh cooked rice and Fried Bananas.

Serves 4.

HAM MOUSSE

1 envelope unflavored gelatin
¼ cup water
2 ribs celery
¼ teaspoon green pepper
6 (or 8) stuffed olives
¾ cup mayonnaise or salad dressing
½ teaspoon salt
½ teaspoon paprika
2 tablespoons horseradish sauce
    Dash of cayenne pepper
1 cup ground ham
½ cup whipping cream

Soften gelatin in cold water. Then place over a pan of boiling water and stir constantly until gelatin has dissolved. Chop up the celery, green pepper and olives fairly fine. Then mix with the mayonnaise, salt, paprika, horseradish sauce, cayenne and ham. Stir in dissolved gelatin. Whip the cream until stiff and mix into ham mixture very gently. Rinse a pint mold with cold water. Pile the ham mousse into mold and chill in refrigerator until firm. This will take 3 to 4 hours. Serve with crackers or melba toast.

Serves 8-10.

LIMA BEAN AND PEAR CASSEROLE

12 cups canned lima beans, drained (butter beans)
3 cans (29-oz.) pears
1½ cups brown sugar
½ cup butter

Dot 3-quart casserole with ¼ cup butter. Cover with half of the beans. Top with half of drained pears, then half of brown sugar. Repeat, ending with lima beans. Distribute remaining butter over top layer. Bake at 275 degrees for 2 hours.

Serves 6 or 8.

TAMALE BAKE

½ pound hot sausage
1 cup minced onion
¾ green pepper, chopped
½ pound ground chuck
1 can (12 ounce) whole kernel corn
½ cup sliced ripe olives (reserve liquid)
1½ cups tomato sauce
1½ teaspoons chili powder
½ teaspoon garlic salt
2 cans (15 ounces each) tamales
⅓ cup tamales liquid
1½ cups grated Cheddar cheese

In large skillet, brown sausage. Remove sausage and drain. Spoon out all but 3 tablespoons drippings from skillet. Add onion and green pepper; sauté until tender. Stir in ground chuck and cook until browned. Drain corn. Add 1 teaspoon corn liquid, ripe olives, 1 teaspoon olive liquid, and sausage to skillet. Mix in tomato sauce, salt, chili powder and garlic salt. Simmer gently for 15 minutes.

Meanwhile, drain tamales; add ⅓ cup tamale liquid to meat mixture. Remove wrappings from tamales. Slice tamales in half lengthwise. Spoon meat mixture into large, shallow casserole and arrange tamales on top. Bake uncovered in 350 degree oven for 15 minutes. Sprinkle with cheese and return to oven until cheese is melted (about 20 more minutes).

Serves 6 or 8.

MASHED POTATO CASSEROLE

8 (to 10) medium potatoes, cooked
1 package (8 ounce) cream cheese
1 cup sour cream, or more
Butter (optional)
Salt and pepper to taste
Seasoned salt

After mashing potatoes, add cream cheese, sour cream, butter, salt and pepper. Whip with electric beater. Grease a 9x13-inch casserole or a 2-quart round casserole. Dot with butter and add potatoes. Sprinkle with Seasoned salt. Bake at 350 degrees for 20 minutes. Cover. Refrigerate.

Serves 8.

NOTE: *Fix the day before you want to serve.*

SQUASH CASSEROLE
DELLA LOWE

4 cups yellow squash
1 large onion
2 cups grated carrots
1½ cups bread crumbs
Dash nutmeg
Dash garlic powder
Salt to taste
1 tablespoon Worcestershire sauce
1½ cups sour cream
½ cup margarine, melted

Slice squash and onion thin; cook until tender. Drain and add grated carrots. Mix bread crumbs, nutmeg, garlic powder, salt, sour cream, margarine and Worcestershire. Combine with vegetables in baking dish. Top with buttered bread crumbs. Bake at 350 degrees for 20 to 30 minutes.

Serves 6.

APPLE, MACARONI 'N' CHEESE

½ pound bacon
1 onion, diced
½ pound elbow macaroni, cooked
1 can (8 ounce) tomato sauce
2 cups applesauce
¼ pound shredded cheese
¼ teaspoon curry powder
⅛ teaspoon dry mustard
½ teaspoon Worcestershire sauce
Salt and pepper to taste

Fry bacon until crisp; drain on paper towels and reserve 4 or 5 slices for garnish. Crumble remaining pieces. Drain off all but 2 tablespoons bacon drippings. Sauté onions in bacon fat. Combine all ingredients; season with salt and pepper. Turn mixture into a 2 quart casserole. Bake at 350 degrees for 25 minutes. About 5 minutes before cooking is completed, arrange reserved bacon slices on top of casserole.

Serves 4 to 6.

CHEESE DUMPLINGS IN TOMATO SAUCE

1 can (10½-ounce) tomato soup
1 cup water
Pepper
2 cups Bisquick
1 cup grated American cheese
1 tablespoon grated onion
¾ cup milk

Heat tomato soup, water and pepper to taste in a saucepan. Lightly mix Bisquick, cheese, onion and milk to make a soft dough. When soup boils, drop in dumpling dough from a teaspoon. Cover tightly and cook slowly. Do not uncover for 20 minutes.

Serves 8.

HAM AND EGG SOUFFLÉ

4 tablespoons butter or margarine
4 tablespoons flour
1 cup milk
1½ cups cooked ground ham
½ teaspoon dry mustard
Salt
Dash black pepper
7 eggs, separated

In a saucepan, melt butter and stir in flour. Blend in milk and cook, stirring until thickened. Add ham, mustard, salt and pepper. Continue to cook and stir until hot. Remove from heat and beat in egg yolks. Whip whites until they hold short, distinct, moist peaks. Fold in half of the whites thoroughly into the sauce; fold in remaining whites as thoroughly as you like. Pour into a well-buttered 2½-quart soufflé dish. If you want a topknot, draw a circle about an inch or so from the rim of soufflé with tip of spoon or knife. Bake at 375 degrees for 35 minutes.

Serves 6.

VARIATION: Instead of ham and mustard, use cooked chopped chicken livers seasoned with ½ teaspoon tarragon or use drained, minced clams seasoned with ¼ teaspoon thyme.

NOTE: *This is a hearty main dish for supper and is a very good brunch dish.*

ENDIVES AND HAM AU GRATIN

½ cup butter or margarine, divided
⅓ cup lemon juice
2 tablespoons hot water
6 Belgian endives, roots trimmed
¼ teaspoon salt
¼ cup all-purpose flour
   Dash cayenne pepper
2 cups milk
¾ cup grated sharp Cheddar cheese
6 thin slices boiled ham
   Paprika

About one hour before serving:
   In a large skillet, melt ¼ cup butter or margarine. Add lemon juice, hot water and endives; sprinkle with salt. Simmer covered 30 minutes or until tender yet crisp, adding hot water if necessary. Meanwhile, preheat oven to 450 degrees. In saucepan, melt ¼ cup butter or margarine. Remove from heat; stir in flour, cayenne and milk; bring to boil, stirring. Reduce heat. Add ½ cup grated cheese. Simmer, stirring over low heat, until thickened and smooth. Drain endives; wrap each in a ham slice, with ends uncovered. Arrange in 10x6x2-inch baking dish. Cover with cheese sauce; sprinkle with ¼ cup grated cheese; dust with paprika. Bake 15 minutes.

Serves 3 or 4.

GNOCCHI

(PASTA)

½ cup butter
½ cup farina
½ cup cornstarch
½ teaspoon salt
4 cups hot milk
1 cup grated Parmesan cheese
4 egg yolks, well beaten

Melt butter in the top of a double boiler. Mix together farina, cornstarch and salt and stir into the melted butter. Gradually add the hot milk and cook the mixture over direct heat, stirring vigorously, until it is very thick. Set the pan over boiling water and cook the mixture for 5 minutes longer. Stir in the Parmesan cheese; remove from the heat and stir in egg yolks thoroughly. Spread the mixture ¾ inch thick in an 8-inch square dish. Chill until firm. Cut the gnocchi into small circles or squares and arrange on a buttered baking sheet. Put a bit of butter on each; sprinkle them with grated Parmesan, and bake at 450 degrees for 10 minutes or until the tops are golden brown.

Serves 8.

MUSHROOM SOUFFLÉ

5 tablespoons butter or margarine
1 pound mushrooms, chopped
3 shallots or green onions (white part only), finely chopped
5 tablespoons flour
⅓ cup sherry or Madeira
¾ cup milk
1 teaspoon salt
9 eggs, separated

Melt butter in a saucepan. Add mushrooms and shallots and simmer rapidly, stirring until all liquid has cooked away. Stir in flour; blend in sherry, milk and salt. Cook, stirring until thickened. Remove from heat and beat in egg yolks. Whip egg whites until they hold short, distinct peaks. Fold about half of the whites very thoroughly into the sauce. Fold in remaining whites as thoroughly as you like. Pour into a well-buttered soufflé dish. Run tip of spoon or knife around top within an inch or two of the rim if you want the soufflé to form a topknot. Bake at 375 degrees for 40 minutes.

Serves 6.

SCRAMBLED EGGS EN CROÛTE

6 medium water rolls, with ¾ of the insides scooped out
Melted butter
12 eggs
5 tablespoons butter
¼ cup heavy cream
Salt
White pepper
Paprika
Fresh parsley

Brush rolls with melted butter and toast at 350 degrees until golden brown.

Beat eggs until the whites and yolks are well mixed, but not frothy. Heat 3 tablespoons butter in a heavy skillet, add the eggs and cook them, stirring constantly, over low heat. As the eggs begin to set, add 2 tablespoons butter and cream. Season the eggs with salt and white pepper to taste. Stuff the toasted rolls with scrambled eggs; sprinkle with paprika and garnish the tops with fresh parsley.

Serves 8.

NOODLES ROMANOFF

1 cup cottage cheese
1 cup sour cream
2 cups hot boiled noodles
1 teaspoon chopped onion
1 small clove garlic, crushed
1 teaspoon Worcestershire
½ teaspoon salt
¼ cup grated cheese

Mix cottage cheese, sour cream and noodles. Add onion, garlic and seasonings. Place in buttered casserole. Sprinkle with cheese and bake 40 minutes in 350 degree oven.

Serves 4.

GREEN RICE

½ cup olive oil
1 onion, chopped
½ clove garlic
1 cup raw rice
1 heaping cup grated cheese
1 heaping cup chopped parsley
1 cup milk
2 eggs, beaten
Salt to taste

Cook the rice. When it is cool, mix with remaining ingredients. Bake at 350 degrees for 30 to 40 minutes, until liquid is absorbed. Serve with creamed or Newburg shrimp, crab or chicken.

Serves 6.

Breads & Sweet Breads

FRENCH BREAD MUSTARD SLICES

½ cup butter or margarine, softened
¼ cup parsley
2 tablespoons chopped green onions
2 tablespoons prepared mustard
1 tablespoon sesame seeds, toasted
1 teaspoon freshly squeezed lemon juice
1 loaf French bread

Combine all ingredients except bread; blend well. Slice bread; spread butter mixture on both sides of slices. Reassemble into loaf; wrap loosely in foil. Heat at 375 degrees about 10 to 15 minutes.

Yields 10 to 12 slices.

CRANBERRY NUT BREAD

1   egg
¼   cup sugar
⅓   cup sour cream
2¼   cups all-purpose flour
1   teaspoon baking soda
1   teaspoon salt
1   teaspoon baking powder
3   tablespoons grated orange peel
½   cup nuts
1   cup cranberries, coarsely chopped

In a large mixing bowl, beat egg. Add sugar and mix well. Carefully stir in sour cream. Sift together flour, baking powder, baking soda and salt. Add to creamed mixture, stirring only until moistened. Add orange peel, nuts and cranberries. Turn onto buttered 9x5x3-inch loaf pan. Bake in preheated 350 degree oven for 55 to 60 minutes.

Yields 1 loaf.

BRAN FLAKES GRIDDLE CAKES

1   cup flour
¾   teaspoon salt
2½   teaspoons baking powder
1   tablespoon sugar
1   egg, well beaten
1¼   cups milk
1   cup bran flakes, slightly crushed
3   tablespoons melted butter

Sift flour, salt, baking powder and sugar together. Combine egg and milk and beat lightly. Gradually add to dry ingredients, beating only until smooth. Add bran flakes, then melted butter and mix lightly. Bake on hot greased griddle.

Yields about 16 4-inch griddle cakes.

BEATEN BISCUITS
BETTY JOHNSON

2   cups unbleached flour
1   teaspoon salt
½   cup cold unsalted butter, cut in pieces
½   cup ice water

Using metal blade of Cuisinart, add flour and salt. Turn on and off twice to aerate mixture. Add butter and process until like cornmeal. With machine running, pour ice water through the feed tube in steady stream; process until it forms a ball; then process for an additional 2 minutes.

Remove dough and roll out on lightly floured surface into a ⅛-inch thick rectangle. Fold in half to form 2 layers. Cut with 1½-inch fluted cutter. Place biscuits on an ungreased cookie sheet. Prick 2 rows of holes with tines of fork. Bake at 350 degrees for 25 to 30 minutes or until golden brown. Remove from oven and split immediately. If centers are soft, return split biscuits to oven for 4 or 5 minutes to assure a crisp base for spreads.

Yields 36 biscuits or 72 split biscuits.

• Y E A S T •

The Fleischmann Company was founded in Cincinnati in 1868. By 1876 it had been granted a patent for the first standardized compressed yeast in cake form. The less perishable granulated dry yeast was developed more than 65 years later for shipment to U.S. Army cooks overseas. The earlier form of yeast was a "sponge" kept by housewives and bakers for their leavening. Until commercial yeast became available, the yeast sponge might be kept for years and was often passed down from one generation to another.

Beaten

• B I S C U I T S •

Beaten biscuits date from the days before baking powder some 200 years ago. Air pounded into the dough expands as the biscuits bake, causing them to rise. The dough was beaten steadily with a hammer or mallet for 20 to 30 minutes until it was shiny and smooth, and then either pinched off into balls or rolled and cut.

SOUR CREAM AND APPLE COFFEECAKE

½   cup margarine
1   cup sugar
3   eggs
2½   cups flour
1   teaspoon soda
1   tablespoon baking powder
¾   cup sour cream
1   cup grated, peeled raw apples, packed
1   cup chopped nuts
1   cup brown sugar
4   teaspoons cinnamon, divided in half
2   teaspoons instant coffee powder

Cream margarine and sugar. Beat in eggs one at a time. Mix and sift flour, baking powder, soda and 2 teaspoons cinnamon. Add to creamed mixture alternately with sour cream and apples. Beat until well blended. Combine remaining ingredients. Spoon half the batter into a greased 9-inch tube pan. Sprinkle ⅔ of the nuts, brown sugar, 2 teaspoons cinnamon, 2 teaspoons dry instant coffee over batter. Cover with remaining batter; top with nut mixture. Bake at 375 degrees for 50 minutes or until done. Cool and remove from pan.

CHRISTMAS COFFEECAKE

1   cup butter or margarine
½   cup granulated sugar
½   teaspoon salt
2   tablespoons grated lemon rind
2   eggs, well beaten
1   compressed yeast cake or 1 package dry yeast
1   cup sour cream
4½   cups sifted all-purpose flour
¼   cup melted butter or margarine
¼   cup brown sugar
¾   cup seedless raisins
¾   cup chopped walnut meats
6   tablespoons granulated sugar
1½   teaspoons cinnamon

Dissolve yeast in sour cream. Cream butter; add ½ cup granulated sugar; cream thoroughly. Add salt, lemon rind, eggs and yeast in sour cream. Blend well. Add flour and mix thoroughly. Cover and chill in the refrigerator for 3 hours.

On a lightly floured board, roll dough to about ¼ inch thickness. Cover bottom of 9x12-inch pan with the melted butter and brown sugar. Spread surface of dough with remaining ingredients which have been mixed together. Roll up as you would a jelly roll, pressing the edges together firmly. Cut crosswise into slices ¾ inch thick, using a sharp knife or floured scissors. Arrange slices on top of butter and brown sugar mixture. Cover with a clean cloth and let rise in a warm place ½ hour until light. Bake at 375 degrees for 35 minutes.

Yields 20 coffeecake wheels.

ROLLED CHEESE BISCUITS

2 cups flour
4 teaspoons baking powder
1 teaspoon sugar
1 teaspoon salt
¾ cup milk or enough to make soft biscuit dough
1 cup grated Cheddar cheese
2 tablespoons shortening

Sift dry ingredients, then work in shortening and add enough milk to make a soft dough. Knead lightly. Roll out on a floured board. Spread lightly with soft butter and cover with grated cheese, a little salt, then paprika. Roll as for a jelly roll and cut in ¾-inch slices. Place cut side on lightly greased pan. Bake at 350 degrees for 10 or 15 minutes.

Yields about 10 biscuits.

NOTE: *These biscuits are delicious served with a fruity chicken salad.*

APPLESAUCE DOUGHNUTS

4 eggs
1 cup firmly packed brown sugar
1 cup smooth applesauce
4½ cups sifted flour
1 teaspoon baking soda
3 slightly rounded teaspoons baking powder
¼ teaspoon *each* cinnamon, nutmeg, salt
5 tablespoons melted butter
    Grated lemon rind

Beat eggs and brown sugar until light and fluffy. Add remaining ingredients. Blend the dough well and chill overnight. Pat out the dough a portion at a time on a lightly floured board and cut out rounds with a floured doughnut cutter. Fry the doughnuts in hot deep lard at 375 degrees and drain them on absorbent paper.

Yields about 36 doughnuts.

NOTE: *These doughnuts freeze well.*

PUMPKIN BREAD
EULA RICHARDSON

3½ cups flour
½ teaspoon salt
3 cups sugar
½ cup chopped dates
1 cup cooking oil
1 can (16 ounce) pumpkin
2 teaspoons soda
1 teaspoon cinnamon
½ cup chopped nuts
4 eggs
⅓ cup water

Combine dry ingredients; dredge dates in flour mixture. Beat eggs well. Add oil, water and pumpkin, then dry ingredients, dates and nuts. Bake in 2 loaf pans (9½x2¾-inch) or 4 small pans at 350 degrees for 1¼ hours. (For larger pans — until a toothpick comes out clean. This test should also be made on the smaller loaves.)

NOTE: *For nut breads or cakes, I always line bottoms of well-greased pans with waxed paper.*

WALNUT-RAISIN BREAD

1   tablespoon vinegar
1   cup milk
1½ cups all-purpose flour
¾   teaspoon salt
½   teaspoon baking powder
1   teaspoon baking soda
½   cup granulated sugar
1   egg, beaten
⅓   cup molasses
¾   cup uncooked rolled oats
¾   cup seedless raisins
¼   cup chopped California walnuts
    Whipped cream cheese, softened

The day before baking bread, add vinegar to milk; let stand overnight. Preheat oven to 350 degrees. Grease well and lightly flour a 9x5x3-inch loaf pan. Sift together flour, salt, baking powder, baking soda and sugar. Then stir in egg, molasses and milk mixture all at once. Fold in oats, raisins and walnuts. Turn at once into prepared pan. Bake 60 to 70 minutes or until cake tester comes out clean. Cool on rack; wrap in plastic wrap or foil. Store overnight. Serve sliced with cheese.

Yields 1 loaf.

NOTE: *Nice in lunch boxes. To make 2 loaves, double ingredients and proceed as directed.*

Desserts

TWO FRUITS PIE

1   baked pie shell
1   cup sugar
4   tablespoons flour
2   cups washed and hulled boysenberries, loganberries, youngberries, or blackberries
1   tablespoon lemon juice
1   tablespoon powdered sugar
2   cups sliced apricots or peaches (canned or fresh)
    Sweetened whipped cream

Combine sugar and flour. Add berries and mash well into sugar mixture. Let come to a boil and cook for 5 minutes or until thick, stirring constantly. Add lemon juice.

Sprinkle powdered sugar over bottom of baked pie shell. Arrange apricots or peaches over pie shell and cover with cooled berry mixture. Chill 2 to 4 hours. Top with whipped cream just before serving.

FRIED BANANAS

4   firm bananas
2   eggs, lightly beaten
1½ cups fresh bread crumbs
½   cup butter
½   cup salad oil

Cut each banana in 4 pieces. Dip in beaten eggs. Roll in bread crumbs. Sauté in butter and oil until golden.

Serves 4.

Oregon Chess Pie

½ cup butter
1 cup sugar
3 eggs
1 teaspoon vanilla
1 cup seedless raisins, simmered in water a few minutes to plump
1 cup coarsely chopped pecans
1 unbaked pie shell

Cream butter and sugar until light and fluffy. Add eggs one at a time, beating well after each addition. Add pecans, raisins and vanilla. Pour into unbaked pie shell. Bake at 350 degrees for 40 minutes. Serve cold with whipped cream or ice cream if desired.

Serves 8.

Almond Rum Pie

⅓ cup pastry flour
Dash salt
⅔ cup sugar
2 large eggs, beaten slightly
8 tablespoons rum
1½ cups half-and-half, scalded
1 baked pie shell, chilled
Currant jelly, melted
½ cup blanched, finely chopped, slightly toasted almonds
Strawberries

Sift flour, salt and sugar together. In the top of a double boiler, mix eggs, rum and half-and-half. Combine flour mixture with egg mixture. Cook over hot water, stirring constantly until mixture is smooth and thick. Cool. Brush bottom and sides of pie shell with currant jelly. Then sprinkle almonds over the bottom. Pour the cooled custard over the almonds. Cover with strawberries brushed lightly with currant jelly. Serve very cold.

Peach Jubilee Pie
Flaming Peach Pie

1 9-inch unbaked pie shell
1 tablespoon flour
1 can (29 ounce) cling peach slices
¾ cup brown sugar, packed down
½ cup sifted all-purpose flour
¼ cup soft butter or margarine
½ teaspoon nutmeg
2 tablespoons light rum

Line a 9-inch pie pan with pastry and rub 1 tablespoon flour over bottom. Drain peaches thoroughly and cover pastry with peaches, building them up slightly on sides.

Blend brown sugar, flour, nutmeg and butter or margarine together and sprinkle over peaches, leaving outside edges uncovered about 1 ½ inches around. Bake at 400 degrees for 25 to 30 minutes until pastry is well browned and topping is crisp and browned. While still warm, sprinkle warm rum (set in pan of hot water to warm it) and ignite. Serve as soon as flames go out.

Serves 6 to 8.

Seedless Grapes in Sour Cream
Dessert Grapes Glacé

1 pound seedless green grapes, picked from stems, washed and well drained
½ cup sour cream
2 tablespoons light brown sugar
4 tablespoons Kahlua

In a medium bowl, mix sour cream, brown sugar and Kahlua; add grapes and toss until well coated. Cover and refrigerate several hours. At serving time, toss grapes again, then spoon into sherbet glasses as a light dessert after a hearty meal.

Serves 4.

KEY LIME PIE

1 baked 9-inch pastry shell
1 envelope unflavored gelatin
1 cup sugar
¼ teaspoon salt
4 eggs, separated
½ cup lime juice
¼ cup water
1 teaspoon grated lime peel
   Green food coloring
   Sweetened whipped cream for topping

Place gelatin, ½ cup of the sugar, and salt in saucepan. Beat together egg yolks, lime juice and water; stir into gelatin mixture. Cook over medium heat until mixture begins to boil, stirring constantly. Remove from heat; stir in grated lime peel. Add food coloring sparingly to tint a pale green. Chill, stirring occasionally, until mixture mounds slightly when dropped from a spoon. Beat egg whites until soft peaks form; gradually add remaining ½ cup sugar. Continue beating until stiff peaks are formed. Fold into gelatin mixture. Whip cream and fold into mixture. Pile into cooled baked pastry shell. Chill until firm. Garnish with additional whipped cream. Garnish with grated lime peel and pistachio nuts.

PEACH MELBA ICE CREAM PIE

COCONUT CRUST:

1 can (3½ ounces) flaked coconut
¼ cup finely chopped nuts
2 tablespoons butter, melted
Coconut crust:

In a small bowl, toss together coconut, nuts and butter. Press firmly and evenly against bottom and sides of a 9-inch pie plate. Bake at 325 degrees for 10 to 15 minutes until golden brown. Cool.

FILLING:

1 quart peach ice cream, slightly softened
1 pint vanilla ice cream, slightly softened

Spoon peach ice cream into crust, spreading to edge of pie shell. Freeze. Spoon vanilla ice cream over peach ice cream. Freeze.

RASPBERRY SAUCE:

1 package (10 ounce) frozen red raspberries, thawed and drained
½ cup sugar
1 tablespoon cornstarch
2 cups sliced fresh peaches, sweetened, or 2 packages (10 ounces each) frozen, sliced peaches, thawed and drained

In a 1-quart sauce pan, combine sugar, cornstarch and syrup. Cook over medium heat, stirring constantly until thickened. Boil two additional minutes. Stir in raspberries. Cool. Just before serving, arrange peaches on pie, cut into wedges and serve with raspberry sauce.

Serves 8.

> • P E A C H   M E L B A •
>
> *The great French chef Escoffier created peach melba* during the 1890s to honor the Australian soprano Nellie Melba. He was captivated by her performance in *Lohengrin,* and served his dessert of peaches, vanilla ice cream and spun sugar between the wings of a swan carved in ice. Sometime later he added the raspberry sauce which has become an indispensable part of this dessert.

ITALIAN COCONUT CREAM CAKE
POCAHONTAS GREADINGTON

2 cups sugar
½ cup oil
½ cup butter or margarine
1 teaspoon vanilla
2 cups flour
1 teaspoon soda
¼ teaspoon salt
½ cup chopped pecans
2 cups coconut
5 eggs, separated
1 cup buttermilk

Cream together sugar, oil and butter or margarine and egg yolks. Add vanilla. Sift together flour, soda and salt. Stir into above mixture. Add coconut, chopped pecans and buttermilk. Beat egg whites until stiff and fold into cake mixture. Pour into 3 greased and floured 8-inch layer cake pans. Bake 30 to 40 minutes in 350 degree oven. Let cake cool completely before frosting.

CREAM CHEESE FROSTING:

8 ounces cream cheese, softened
½ stick margarine, softened
1 box (1 pound) powdered sugar
1 tablespoon vanilla

When cake is cool, cream butter and cream cheese together. Add powdered sugar and vanilla and beat until smooth, and ice a most delicious cake.

APPLE WITH CRUMB TOPPING

6 tart apples, sliced
¾ cup sugar
2 tablespoons water
¼ cup butter or margarine
1 cup quick oats
½ cup brown sugar
½ teaspoon cinnamon
½ cup broken nutmeats
1 teaspoon grated lemon rind

Slice apples into well-buttered, 8-inch baking dish. Sprinkle with granulated sugar and water. Place in oven to heat. Melt butter or margarine and stir in quick oats, brown sugar, cinnamon, broken nut meats and lemon rind. Spread over apples and bake at 350 degrees for 45 minutes until apples are tender. Serve warm with plain or whipped cream.

Serves 8.

THREE FRUITS SHERBERT
MARY ANN JACOBS

3 bananas, puréed
   Juice of 3 oranges and 3 lemons
3 cups sugar
3 cups milk
3 cups heavy cream, lightly whipped

Mash bananas; add fruit juices and sugar. Stir until sugar is dissolved. Have ice cream freezer ready with layer of ice and salt. Pour mixture into freezer; add milk and cream. Pack ice cream freezer with ice and rock salt. Freeze until desired consistency. Remove dasher and pack to ripen an hour or two or store in deep freeze.

Yields 1 gallon.

SOUR CREAM PEACH PIE

1   9-inch baked pie shell
⅔   cup peach syrup
2   tablespoons tapioca
½   cup sugar
1½   cups thick sour cream
½   teaspoon almond extract
7   (or 8) peach halves

Mix together peach syrup, tapioca, and sugar in double boiler. Cook until mixture thickens (15 minutes). Cool. Meanwhile, mix sour cream with almond extract. Combine the two mixtures. Fill baked pie shell with half the mixture. Add peach halves (round side up). Pour on the remainder of the mixture. Garnish with any left over peaches which may be sliced and arranged in a design. Bake at 350 degrees for 40 minutes until set.

Serves 6 to 8.

CRISP THIN COOKIES
CORDELIA JENKINS

½   cup butter or margarine
2   cups brown sugar
2   cups pecans, finely chopped
1¼   cups cake flour
1   teaspoon baking powder
1   teaspoon vanilla
2   eggs
¼   teaspoon salt

Mix in order given. Drop far apart on oiled cooky sheet. Bake in 350 degree oven 8 or 10 minutes. Remove from oven and while warm, remove from tin.

NOTE: *With practice, these cookies can be rolled on wooden spoon handle while warm. It takes practice and patience, but worth the effort.*

PRUNE CAKE
MARY ANN JACOBS

2   cups all-purpose flour
3   teaspoons baking powder
1   teaspoon salt
¼   teaspoon soda
½   cup shortening
1   cup sugar
1   teaspoon ground cinnamon
½   teaspoon ground nutmeg
¼   teaspoon ground cloves
2   eggs, beaten
¼   cup prune juice
½   cup milk
1   cup cooked, chopped prunes
1   cup chopped walnuts

Combine flour, baking powder, salt and soda; set aside. Cream shortening, sugar and spices until fluffy. Add eggs and continue to beat until creamy. Add flour mixture, prune juice and milk, alternately, to creamed mixture. Add prunes and walnuts. Pour into a greased and floured 8-inch square pan. Bake at 350 degrees for 50 to 55 minutes. Frost with Orange Creme Frosting when cool.

ORANGE CREME FROSTING

½   cup butter or margarine
4   cups sifted powdered sugar
4   (to 6) tablespoons cream
1   teaspoon orange extract

Cream butter and powdered sugar. Add cream to make spreading consistency. Add orange extract. Spread on top and sides of prune cake.

Yields enough frosting for one 8-inch square cake.

ANGEL PIE

1   envelope unflavored gelatin
1   cup milk
    Pinch of salt
½   cup sugar
1   cup light cream
3   eggs, separated
1   teaspoon vanilla
1   cup strawberries, sweetened and thickened
⅓   cup sugar
1   teaspoon cornstarch dissolved in 2 teaspoons
    cold water

Soften gelatin 5 minutes in cold milk; add salt, ½ cup sugar and cream. Cook over hot water, stirring occasionally, until gelatin is dissolved. Beat egg yolks slightly; add hot milk gradually. Return to double boiler and cook until mixture coats spoon. Cool. Add vanilla. Beat egg whites until stiff but not dry. Fold into custard. Set in refrigerator until it begins to thicken but is not entirely jelled. Pour into graham cracker crust. Chill until well set. Just before serving, spread berries over top of pie.

To thicken berries: wash, slice and sweeten berries, using ⅓ cup sugar. Let stand 15 or 20 minutes. Drain juice in a small saucepan; place on stove to heat. Stir dissolved cornstarch into juice and cook until thick and clear. Let cool and stir the sliced raw strawberries into sauce. When well chilled, spread over top of chilled pie.

Serves 6 to 8.

GRAHAM CRACKER CRUST

FOR ANGEL PIE

16 regular-sized graham crackers (1¾ cups
    crumbs when rolled fine)
½   cup sugar
½   cup melted butter or margarine
½   teaspoon cinnamon (optional)

Blend well and pat into pie pan. Half cup of crumbs might be reserved to sprinkle on meringue. Bake at 350 degrees for 10 minutes. Let cool.

Yields 1 pie crust.

NOTE: *This type pie crust is especially good for ice box and cream pies. Zwieback, vanilla wafers or corn flakes rolled fine can be used instead of graham cracker crumbs.*

MAPLE NUT ICE CREAM

2½ cups maple syrup
½   teaspoon maple extract
6   egg yolks, well beaten
1   quart milk
1   pint whipping cream
1   cup finely chopped pecans

Heat maple syrup to boiling point. Add maple extract. Pour this syrup slowly into egg yolks, beating constantly. Strain into milk and cook in double boiler until custard coats spoon. Let cool and add whipping cream, whipped until thick but not stiff, and finely chopped pecans. Freeze in crank or electric freezer.

Yields about 2 quarts.

PUMPKIN MARMALADE PIE

2   partially baked 8-inch pastry shells
1   can (16 ounce) pumpkin
1   cup apple butter
1   whole egg
2   egg yolks
½   cup light brown sugar, firmly packed
2   tablespoons cornstarch
1   teaspoon ground cinnamon
¼   teaspoon *each* ground nutmeg and ground
     ginger
1⅔ cups evaporated milk
½   cup orange marmalade
1   cup heavy cream, whipped

Combine the pumpkin and apple butter in a large bowl. Mix well. Add the whole egg, egg yolks and all remaining ingredients except the marmalade. Beat with an electric beater until smooth. Pour half of the mixture in each pie shell. Place in a 425 degree oven and bake for 15 minutes. Reduce heat to 325 degrees and continue baking another 25 minutes or until set. Cool.

Once pies are cooked, wrap one in moisture- and vapor-proof wrap and freeze for future use. To finish the other pie, spoon marmalade over the entire surface of the filling. Whip the cream and spoon over the marmalade just before serving.

EDITOR'S NOTE: *To partially bake a pie shell, press a piece of buttered foil over crust. Bake at 400 degrees for 10 minutes. Remove foil and bake another 2 minutes.*

ALMOND ROCA RUM PIE

1   baked 8½-inch pie shell
4   egg yolks
⅓   cup sugar
⅛   teaspoon salt
2   teaspoons unflavored gelatin
2   tablespoons water
½   pint whipping cream
2   tablespoons Jamaican rum
3   (to 4) ounces Almond Roca or English
     Toffee, coarsely chopped

Beat egg yolks until light. Add sugar and salt. Mix gelatin with water and melt over hot water. Add to mixture, along with cream, whipped stiff, and rum. Cool slightly and pour into cooled pie shell. Cover with coarsely chopped Almond Roca or English toffee. Allow to stand in refrigerator for several hours to set before serving.

Serves 6 or 8.

THE DIVINE PUMPKIN PIE
MARY ANN JACOBS

1   unbaked 9-inch pastry shell
3   eggs
1   cup evaporated milk
1½   cups pumpkin
1½   cups dark brown sugar
½   teaspoon salt
1   teaspoon cinnamon
½   teaspoon cloves
½   teaspoon ginger
1   tablespoon cognac
3   tablespoons butter
1   teaspoon vanilla

Beat eggs and mix with milk. Add remaining ingredients and mix thoroughly. Pour into pastry shell and bake at 325 degrees for 45 minutes to 1 hour.

BREAD PUDDING WITH WHISKEY SAUCE
ANNE KOONTZ INGRAM

1   loaf French bread (dry)
1   quart milk
3   eggs
2   cups sugar
2   tablespoons vanilla extract
1   cup raisins
3   tablespoons melted margarine

Preheat oven to 350 degrees. Soak bread in milk. Crush with hands to make sure milk is soaked thoroughly. Add eggs, sugar, vanilla, raisins and stir well. Pour margarine in bottom of heavy 9x14-inch baking pan. Add bread mixture. Bake until firm, approximately 40 minutes. Cool the pudding. Cube it and put into individual dessert dishes. When ready to serve, add whiskey sauce and heat under broiler for a few minutes.

WHISKEY SAUCE:

1   cup sugar
½   cup butter
1   egg, beaten
2   ounces bourbon, or to taste

To make the whiskey sauce, cream sugar and butter. Cook in a double boiler until very hot and sugar is dissolved. Add beaten egg and whip very fast so egg doesn't curdle. Cool and add whiskey.

Serves 8.

PENNSYLVANIA DUTCH CHEESECAKE

1   cup butter
1   cup sugar
2   cups cottage cheese
4   eggs, separated
¼   cup sherry
    Grated rind of 1 lemon
¼   teaspoon nutmeg
    Pastry for deep dish pie

Cream together butter, sugar and cottage cheese. Add slightly beaten egg yolks, sherry, grated lemon rind and nutmeg, stirring until smooth and well blended. Beat egg whites until stiff; fold them into the mixture and bake in a deep pie dish lined with pastry at 450 degrees for 30 minutes.

NOTE: *Maybe the "Dutch" brought this dish with them from Germany along with their sense of color and their love of pork. It makes a treasure that looks quite like a pie and is very likely to arouse curiosity as well as enthusiasm.*

CREOLE ICE CREAM

½   cup sugar
1   pint half-and-half, scalded
6   egg yolks, beaten well
1   cup maple syrup
1   tablespoon vanilla
1   cup toasted almonds, chopped
1   quart whipping cream

Caramelize sugar to nice brown and gradually stir scalded half-and-half into it. Cook over lowered heat until caramel is dissolved. Combine beaten egg yolks and maple syrup. Mix thoroughly and add to scalded cream. Cook in double boiler until custard coats spoon. Let cool. Strain. Add vanilla and chopped toasted almonds. Fold in whipped cream and freeze.

OATMEAL SPICE CAKE

1 cup rolled oats
1 cup hot water
½ cup butter or margarine
1 cup brown sugar, firmly packed
½ cup granulated sugar
2 eggs
1 cup flour
½ teaspoon *each* baking powder and salt
1 teaspoon *each* cinnamon and soda
½ teaspoon ground cloves
½ cup mashed ripe bananas
½ cup *each* chopped nuts and chopped dates

Put rolled oats in a bowl; pour in hot water, stir and cool for about 30 minutes. Cream butter with sugars, blend in eggs. Beat until smooth. Sift flour, measure and sift again with cinnamon, soda, baking powder, salt and cloves; slowly add to creamed mixture, mixing after each addition. Mix in banana. Blend in oats, nuts and dates. Pour into a greased pan (9x13-inch). Bake at 350 degrees for 30 minutes. Cool. Cut in squares to serve from pan.

Serves 16.

NOTE: *This is a moist cake with a date flavor. No icing is necessary.*

CHESTNUTS IN CREAM

2 pounds chestnuts
1½ pints cream
2 tablespoons butter
8 truffles, thinly sliced
1 jigger cognac or brandy

Remove a little strip, ¼ inch wide, from the rounded part of each chestnut and roast the chestnuts at low level, high heat, for 45 minutes, turning once. Peel while hot. Put in covered earthenware casserole. Pour cream over the chestnuts. Add butter and truffles and cover. Bake at 300 degrees for 45 minutes. Minutes before serving, pour a large jigger of cognac or brandy over the chestnuts.

Serves 6 to 8.

NOTE: *Chestnuts can be obtained in cans, which saves a lot of time and tedious preparation.*

CHOCOLATE MOUSSE

4 egg whites
1 cup sugar
½ cup water
¼ teaspoon cream of tartar, dissolved in 1 teaspoon water
12 ounces semi-sweet chocolate morsels, melted and cooled
1 pint heavy cream, whipped
1 teaspoon vanilla
2 tablespoons brandy

In a small saucepan, combine sugar, dissolved cream of tartar and water. Cook mixture until it reaches soft ball stage (236 to 238 degrees on candy thermometer). Add cooked sugar mixture in a thin stream to egg whites, blending at medium speed until cool. Mix vanilla, brandy and whipped cream. Fold cooled chocolate into whipped cream mixture.

Pour in mold and refrigerate several hours before serving. Decorate with swirls of whipped cream and shaved or grated chocolate.

Serves 8.

Dessert Drinks

GUADELOUPE MILK PUNCH

¾ cup light rum
3 tablespoons sugar
3 cups milk or half-and-half
   Grated nutmeg
   Ice cubes

Put rum, sugar and milk in a shaker with a cup of ice cubes and shake well. Strain into 12-ounce glasses. Sprinkle each with nutmeg and serve.

Serves 6.

FRESH ORANGE FREEZE

1 pint orange sherbet
2 cups orange juice
2 cups crushed ice
1 orange, thinly sliced (optional)

Combine orange sherbet, orange juice and crushed ice in blender; blend until thick and frosty. Serve immediately in tall chilled glasses. Garnish with orange slices if desired.

Serves 6.

PEACH COOLER

4 eggs, separated
⅛ teaspoon salt
¼ cup sugar
1 package (12 ounce) frozen sweetened peaches, thawed, or 1½ cups sweetened, sliced fresh peaches
1 tablespoon freshly squeezed lemon juice
⅛ (to ¼) teaspoon almond extract
2 cups chilled milk
1 pint vanilla ice cream
   Whipped cream (optional)
   Peach slices (optional)

Beat egg whites and salt until they hold peaks. Add sugar gradually; continue beating until stiff and glossy. Purée the peaches in a blender. Combine egg yolks, peaches, lemon juice and almond extract, mixing well. Add milk and ice cream, blending until smooth. Fold in egg whites. Serve in tall, chilled glasses. Garnish with whipped cream and peach slices, if desired.

Serves 8 to 10.

A DESSERT DRINK

1 jigger brandy
2 scoops vanilla ice cream
½ jigger Galliano
½ scoop crushed ice

Place all in blender; blend well. Serve in white wine glasses or champagne glasses.

· E I G H T I E S ·

The Eighties

CURRIED CHICKEN PATÉ
BETTY JOHNSON

1   whole chicken breast or 1¼ cups leftover chicken (or turkey), cut in 1-inch pieces
1   shallot
1   medium apple, peeled and cored
½   cup butter, cut in pieces
½   teaspoon *each* salt and pepper
1   tablespoon lemon juice
1   teaspoon mild curry powder

Add chicken, shallot and apple to Cuisinart with metal blade, turning on and off until mixture is finely chopped. Add remaining ingredients. Turn Cuisinart on and off several times. Then process until smooth. Taste and season. Serve with Beaten Biscuits.

WHEAT GERM STUFFED TOMATOES

4   large tomatoes, 3 inches in diameter
1   avocado
½   cup wheat germ
½   cup chopped celery
2   tablespoons finely chopped onion
2   tablespoons chopped parsley
2   tablespoons lemon juice
½   teaspoon salt
⅛   teaspoon pepper

Cut ¾ inch from tops of tomatoes. Scoop out pulp, leaving shells intact. Dice tops and pulp. Drain. Combine tomato, diced avocado; add parsley and other ingredients. Mix well. Spoon into tomato shells. Garnish with parsley or herbs.

Yields 4 servings.

BARLEY SALAD VINAIGRETTE

1   cup Quaker Quick Pearled Barley
1   teaspoon salt
3   cups boiling water
2   cups mushroom slices
1   cup thin carrot slices
¼   cup green onion slices
½   cup vegetable oil
⅓   cup lemon juice
1½ teaspoons garlic salt
1   teaspoon prepared mustard
½   teaspoon tarragon leaves, crushed
⅛   teaspoon pepper

Cook barley in salted boiling water according to package directions. Drain. Cool. Combine barley, carrot and onion. Add combined remaining ingredients; mix well. Chill about 3 to 4 hours; serve on lettuce.

Yields 6 to 8 servings.

CLEORA'S AVOCADO RING MOLD

5   tablespoons unflavored gelatin
6   tablespoons lemon juice
2   tablespoons vinegar
½   cup mayonnaise
6   cups avocado pulp
    (about 9 large avocados, puréed in blender)
2   tablespoons grated onion
1   cup sour cream
¾   cup heavy cream, whipped
4   teaspoons salt
2   teaspoons dill weed
1   teaspoon thyme
    Green food coloring

Soak gelatin in lemon juice and vinegar 5 minutes. Set in a small pan of hot water and stir until dissolved. Add mayonnaise, avocado, onion, sour cream, whipped cream, salt, dill weed and thyme. Blend thoroughly. Add few drops green food coloring to give desired color. Pour in oiled 3-quart ring mold. Place in refrigerator several hours (overnight is best). Unmold and fill with chicken salad or seafood salad of your choice.

Serves 12 or more.

Breads

JALAPEÑO CORNBREAD
MARY ANN JACOBS

⅓   cup bacon fat
1   cup yellow cornmeal
1   teaspoon salt
¾   teaspoon soda
1   cup buttermilk
2   eggs
1   large onion, chopped very fine
2   (or 3) teaspoons jalapeño peppers, chopped very fine
1   can (12 ounce) cream-style corn
½   pound grated sharp cheese (or more)

Put bacon fat in cast iron skillet to melt in 400 degree oven. Mix cornmeal with salt and soda. Combine remaining ingredients except for cheese. Mix wet and dry ingredients and stir in melted fat. Mix well and pour ½ batter into skillet. Sprinkle cheese over this. Pour balance of batter on top and more grated cheese (optional). Bake in 400 degree oven 20 minutes or until done.

Serves 6 to 8.

BACON POPOVERS

1   cup sifted flour, sifted with
½   teaspoon salt
3   eggs, lightly beaten
1   cup milk
2   tablespoons melted butter
½   cup cooked, crumbled bacon

In a large bowl or electric mixer, combine flour and salt, lightly beaten eggs, milk and melted butter. Beat the batter until it is smooth. Stir in bacon. Grease iron popover pans and heat until they are sizzling hot. Fill cups half full with the batter and bake the popovers at 450 degrees for 20 minutes. Reduce the temperature to 350 degrees and bake for about 20 minutes more or until they are brown and crisp.

Yields 11 popovers.

SALT FREE HEALTH BREAD

1   cup skim milk
1   envelope yeast
1   cup water
3   tablespoons sugar
⅓   cup safflower oil
2   teaspoons salt substitute
5   (to 6) cups stone-ground flour
½   cup defatted wheat germ

Heat milk; cool to lukewarm. Dissolve yeast in water; add to cooled milk . Add sugar, safflower oil, salt substitute. Stir in flour and wheat germ on floured board. Knead stiff dough until smooth; place in greased bowl; cover and let rise to double in bulk. Punch down and let rise again to double in bulk. Divide into 2 loaves. Place in greased loaf pans. When double in bulk, bake at 375 degrees for 50 minutes.

Yields 2 loaves.

CROISSANTS

1   cup milk
¼   cup yeast
1½ teaspoons salt
1   egg
4   cups wheat flour
¾   cup butter
1   egg for brushing

Dissolve yeast in a little cold milk. Add the rest of the milk, salt, and egg (lightly beaten). Add flour and mix to a light dough. Place on a cookie sheet and roll into oblong shape. Cut butter (which must be cold but not refrigerator cold) into slices and put these on half of the dough. Fold the other half over and seal the edges. Roll again into a rectangle. Fold three times, seal and roll into a rectangle. Repeat twice. Let it stand in a cool place for about 1 hour. Roll into 2 circles and divide each in pie-shaped pieces. Beginning at round edge, roll up. Place on cookie sheet and let rise in a.cool place for 1 hour. Brush with egg and bake at 475 degrees for 7 to 8 minutes.

The

• C R O I S S A N T •

The method for making croissants was established at the end of the 16th century by a French chef named Saupiquet. There are many variations but all employ the use of butter, folded into the dough in layers. Steam released from the butter during baking causes the pastry to rise in the tissue like layers. Pastry chefs have always been persons of great importance in France, where they established the earliest known trade union in 1270. By the mid 16th century French pastry chefs were granted titles and special privileges by royal decree.

Main Dishes

CRAB AND CHEESE CRÊPES EN CASSEROLE

CRÊPES:

4   eggs
1   cup milk
1   cup flour
2   tablespoons butter, melted
½   teaspoon salt

For crêpes, combine eggs, milk, flour, butter and salt in an electric blender; process for a few seconds, or until smooth. (Without blender: beat eggs with milk; stir into sifted dry ingredients. Beat until smooth; stir in melted butter.) Heat a lightly buttered 7-inch skillet. Put 2 tablespoons batter into pan for each crepe. Rotate pan to spread batter evenly. Cook over medium high heat until delicately browned around edge. Turn with wide spatula. Cook second side about 20 seconds. Place on cookie sheet or stack on plate until all crêpes are cooked.

FILLING:

½   pound fresh mushrooms, sliced
    Butter
½   cup flour
½   teaspoon salt
¼   teaspoon white pepper
¼   teaspoon paprika
1¾   cups half-and-half
¼   cup dry white wine
2   packages (6 ounce) frozen crabmeat, thawed and diced
2   wedges (1½ ounce) Gruyere cheese, grated (about 1 cup)
1   tablespoon minced chives
1   tablespoon parsley

For filling, cook mushrooms in 2 tablespoons butter; set aside. Melt ⅓ cup butter in a heavy pan; blend in flour, salt, pepper and paprika. Gradually add half-and-half. Cook, stirring constantly, until thickened and smooth. Stir in wine, crabmeat, cheese, chives and parsley. Heat. Put 2 tablespoons filling on each crêpe. Roll up crêpe; secure with a wooden pick. Arrange filled crêpes in a buttered jelly-roll pan. Bake at 350 degrees about 10 to 12 minutes or until heated and bubbly. Garnish with parsley.

Yields 16 filled crêpes, 8 servings.

CURRIED LAMB WITH BANANAS

4   pounds lean shoulder of lamb, cut in 1½ inch pieces
2   tablespoons butter
2   large onions, chopped fine
2   large cooking apples, cored and chopped fine
1   large clove garlic, minced
½   cup flour
¼   cup curry powder
3   cans (10½ ounces) chicken broth
    Salt and pepper
1   cup heavy cream
    Lemon juice to taste
2   ripe, but not soft, bananas, peeled and quartered

Sauté lamb in butter; add onions, apple and garlic. Continue cooking until all liquid is evaporated. Sprinkle with flour and curry powder. Stir until well coated. Stir in chicken broth. Bake at 375 degrees for 1 hour or until tender. Add cream and lemon juice. Season with salt and pepper. Then add sliced bananas. Bring to a boil just before serving.

Serves 8.

NOTE: *Serve with cooked dry rice, chutney, chives or scallions, raisins soaked in cognac, chopped peanuts or chopped almonds, or fresh or toasted coconut.*

Sauces

COINTREAU BARBECUE SAUCE

1   fifth burgundy
4   medium onions
2   ribs celery
2   cans (10½ ounce) beef bouillon
3   cans (6 ounce) tomato paste
    Salt, pepper and Tabasco sauce to taste
2   tablespoons Cointreau

Combine all ingredients, except Cointreau, in a saucepan. Cook until reduced by half. Add Cointreau.

NOTE: *Excellent for steaks, hamburgers and spareribs and for either outdoor or indoor broiling. Extra sauce keeps well in refrigerator.*

HOT LEMON SAUCE FOR GINGERBREAD
LOUISE PACETTI

⅔   cup sugar
3   tablespoons cornstarch
1½ cups boiling water
2   tablespoons butter
    Grated rind of 1 lemon
2   tablespoons lemon juice
½   teaspoon vanilla
    Dash of salt

Mix sugar and cornstarch; add slowly to boiling water; cook until thick. Add other ingredients. Serve hot over gingerbread.

Desserts

GRAND MARNIER SOUFFLÉ

4   tablespoons *each* flour and butter or
    margarine
1   cup light cream
    Dash of salt
6   eggs, separated
¾   cup sugar
    Grated peel of 1 orange
¼   cup Grand Marnier
    Whipped cream
    Grand Marnier

In a saucepan, melt butter and blend in flour. Stir in cream and salt; cook, stirring until thickened. Remove from heat. Beat in yolks, ½ cup sugar, orange peel and Grand Marnier. Whip whites until they hold soft peaks, then beat in remaining sugar until they hold short distinct soft peaks. Fold in half the whites very thoroughly. Fold in other half as thoroughly as you like. Pour into a buttered and sugar-dusted 2-quart soufflé dish. Fit a lightly buttered foil collar around dish. It should extend about an inch above rim. Bake at 375 degrees for 15 minutes, then remove collar. Do not remove from the oven. Continue baking for 20 to 25 minutes. Over each serving, spoon whipped cream flavored to taste with Grand Marnier (or flame each serving with a spoonful of the warmed liqueur).

Serves 6.

VARIATIONS: *You can flavor this soufflé with Cointreau or Curacao instead of Grand Marnier. Or you can omit the orange peel and flavor the soufflé with Kahlua, creme de cacao or other favorite, suitably flavored liqueur.*

MACADAMIA CHESS PIE

1   baked pie shell
1   cup sugar
½   cup butter
2   eggs, beaten
2   egg yolks, beaten
1   teaspoon grated lemon rind
    Juice of 2 lemons
1   cup macadamia nuts, coarsely chopped
1   cup golden raisins
    Whipped cream

Cream butter and sugar. Add eggs and yolks, lemon juice and lemon rind. Place in saucepan over low heat. Add nuts and raisins which have been plumped by simmering in very small amount of water. Let cook until thickened, stirring constantly. Let cool and pour into baked pie shell. Chill and serve with dollop of whipped cream.

PINEAPPLE-WALNUT CAKE

½   cup butter or margarine
1½ cups sugar
2   eggs, lightly beaten
2   cups flour
½   teaspoon salt
2   teaspoons soda
1   can (1 lb., 4½ ounces) crushed pineapple
¾   cup chopped walnuts
1   cup brown sugar, firmly packed

Cream butter with sugar; beat in eggs until smooth. Sift flour; measure and sift again with salt and soda. Blend dry ingredients with creamed mixture; mix in the pineapple, including liquid. Spoon into a greased 8x12-inch baking pan. Combine walnuts and brown sugar; sprinkle over top. Bake at 350 degrees for 45 minutes. Serve warm or cold from pan.

Serves 12.

CHEESE DESSERT
OR SOUSED CAMEMBERT WITH ALMONDS

1   whole, ripe Camembert
    White wine
½   cup butter
    Finely chopped, toasted almonds

Soak Camembert overnight in enough white wine to cover. Drain; scrape off discolored portion (but not all the crust) and mix the cheese with butter. Work until perfectly smooth. Now chill for easier handling, and form into the original shape of the cheese. Cover top, bottom and sides with toasted almonds. Chill again, but remove from refrigerator about a half hour before serving. Hot toasted crackers should accompany this dish.

CARROT PICNIC CAKE

1½ cups unsifted flour
1   cup sugar
¼   teaspoon *each* nutmeg and ginger
1   teaspoon soda
    1½ teaspoons cinnamon
½   teaspoon baking powder
½   teaspoon salt
2   eggs
1   can (8 ounces) crushed pineapple, undrained
½   cup cooking oil
1   teaspoon vanilla
1   cup grated carrots
½   cup chopped nuts

Combine all dry ingredients in a large bowl. Add eggs, pineapple, oil and vanilla. Stir in carrots and nuts. Bake in well-oiled and floured bundt or stem pan at 350 degrees for 45 to 50 minutes.

White Chocolate Cake

¼ pound white chocolate
½ cup boiling water
1 cup butter
2 cups sugar
4 egg yolks
1 teaspoon vanilla
2½ cups cake flour
1 teaspoon baking powder
¼ teaspoon salt
1 cup buttermilk
4 egg whites, stiffly beaten
1 cup chopped pecans
1 cup shredded coconut

Melt chocolate in boiling water; cool. Cream together butter and sugar; beat in egg yolks, one at a time, beating well after each addition. Add melted chocolate and vanilla. Sift together flour, baking powder and salt; add to chocolate mixture alternately with buttermilk. Do not overbeat. Fold in beaten egg whites; gently stir in nuts and coconut. Bake at 350 degrees for 30 to 45 minutes in 3 greased layer cake pans. Ice with coconut frosting.

Coconut Frosting

2 cups sugar
½ cup water
½ cup white corn syrup
2 egg whites, beaten frothy
   Pinch salt
1 teaspoon vanilla
1 (to 2) cups grated coconut

Cook sugar, water and corn syrup until it reaches soft ball stage (238 degrees). Pour slowly into egg whites and beat until stiff; add salt and vanilla. Spread on cake layers; sprinkle coconut between layers and over cake.

Pumpkin-Orange Chiffon Pie

1 baked 9-inch pie shell
1 cup sugar
1 envelope unflavored gelatin
1½ teaspoons pumpkin pie spice
3 egg yolks
½ cup milk
1¼ cups canned, cooked pumpkin
1 teaspoon grated orange peel
¼ cup orange juice
3 egg whites
   Sweetened whipped cream
   Grated orange peel

For filling, stir together ½ cup sugar, gelatin and spice in a saucepan. Beat together egg yolks and milk. Add to saucepan. Cook over medium heat, stirring constantly, until mixture comes to a boil. Stir in pumpkin, orange peel and juice. Chill until partially set. Beat egg whites until frothy; gradually add remaining ½ cup sugar and beat until stiff peaks form. Fold into pumpkin mixture. Pour into prepared pie shell. Chill until firm (at least 6 hours). Serve with sweetened whipped cream, garnished with grated orange peel.

Serves 6.

Prune Sour Cream Pie

1 8-inch unbaked pie shell
2 eggs, slightly beaten
⅔ cup honey
⅔ cup sour cream
¼ teaspoon salt
2 tablespoons lemon juice
2 cups cooked, chopped prunes

Combine eggs, honey, sour cream, salt and lemon juice. Stir in prunes. Pour into pie shell. Bake at 450 degrees for 10 minutes. Reduce heat to 375 degrees and bake 30 to 40 minutes longer.

PEACH BRANDY POUND CAKE

3   cups sugar
1   cup butter or margarine, softened
6   eggs
3   cups all-purpose flour
¼   teaspoon soda
    Pinch of salt
1   cup sour cream
2   teaspoons rum
1   teaspoon orange extract
¼   teaspoon almond extract
½   teaspoon lemon extract
1   teaspoon vanilla extract
½   cup peach brandy

Combine sugar and butter; cream until light and fluffy. Add eggs one at a time, mixing well after each addition. Combine dry ingredients and add to creamed mixture alternately with sour cream, beating well after each addition. Stir in remaining ingredients. Pour batter into a well greased and floured 10-inch bundt pan or tube. Bake at 325 degrees for 1 hour and 20 minutes.

Index

Conversion Chart
American to British

American	British	Metric
BUTTER AND SOLID FATS:		
1 tablespoon	½ oz	15 g
2 tablespoons	1 oz	30 g
4 tablespoons	2 oz	60 g
8 tablespoons (½ cup or 2 sticks)	4 oz	115 g
16 tablespoons 1 cup or 2 sticks	8 oz	225 g
32 tablespoons (2 cups or 4 sticks)	32 oz	450 g
FLOUR (UNSIFTED)		
1 tablespoon	¼ oz	8.75 g
¼ cup (4 tablespoons)	1¼ oz	35 g
½ cup	2½ oz	70 g
1 cup	5 oz	140 g
3½ cups	16 oz (1 lb)	490 g

NOTE: 1 cup sifted flour = 1 cup unsifted flour minus 1½ tablespoons.

American	British	Metric
SUGAR (GRANULATED)		
1 teaspoon	⅙ oz	5 g
1 tablespoon	½ oz	15 g
¼ cup (4 tablespoons)	1¾ oz	60 g
½ cup	3½ oz	100 g
1 cup	6¾ oz	200 g
2⅓ cups	16 oz (1 lb)	480 g

LIQUIDS

AMERICAN	BRITISH	FLUID OUNCES	NEAREST METRIC EQUIVALENT (DL. = DECILITER)
2 tablespoons	2 tablespoons	1	¼ dl.
¼ cup	4 tablespoons	2	½ dl.
½ cup		4	1 dl.
⅔ cup	¼ pint or 1 gill	5	1½ dl.
¾ cup		6	1¾ dl.
1 cup or ½ pint		8	2¼ dl.
1¼ cups	1½ pints	10	2¾ dl.
2 cups or 1 pint		16	4½ dl.
2½ cups	1 pint	20	5½ dl.
4 cups or 1 quart		32	9 dl.
4½ cups	1⅓ pints plus 1 oz.	36	1 litre

OTHER EQUIVALENTS

	AMERICAN	BRITISH	METRIC
Brown sugar	2⅓ cups	1 lb	450 g
Confectioner's sugar	4 cups	1 lb	450 g
Nuts, ground	¾ cup	4 oz	115 g
Bread crumbs, fresh	2 cups	4 oz	115 g
Bread crumbs, dry	¾ cup	4 oz	115 g

For baking, 1 cake yeast = 30 g fresh yeast.
1 envelope = 7 g dry yeast.

OVEN TEMPERATURES

FAHRENHEIT (F°)	GAS MARK	CENTIGRADE (C°)	OVEN HEAT
250	½	120	very slow (very cool)
300	2	150	slow (cool)
325	3	165	moderately slow (moderately cool)
350	4	180	moderate
375	5	190	moderately hot
400	6	205	hot
450-500	8-10	230-260	very hot

For other temperatures, to convert Fahrenheit to Celsius subtract 32 degrees and multiply by 5, then divide by 9.

TERMINOLOGY DIFFERENCES BETWEEN BRITAIN AND AMERICA

AMERICAN	BRITISH
small zucchini	caurgette
eggplant	aubergine
large zucchini	marrow
scallions	spring onions
jumbo shrimp	prawns
superfine sugar	castor sugar
confectioner's or powdered sugar	icing sugar
ground	minced
pitted	stoned
strips	rashers
light cream	single cream
heavy whipping cream	double cream
shortening	hardened vegetable oil
jelly	jam
tomato paste	tomato purée

EDITORIAL

Sally Dennison, Ellen Fly, Carol Haralson, Michael Hightower, Paulette Millichap, Alice Price, Faye Schuett, Dudley Thomas, Ann Weisman.

FOOD CONSULTANTS

Ellen Fly, Caroline Brune, Cheryl Dobbins

PRODUCTION

Carol Haralson, Carl Brune, Karen Slankard

TYPOGRAPHY AND MANUSCRIPT PREPARATION

Susan Coman, Coman and Associates; Beth Britt; Martha Long; Typo Photo Graphics, Inc.

Special thanks to Mr. & Mrs. Frank J. Hightower, Christine Booth, Patty Floyd, Elizabeth McCullough, Kaye Sorensen, and Vanda Simmons.

Historical photographs and cookery implements for photographic illustrations were loaned courtesy of Cleora Butler, Kevin Byrne, Colonial Antiques, Mrs. George Dennison, Peggy Farmer, Carol Haralson, Miss Jacksons of Utica Square, Paulette Millichap, Chris Knop Kallenberger, Jan Stevens and The Snow Goose, The Tulsa Garden Center and Ann Weisman.

Information for historical notes was obtained in part courtesy of Hi Gottesman, Boyle-Midway, Inc.; Betty Cronin, Campbell's Soup, Inc.; Cuisinarts, Inc.; Phyllis Elias, Earl's Health Foods; Michael Mudd and Barbara Grellet, General Foods; David Hanover, Hanover's Meat Market; Debbie Foster, H. J. Heinz Company, Inc.; Dave Bollette, Hobart Corp.; Diane Dickey, W. K. Kellogg Co.; Marie Holen, Land O'Lakes, Inc.; Mrs. Edith Masten, Thomas J. Lipton Co.; Ron Dean, Mecca Coffee Co.; Dave Stivers, Nabisco Brands, Inc.; Beth Kathan, John Oster Co.; Lisa Carlson, Pillsbury; Carol Owen, Reynolds Metals Co.; Wayne Smith, Sunbeam Appliance Co.; and Darby Cassidy, Webster Industries, Inc.

This book was printed on seventy-pound Williamsburg Text
and eighty-pound Lustro Offset Enamel Dull
by Eastern Press, Inc., of New Haven, Connecticut.

The typeface is Simoncini Garamond,
set by Typo Photo Graphics, Inc.
and Coman & Associates of Tulsa, Oklahoma.
Photographs reproduced as duotones are laser-scanned
using 200-line screens.